THE SCOTTISH HIGHLANDS

THE
Scottish Highlands

W. H. MURRAY

THE SCOTTISH MOUNTAINEERING TRUST

EDINBURGH

First published in Britain in 1976 by
THE SCOTTISH MOUNTAINEERING TRUST

Copyright © 1976 by the Scottish Mountaineering Trust

Designed, produced and sold for the Scottish Mountaineering Trust
by West Col Productions, 1 Meadow Close, Goring on Thames,
Reading, Berks, RG8 0AP

SBN 901516 83 X

Set in Monotype Plantin Series 110 and Grotesque 215
and printed in Great Britain by Billing & Sons Limited,
Guildford, London and Worcester

Contents

Illustrations

DIAGRAMS AND MAPS by *James Renny*

Acknowledgements

In writing this book, I have been deeply indebted to at least 200 authors and editors, whose books, articles, journals, and magazines are listed in the bibliography. I have a particular need to give my thanks for help to twelve members of the Scottish Mountaineering Club. They are G. Scott Johnstone, of the Institute of Geological Sciences, who gave me wide-ranging critical advice on geology; W. D. Brooker, for information on past and present mountaineering history; Dr Adam Watson, for detail on grouse; B. H. Humble, for information on the Cairngorms; Hamish MacInnes, Neil Quinn, and Graham Tiso for comment on ice-climbing techniques and equipment; J. C. Donaldson for listing the Munros and their heights; T. Weir and D. J. Bennet for contributing photographs; W. B. Speirs for information on skiing and his patience as general editor; and to James Renny for drawing all the maps and diagrams with meticulous care and long labour.

My thanks are due also to Richard Grieve of Kinlochleven for his photograph of the Crowberry Ridge; to Derek Ratcliffe of the Nature Conservancy for advice on mountain plants; and to Dr Hilary H. Birks and Dr H. J. B. Birks for writing an article on the Highlands' arctic-alpine flora.

Introduction

The mountains dominate the Highlands. This book is primarily for those who delight in hills, whether by travelling through them, climbing up them, or exploring all their recesses. The enjoyment of the Highlands can be enhanced by a good understanding of the way they were originally shaped by natural forces, how their wildlife and plant life arrived and spread and developed, and how that natural scene has been profoundly modified by man's activities.

This book is a guide to the Highlands in depth, rather than a detailed account of their multitudinous facets and routes of approach. It does not in any way supplant the Scottish Mountaineering Club's District Guides, which deal with the detail most thoroughly. It is background reading by which they and the mountain environment they describe may be better appreciated. Five chapters on the Highland districts, South, Central, Cairngorms, West, and North, are designed to show what is best in each; they give an indication of the better routes up the better-known hills, but for the detail of these, and of the innumerable routes and points of interest not mentioned, it is necessary to refer to the District and Rock Climbing Guides, and to Ordnance Survey maps. On one subject – the history of Scottish mountain climbing – the rule has been changed, and the detail given here instead of there.

I recommend Bartholomew's half-inch maps for travel by road or track. For hill-walking and mountaineering, only the O.S. sheets are of large enough scale for safety. They are of three current series: 1:63,360 (1″ to 1 mile); 1:50,000; and 1:25,000.

The recent imposition of the metric system for the country's traditional units of measurement might have been accepted on these pages by quotation of metric equivalents alongside the accustomed linear figures. This was found to congest the text insufferably. The metric figures for mountain heights have, therefore, been relegated to appendix I.

The spellings of place names have been taken from the Ordnance Survey maps, except where these are so clearly wrong that they cannot be accepted (for example, Isle of Rum, not the O.S. Rhum). The use and non-use of capital letters in place-names has too long been a problem afflicting visitors from the south, yet is simply resolved. Thus Glen Coe refers always to the glen, but Glencoe to the village or the Glencoe hills. Likewise Cairn Gorm is the mountain but the crystals found on it are Cairngorm stones, and the district or mountain group is the Cairngorms.

1   Physical Description

The Scottish Highlands are an eroded plateau, which 20–30 million years ago was lifted up as part of Scandinavia. The land then stood higher than now and extended 120 miles farther west to the continental shelf beyond St Kilda. Erosion by water carved the tableland into several hundred hill-shapes. It parted from Scandinavia 10–15 million years ago when the western margin of Eurasia subsided. The forested plain linking Scotland with Norway submerged under the North Sea (although not for the last time), while the western half of the Highlands sank into the Atlantic, from which hill-tops stuck out as islands. The westward-running glens became fiords. Southwards, the Central Lowland depression – a rift valley formed by a much earlier subsidence – divided the Highlands from the Southern Uplands and gave the Grampian mountains a clearly marked base line, now known as the Highland Line. Its course runs north-east from Arran on the Firth of Clyde to Stonehaven.

Definition. The Highlands may thus be defined as the hill country north of Scotland's Lowland waist, including the Hebrides. No definition less wide could cover the ground of the Highlands' natural history, but for the practical purposes of Highland walking and exploratory travel a more restricted definition is wanted. The Outer Hebrides, much of the Inner, and almost all of Caithness, lie too low to the sea to qualify here as Highland country. Likewise the north-east seaboard, which carries broad lowland belts around the Moray Firth, Banffshire, and Aberdeenshire. All are excluded from the descriptive chapters of this book, but exception is made in favour of four islands: Arran, Mull, Rum, and Skye. Their hills rise so high and so close to the mainland that everyone exploring the Highlands will want to go there. They are truly Highland in character. This more restricted Highland area comprises over 14,000 square miles of hill country. It contains 543 hill-tops rising to 3,000 feet or more, of which 282 are classified as separate mountains called *Munros*, named after Sir Hugh T. Munro the third president of the Scottish Mountaineering Club, who first listed them in 1891. Twelve tops rise above 4,000 feet, of which seven rank as Munros (see Table, p. 247).

Quality. The Scottish Highlands have a natural beauty unique of its kind, yet the basic ingredients of loch, river, woodland, sea, and mountains, are common to other highland countries. The sea is the one element not common to most. The distinctive landscape quality of the Highlands is caused in part by climate, in part by the underlying rock, and in part by the geological accidents that laid down the structure and imposed the site – sufficiently long ago for all components to come to good proportion. Topography is widely varied – contrast Skye with the Cairngorms, or Argyll with Sutherland – and this variety is compounded by light and colour in equal diversity, due both to seasonal climatic change and to vegetation. The whole land is wrapped by an Atlantic atmosphere, soft over the most part but drying eastward; notoriously wet and windy on the hills, which in winter are struck by blizzards. All is made tolerable by the ever-present chance of swift change to sun and sparkling air. The reward is a richness and subtlety of landscape colour that drier lands do not have. The colour is from the plant-life that clothes the hills and glens, from the reflecting waters, the rushing burns, and the atmosphere itself.

The Highlands still retain a larger element of wilderness character than may be found in other European countries south of Scandinavia. Wilderness here does not mean unchanged by the hand of man, for there is no land of that kind in Britain below the mountain-tops, but rather land free of man-made intrusions. Highland and Island industries have not been of a kind to mar natural beauty until recent years, so that enough unspoiled country is left to delight the eye. These are some of the qualities that distinguish the Highlands. The quiet in which they can best be enjoyed is found most readily among the hills.

Construction. The mountains have two peculiarities of structure. The first is that they are cut from a plateau, and the second, that the cutting is done to a criss-cross pattern. The first means that the higher tops keep a uniformity of height not always obvious from below, but quickly apparent from the summits. The view from Ben Nevis is thus often likened to a sea of peaks, and like every sea it proves the rule by throwing up an occasional roller bigger than average, notably the Cairngorms, or the Ben Nevis group, or the Affric–Strathfarrar hills. The second peculiarity is likewise concealed when a first glance is bestowed on a relief map. A state of chaos appears. Valleys and ranges run in all directions. But closer study reveals a pattern of north-east to south-west graining furrowed transversely north-west to south-east. This pattern is the Highlands' structural feature. The north-east to south-west grain is readily picked out, most strongly in west Argyll. This dominant structure of folds and faults, giving roughly parallel glens with mountains between sliced out as long ridges, dates from 400 to 500 million years ago during the Caledonian orogeny, when a great mountain chain rose as described in the next chapter. The transverse glens are quite independent of that first structure. They were caused after the Caledonian mountains had been eroded down to a plain, and the land elevated as a new tableland dropping in steps to the south-east. The new rivers ran down the slope, which was solid rock free of faults and folding. They carved glens called consequent valleys, for example, the Lairig Ghru, Glen Spean, Glen Nevis, Glen Coe, until they were intercepted by the older rivers of the Caledonian structure. When the older rivers lay in faults they eroded their beds faster than the newer rivers and so in course of time captured and redirected them. For example, Glen Coe formerly channelled a river that took its source in Ardnamurchan and flowed east across Rannoch Moor to the North Sea. Its waters were intercepted by a river running south-west along the fault lines of what are now Loch Linnhe and Loch Leven. The river Coe was thus left with insufficient water to clear its eastward course when tributaries blocked its glen with a deltaic cone, which became a watershed turning all drainage back to the west. Similarly, the river Spean formerly flowed east to the Spey, and the rivers Nevis and Leven to Loch Rannoch. Such instances can be multiplied across the country. The entire Highland plateau was thus thoroughly carved up and shaped to mountainous form. An outstanding example of a north-east to south-west fault is the Great Glen; and of folding, Loch Tay or most of the big sea-lochs of Argyll. An example of a consequent valley is the Garry–Tummel–Tay, which starting from the Grampian spine crosses the strike of all Highland rocks and even the Lowland fault at Strathmore near Perth.

Seaboard. In addition to these basic structures, the Highlands have a number of other features of great importance. The first and most striking is the riven coastline from the Clyde to the Kyle of Tongue. The Highlands have no eastern coast, except to the north and west of the Dornoch Firth and Cromarty Firth. The extraordinary character of the west coast is shown by its length: 260 miles as the crow flies but well above 2,000 in outline, not counting minor indentations. When the older coastline submerged, the waters flooding in to the glens created not only the 550 Hebrides, but upwards of 40 mainland sea-lochs. These did not appear all at once: their numbers were increased by later Ice Age glaciers, which deepened valleys and cut through the isthmuses of some big peninsulas like Skye, Mull, Jura-Islay, and probably Arran. Others were lost when moraine debris silted up the mouths of sea-lochs, like Loch Lomond, Loch Eck, and Loch Awe – and were both lost and gained when sea and land rose unequally after the melting of local and polar ice.

The Great Glen. A geographical feature unique in the Highlands is the Great Glen, which splits Scotland diagonally. This originated as a fault-line between the Moray Firth and the Firth of Lorn, where after the close of the Caledonian orogeny the north block of what is now Scotland is believed to have moved 65 miles south-west in relation to the south block. The bed is filled for 45 miles by Loch Ness, Loch Oich, and Loch Lochy, and the remaining 22 miles by their rivers, from which the Caledonian Canal was cut. The Great Glen separates the Highlands into two contrasted regions: to its south-east, the Grampian region, all of inland character, save Argyll; to its north, the Atlantic region, usually called the North-West. Each is covered most largely by the same kind of metamorphic rocks (crystalline schists, flaggy gneisses, and quartzite) but of different age: the Moine series to the north and Dalradian to the south. The two regions are unalike.

North–West Region

The North-West's mountain spine or watershed extends 150 miles north to south, and keeps exceedingly close to the west coast. The Atlantic flanks, rising 2–3,000 feet, are short and steep, whereas the eastern slopes are long, interrupted by other hills, and give a relatively monotonous scene because their schists have uniformity of structure. The rivers draining west are accordingly short and lively, most furious during a spate, for quite apart from their steeper ground they catch the first heavy rainfall coming in from the Atlantic. The watershed in some places is only $1\frac{1}{2}$ miles from the sea, for example at the head of Glen Pean, whose westward river has only a three-mile run, while the eastward (by way of Loch Arkaig) goes 65 miles. The more usual river-lengths vary from 5 to 25 miles westward compared to 30 and 40 miles eastward.

The west seaboard carries the most striking mountain shapes of Scotland, for they include not only the sandstone and quartzite cones, towers, and ridges of Sutherland and Wester Ross, but the gabbro and basalt pinnacles of Skye and Rum. It is for the most part much barer country than the Highlands to south and east, for the North-West coast is the windiest of the British mainland, and its soil poor. Nearly all travellers notice a change in atmosphere after crossing the Great Glen. The farther they go north the more distinct it becomes: it is that of a seaward peninsula, a lighter, more bracing air, a new freshness in colour and light. The North Highlands are, in fact, the main Atlantic promontory of Scotland, and to enter from the south is to enter a new country.

Grampian Region

The Grampian region, which has much the same length with greater breadth, shows the north-east to south-west grain line with greater emphasis. Intruding into its main body of crystalline schists are large areas of Caledonian granite forming much of the Cairngorms and mountains to the south-west between Lorn and Lochaber. Around Glen Coe and on top of Ben Nevis sit the lava cores of two big cauldron subsidences, exposed by 300 million years of denudation. The Grampian's greater diversity of rock gives a more richly varied scenery, rarely as spectacular as the best of the North-West, but with other merits that the North-West cannot rival. The Cairngorms have no aspiring peaks like the Cuillin or Torridon hills, yet their rolling plateau bitten by huge, rock-walled corries, their long passes between the Spey and the Dee, their forested approaches, have a majesty unrivalled anywhere else in Scotland. No glen of the North-West can match Glen Coe as a rock canyon, or the Tummel valley for spacious woodland beauty. No wooded defile can equal Glen Lyon, or wooded river gorge compare with the Himalayan quality of upper Glen Nevis. There is no cliff architecture even in Skye shaped to such magnificent form as that of Ben Nevis above the Allt a' Mhuilinn. Such comparisons may be invidious, in the sense that North-Western qualities unmatched southward can equally well be listed, but a point has to be appreciated – that the central, east, and south Highlands have their outstanding landscape qualities more widely spread over bigger tracts of hill country, where they are less easily found unless one knows where to go. In the North-West they are concentrated along the seaboard, cannot be missed, and thus give a more powerful impression of quality.

The Grampians have a double watershed, given Y-shape by Strathspey. The principal watershed is the western, 150 miles long. Starting on the Monadh Liath between the upper Findhorn and the Great Glen, it bends sharply east at Creag Meaghaidh, rounds the head of Loch Laggan, then swings south-west on a sinuous course to the Black Mount of Argyll, and finally tails off down Loch Lomond's east side to the Lowland fault. The eastern or Cairngorm spur runs 75 miles from Glen Fiddich Forest above Dufftown through the high Cairngorm tops to the Drumochter pass. The rivers of the western spine again have a short westward run, while eastward they take long courses draining huge territories. The sources of the Tay range across Scotland from the Braes of Angus to Lorn. On the arms of the Y (the Monadh Liath and the Cairngorms) the principal drainage is north and east by long and famous salmon rivers: the Findhorn, Spey, Deveron, Don, and Dee.

There are very marked differences of configuration between the Cairngorms and the rest of the Highlands. The rest have a typical hill-scene of well-defined ridges, often with pointed peaks and craggy sides, and they are flanked by glens or moors bearing freshwater lochs. The Cairngorms by contrast are typified by more gently rounded flanks and summits, almost featureless were it not for the interspersed corries. Rock-structure, and a different glacial action, account for part of the contrast, but no less important is the west's heavier rainfall giving stronger erosion, especially on the steeper western flanks. Equally remarkable is the scarcity in the Cairngorms of glen lochs.

The Lochs are one of the principal landscape assets of the western half of the Highlands. They abound in both the old grain lines and transverse valleys, providing the combination of water and fringing trees that do most justice to the hill-shapes above. In spring and autumn the waters reflect the green or gold of the flanking vegetation and the glint of rain-washed rocks. Their surfaces continually alter colour according to the sky, from black to white, or gun-metal to royal blue. They are greatly to be prized for the life they bring to any mountain scene. Yet hardly any can be found east of a line drawn from Inverness to Perth.

The Highland lochs are of three main kinds: glen lochs, rock lochans, and moraine lochans. Numerous as glen lochs are, they are fewer than the others, which number many thousands. The glen lochs lie in big rock basins either deepened or excavated by glacier-action, usually in faults or folds that had first been eroded by river-action. It is fair to regard them as of recent origin, for any basins caused by faulting or folding of rocks must have been filled in long before the Ice Age. Some of them are of extraordinary depth. Loch Ness in the Great Glen has been sounded to more than 900 feet, Loch Morar to more than 1,000 feet, and Loch Lomond to more than 650 feet. Famous examples in the old grain lines are Loch Awe, Loch Shiel, Loch Affric, Loch Ericht, and Loch Tay; and in trans-verse furrows, Loch Katrine, Loch Rannoch, Loch Arkaig, Loch Garry, and Loch Maree. Every one of these is associated with the finest inland scenery in the Highlands.

Rock lochans lie in ice-scoops, where the glaciers gouged out shallow hollows in resistant rock. They naturally abound on the gneiss platforms of the North-West Highlands, gneiss being one of the tougher rocks, and on the metamorphic rocks of the Central Highlands. The most astonishing sight of them may be had from the summit of Foinaven, 2980 feet, in Sutherland. They star the moor to the south-west like a Milky Way, for several hundred are crowded into 120 square miles. Equally good is the view from Suilven over the Glencanisp and Inverpolly Forests of Assynt, for though the lochans there number only a couple of hundred they appear countless, and are circled by the mountains of Canisp, Cul Mor, and Stack Polly. Some of these rock-lochans are by no means small. The Cam Loch, which moats Suilven, curves 8 miles in the most sinuous of Highland waterways. Its neighbour, Loch Sionascaig, has a shore-line of 17 miles in a 3-mile length, spattered with islets. The moor-lands of the West and Central Highlands are likewise adorned, although not on this lavish scale. The rock lochans are plentifully dispersed on mountain ridges, and on flanks under the summits. Examples are especially numerous in Wester Ross on the hills between Little Loch Broom and Loch Maree, and again between Glen Torridon and Loch Carron. Splendid examples in Skye are Loch Lagan and Loch Coire a' Ghrunnda, cupped in gabbro to either side of Sgurr Alasdair.

Moraine lochans are small lochs dammed behind the rubble, rocks, and stones dropped by retreating glaciers. They are found throughout the Highlands in hollows from high corries to low glens. Examples from the Cairngorms are Loch Callater, Loch an Eilein, and Loch Morlich; in central Mull, Loch Ba; in Wester Ross, Toll an Lochain under the cliffs of An Teallach, or Loch Coire Mhic Fhearchair on Beinn Eighe. Neat distinctions cannot always be drawn between these three different kinds of loch, for the criteria overlap. Loch Coruisk in the Cuillin lies in a rock basin 125 feet deep, but the upper layer is retained by a moraine barrier. Loch Lomond too is thus dammed; so too the south end of Loch Awe, Loch Shiel, Lock Muick in the Cairngorms, and many another. All of them owe shape and size if not their very being to ice action. Their multitude is a legacy to be prized along with the mountains, glens, rivers, and sea-lochs as a characteristic element of the Highland scene. Weather and its agents have made them all.

Climate

The climate of Scotland is determined by latitude and its site between a great ocean and a great continent. Its notoriously changeful weather is a consequence of a continual double interchange between continental and oceanic air-streams and between distant polar and tropical air masses that give rise, where they meet, to the rapid succession of fronts and depressions passing over the British Isles. Highland weather is dominated by the passage of these Atlantic depressions, and by the prevailing westerly winds that blow across the warm waters of the Gulf Stream's North Atlantic Drift. These have less effect on the east Highlands than the west. The contrast in rainfall is very great. On the west coast, where moist winds have to take an abrupt rise over the mountains, the annual rainfall is 60 inches on the coast and 120 or more on the Highland spine between Central Ross and Arrochar, for precipitation is determined not by closeness to the sea but by height above it. Thus the summit of Ben Nevis has a mean annual rainfall of 157 inches, more than twice that of Fort William (77 inches), which is only 4 miles away at sea-level. The east coast by contrast has under 30 inches, and the Cairngorm and Monadh Liath plateaux only 60 to 90 inches.

There is little difference in summer temperatures between east and west, but in winter the west is warmer by $1\cdot11\,°C$ ($2\,°F$); this is sea-level temperature. There is an abrupt drop in temperature for the heights above sea-level, giving much snow and ice on the tops and their upper flanks in winter. The Cairngorms, although they have a smaller annual precipitation than the West Highlands, have heavier snowfalls, for these often come on easterly and south-easterly

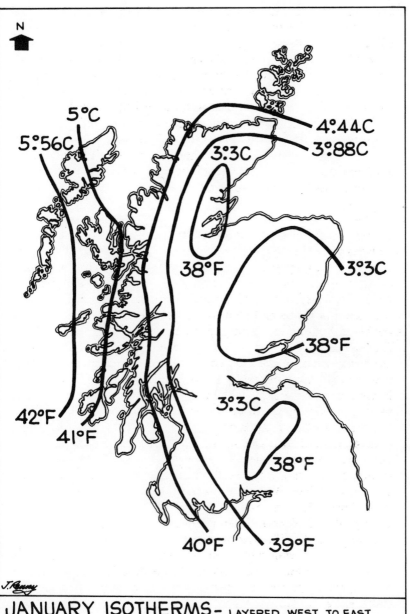

JANUARY ISOTHERMS – LAYERED WEST TO EAST
IN RESPONSE TO NORTH ATLANTIC DRIFT AND WEST WINDS.

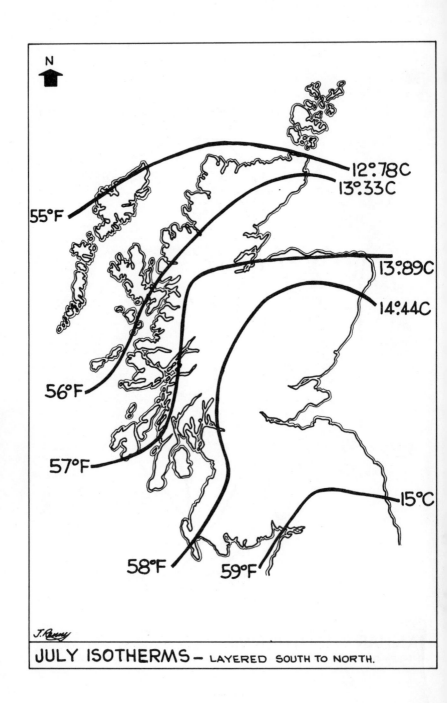

N

12°.78C
13°.33C
55°F
13°.89C
14°.44C
56°F
57°F
15°C
58°F
59°F

J. Renny

JULY ISOTHERMS — LAYERED SOUTH TO NORTH.

winds, which are prolonged. The one western exception to this general rule is Ben Nevis, 4406 feet, which has a mean annual temperature below freezing point. Its north face snow-beds are virtually permanent.

The increase of rainfall with altitude is so uniformly abrupt that rain maps and relief maps look much alike. An isotherm map for a hill based on annual mean temperatures would have contours showing a 3° to 5°F drop in temperature for each 1,000 feet gained. Likewise, wind velocities above 3,000 feet are usually more than double their low ground strength. When these factors are all taken into account – and they must be continually borne in mind by the hill-walker – it follows that weather conditions prevailing on the low country close beneath the mountains can mislead anyone lacking bitter experience. Cold by itself does not seem menacing, nor does a gale wind, but the two together have deadly effect on living things, especially the human body. Warm and windproof clothing has to be carried by all who go on to Scottish mountains. So changeable is the weather that winter conditions and blizzard may occur on any summer day.

The best, that is the driest and sunniest, season of the year is from mid-March to mid-June. East winds then prevail, and although the continental air stream prevents temperature from rising much, the lengthening daylight hours give much sun, reaching an optimum in June. Always there are recessions. The first week of May has been so consistently bad through the years that its cold weather and snow-falls are called 'the lambing snows' in the west. July and August are warm but wetter. In September and October temperature gradually falls, not uncommonly with better weather.

The islands are cooler than the mainland in summer, and warmer in winter. Rainfall is much the same as the West Highlands (60 to 120 inches), but snowfall is less. The shore line is almost free of snow, and the mountains neither receive as much snow as the mainland nor hold their snows as long, because the Highland spines take the lion's share of easterly deposits and thereafter the return to warmer westerlies quickly strips the island hills. The more important aspect of island weather is wind, which blows with more constant affliction than over the mainland. Except at sheltered sites, island trees (like those of Sutherland) are more stunted than elsewhere, because the leaves are over-ventilated, become parched, and fall early. Water-logging of the ground by heavy rain has similar effect by causing plants to work overtime in transpiration (giving off water).

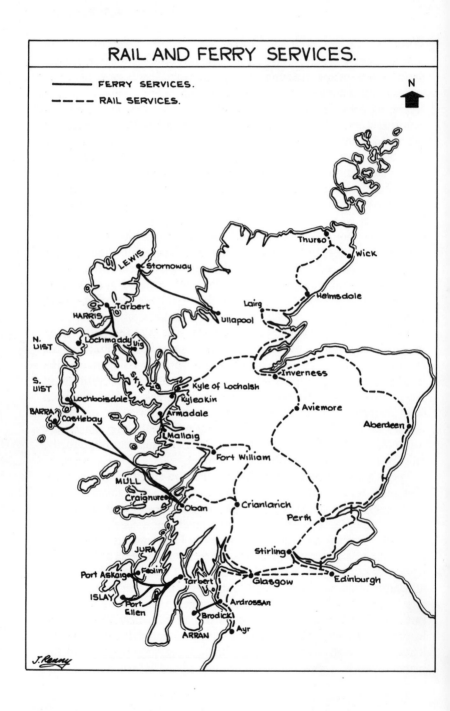

RAIL AND FERRY SERVICES.

FERRY SERVICES.
RAIL SERVICES.

N

Woodland

It follows that the eastern Highlands, with drier weather and better drainage, grow much more heather, and trees of greater variety and stature, than the west. Strath Spey and the Mar and Balmoral Forests are famous for their Scots pines, whose dark green is relieved by well-grown stands of birch, larch, and Douglas fir. The glens of Atholl and the Tummel valley between Loch Rannoch and Pitlochry are richly wooded in larch, pines, birch, oak, ash, chestnut, holly, alder, cypress, and many others. On the south shore of Loch Rannoch, the Black Wood is one of the biggest remaining fragments of the old Caledonian forest, which was predominantly oak and birch in the west, and pine and birch eastward. The old forest was destroyed by man between the ninth and eighteenth centuries. The Highlands owe much present woodland to the enlightened policies of last century's landowners. They planted for beauty, and this has been one of the merits of private ownership as distinguished from state ownership. The difference in standards is most striking in the west, where the private woodlands of Loch Lomond, the Trossachs, Loch Fyne, Loch Awe, Lorn, Torridon, Gairloch, Glen More at Loch Broom, and others may be compared with the commercial plantations of the Forestry Commission. We owe a great debt for surviving woodland beauty to men of a past age. Their plantings have suffered during this century from neglect and war. The Forestry Commission is now the biggest landowner in Scotland, especially in the south-west Highlands, where its sitka spruce is ousting the native hardwoods (oak, birch, rowan) to a degree causing impairment of landscape.

The Highlands divide most naturally into five mountain districts: South, Central, Cairngorms, West, and North. Each has its own character, widely differing from the others.

More detailed accounts follow in Chapters 5 to 9.

Access

Transport services by road, rail, air, and sea, have in recent years been subject to so much annual change that detail of the services, as distinct from the main routes, can be reliably found only by reference to an annual publication. This urgent need has been filled by the Highlands and Islands Development Board, 27 Bank Street, Inverness, whose *Getting Around the Highlands*, and *Comprehensive Transport Timetable* are published in April each year, and available from stationers.

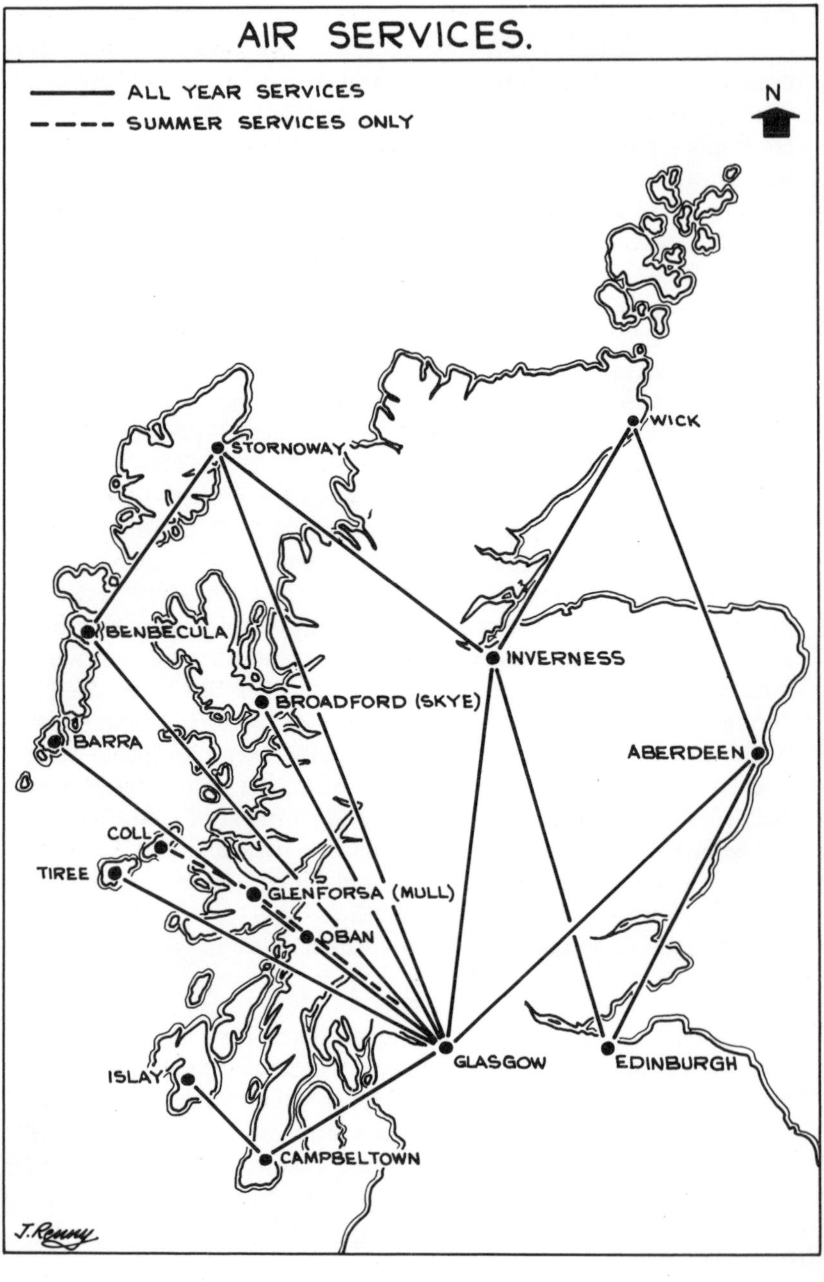

AIR SERVICES.

ALL YEAR SERVICES
SUMMER SERVICES ONLY

N

STORNOWAY

WICK

BENBECULA

INVERNESS

BROADFORD (SKYE)

BARRA

ABERDEEN

COLL

TIREE

GLENFORSA (MULL)

OBAN

GLASGOW

EDINBURGH

ISLAY

CAMPBELTOWN

J. Renny

Roads. Highland roads are now well surfaced. A brief account of access roads to each district, and the main footpaths within it, is given in the District chapters 5 to 9. Local bus services appear in *Getting Around the Highlands*.

Rail. Four railway lines, from Glasgow, Edinburgh, and Inverness, pass through the Highlands (see map p. 22):

(1) The West Highland line from Glasgow by way of Loch Long, Crianlarich, and Bridge of Orchy across the east side of Rannoch Moor to Fort William, Glenfinnan, and Mallaig. This line is scenically the best that Scotland offers.

(2) Glasgow and Edinburgh to Inverness by way of Perth, Strath Tay, Drumochter, and Strath Spey.

(3) Inverness to Kyle of Loch Alsh by Strath Bran and Glen Carron.

(4) Inverness to Thurso in Caithness by Bonar Bridge and Lairg.

The West Highland line has a branch from Tyndrum to Oban through Dalmally and the Pass of Brander. The Edinburgh to Aberdeen line, although not within the Highlands, passes through Strath More below the Braes of Angus.

British Rail have Passenger Train Enquiry Offices at Queen Street Station, Glasgow, at Central Station, Glasgow (for the Clyde), and at Waverley Station, Edinburgh.

Air. BEA operate daily air services from Glasgow and Edinburgh to Inverness, Aberdeen, and Wick. Their Scottish offices are at 122 St Vincent Street, Glasgow, and 135 Princes Street, Edinburgh.

Loganair operate week-end flights from Glasgow to Oban and Mull from June to September, and thrice weekly flights to Skye and Inverness, reduced in frequency during the winter. Their office is at Glasgow Airport, Abbotsinch, Paisley, Renfrewshire.

Ferries. Steamer and car-ferry services to the islands are run by Caledonian MacBrayne Ltd. Timetables may be had from them and bookings made at The Pier, Gourock, Renfrewshire.

Accommodation

The HIDB publish annually two guides to accommodation: *Where to Stay in Scotland*, which covers all Scotland, and *Hotel, Guest House, and B & B Accommodation*, which covers the Highlands and Islands. The latter booklet is cheap, well produced, and light enough for a rucksack.

2 Origin of the Highlands

The position of Scotland on the surface of the earth is very different now from what it was when her crustal rocks were formed. It has long been known that the continents float on the deeply underlying mantle. If a great load is put on top, like a mountain chain or a big ice-cap, it locally depresses the crust, and its removal by erosion or melting allows the crust to lift up. The further hypothesis that the continents drift sideways as well won acceptance more slowly. The first evidence found was the geological match of the American Atlantic coasts with those of Europe and Africa – a match in land-form, rock, and fossils. This gave rise to the theory of continental drift put forward in 1910 by Alfred Wegener. Most geophysicists felt that conclusive proof was still wanted, and this has now come from two sources: the magnetization of minerals in rocks (paleomagnetism), by which the changing position of the crust relative to the North Pole has been charted, and from the exploration of the ocean floor, which has disclosed the mechanics or mode of drift (plate tectonics). Finally, the drift has been approximately dated and particular rates measured.

The evidence for continental drift from paleomagnetism, global plate tectonics, and other branches of geology is so clear that the interpretation of earth history, which had assumed fixed positions for continents and ocean basins, is being radically revised. The evidence gathered over the last twenty years has advanced Wegener's theory to the point that his term Continental Drift is no longer adequate. It is not just the continents that drift. The movement is of great plates of the crust bearing continents and/or ocean basins. Hence the name plate tectonics for this study is replacing while including that of continental drift. The study reveals that when the Americas were united to Eurasia and Africa, Scotland was part of Newfoundland. The proof from paleomagnetism that since Pre-cambrian times the continents have changed widely in position relative to the poles can be simply stated. At the equator, a magnetic needle lies horizontally, at the poles vertically, and in between at an intermediate angle. Likewise, particles of iron oxide settling in a sediment or a lava-flow align themselves on the poles and are fixed in the hardening rocks. Their evidence across the earth is identical. Either the poles have moved or the continents: if the poles, then the magnetic mineral alignments for all continents at a given time would be the same; if the continents, then their pole alignments at a given time would differ. The latter has been proven true. The evidence shows that the Pacific Ocean was for long centred on the North Pole, and Scotland on the equator during the Devonian period.

When the ocean floors were explored, a global range of high mountains was charted, and the discovery made that the ridge-crests were fissured to profound depth. In plate tectonics the plates are the blocks of the crust that diverge along the submarine ridge-crests, where magma continually wells up, cools, and forms new crust. The plates at the two sides pull apart from the ridges or sink out by drag. Great clefts may also develop under continents and ocean floors, which then drift apart while a new ocean spreads, for example, the Red Sea where Arabia has parted from Africa. The eight principal plates are North America, South America, Eurasia, Africa, India, Australia, the Pacific, and Antarctica. There are several minor plates, like the Caribbean, and others. The geophysicists have found identical matches between the Precambrian radiometric age dates, lithologies, rock-structures, and fossils on the shores or continental shelves of these plates. The sequence of the drifts has been approximately dated in the radiometric and relative time scales. They began 200 million years ago in the Mesozoic era. The rate of drift between Europe and North America is about half an inch a year in recent millennia.

The portions of crust that now form Scandinavia, Greenland, and the Scottish Highlands lay together on the Eurasian plate, east of the split line. The rocks of the Scottish fragment had nearly all been formed long before the drift started. The only new rocks to follow the drift were Mesozoic sediments and the Tertiary lavas and granites, most of which had vanished by denudation before Britain was parted from Europe.

The history of the Highlands starts with its oldest rock, the northern gneiss. The oldest rocks everywhere on earth are gneisses (the earliest found thus far being dated by radiometric methods to nearly 3,600 million years). The Lewisian gneisses of north Scotland are of two age groups, 2,600–2,200 million years, named Scourian (after the district of Scourie in west Sutherland), and 1,600 million years, named Laxfordian (after the neaby Laxford river). They probably

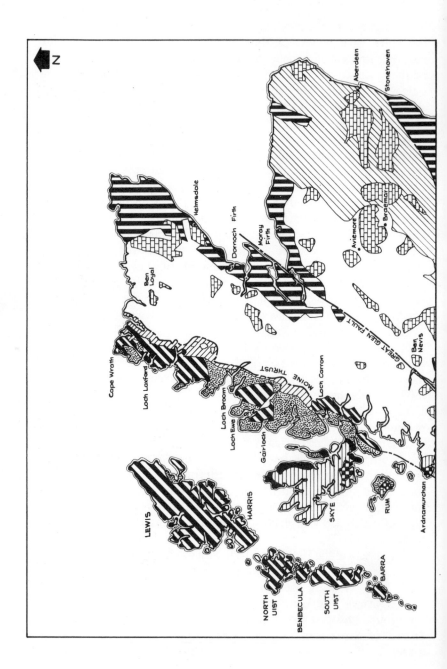

N

Cape Wrath
Loch Laxford
Ben Loyal
Helmsdale
Dornoch Firth
Moray Firth
Aberdeen
Stonehaven
Braemar
Aviemore
GREAT GLEN FAULT
Ben Nevis
Loch Broom
Loch Ewe
Gairloch
MOINE THRUST
Loch Carron
Ardnamurchan
RUM
SKYE
BARRA
SOUTH UIST
BENBECULA
NORTH UIST
HARRIS
LEWIS

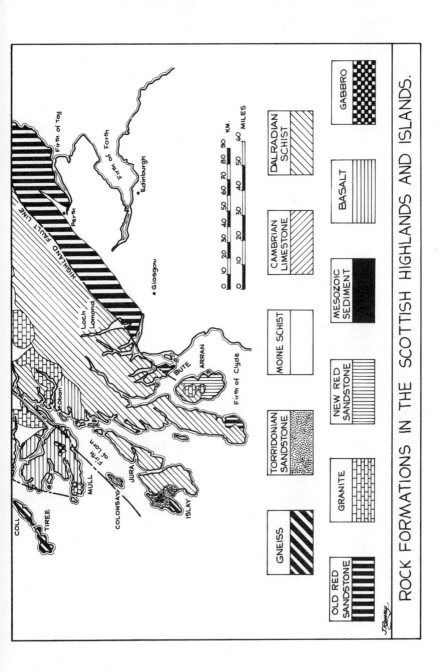

ROCK FORMATIONS IN THE SCOTTISH HIGHLANDS AND ISLANDS.

underlie all rocks of the Highlands. This ancient gneiss extends over great areas of northern Europe from the Urals westward through Greenland, and continues across northern Canada, where it occupies two million square miles between the Arctic and the Great Lakes. The Highlands were part of that old north land, much of which slowly sank under the sea while vast quantities of its surface were washed off to accumulate as sand and mud. The Torridonian sandstone was thus formed from eroded gneiss 900–750 million years ago, but not as a marine deposit. The rock formed along a continental seaboard from which it passed out under the sea laterally. The overlapping of its strata and the absence of fossils other than plankton show that the land from which it came lay to the north-west and was lifeless desert. Ripple-marks, sun-cracks, and rain-pits show that the sands were deposited in shallow lakes, deltas, and estuaries, while the accumulation of more than 16,000 feet of rock-strata proves that the mass progressively sank, punching the crust deep into the underlying mantle. Finally, a mountain land of red Torridonian sandstone was raised up by crustal warping.

At the same period of time a huge neighbouring rock area of the same sediments (of gneiss) was laid down in shallow sea and then metamorphosed by heat and pressure to form the Moine schists, which in Knoydart have been radiometrically dated to 740 million years. They may be as much as 20,000 feet thick at Fannaich. Like the Torridonian rocks, with which they were originally equivalent, at least in part, they occupied a vastly greater area than now, but unlike the Torridonian were later folded as an Alpine range. These two rock areas were to be forced close together by two subsequent thrust movements (pre- and post-Cambrian).

In course of time the Moine-Torridonian land-mass was reduced to a plain by erosion. A gradual down-warping of the continental mass – possibly along the edge of Canada's Laurentian Shield – allowed a Cambro–Ordovician shelf sea to cover much of Britain and Scandinavia. The old gneiss lands still rose to the north. They supplied by water-transport during the next 100 million years a bulk of sandy sediments so great that their accumulation on the sea-floor had become three miles thick at the start of the Caledonian orogeny.

The Caledonian mountain-building period lasted approximately 130 million years and created a continent known as the Old Red Northland. It included all Scotland from the Southern Uplands northward, Scandinavia, and Greenland – where the mountain chain now heavily dissected runs parallel to the east coast – while farther west its ribs run from Newfoundland south to New York State. The Caledonian mountains rose on a broad front to possibly Himalayan scale. They were built of the sediments of the Cambrian sea-floor, including the underlying Moine rocks. The soft sands and mud by deep burial and stress were metamorphosed into the quartz-ites and crystalline schists that today cover the Central and South Highlands to a depth of at least 13,000 feet – their real thickness may be up to three times as much. They are named Dalradian schists after the first Scots kingdom of Dalriada. The originally flat beds were thrown into mountainous overfolds and often so intensely contorted that older schists overlie younger while enormous masses of magma were intruded to crystallize as granite. Such granite intrusions through both the Moine and Dalradian schists are now exposed to form the Cairngorm plateaux and the territory between Loch Awe and Loch Ericht. The latter outcrop forms a belt 10 miles wide by 40 long including Ben Cruachan, Ben Starav, Clachlet, and the Moor of Rannoch, all of different ages within the Caledonian orogeny. The Moor of Rannoch granite is radiometrically dated to 415 million years and is typical of an older intrusion, whereas the Cruachan granite is younger and belongs to a series of subsidences of which Glen Coe and Ben Nevis (to be described later) are the best examples. Numerous smaller intrusions include Ben Loyal.

This mountainous continent was arid land unprotected by vegetation. At the time of its rising no plants had evolved from the sea in high enough form to invade the land. That important event was to happen in the latter part of the orogeny. Meantime, the barren mountains were attacked by torrential rains and the valleys by floods, which deposited Old Red sandstone in basins and estuaries and shallow seas to a depth of nearly 20,000 feet (Kincardineshire). Gigantic boulder-beds were formed and later consolidated as conglomerates or puddingstone, which may be seen in great quantity on the cliffs behind Oban. In all, three such deposits were made during the Devonian period (Lower, Middle, and Upper Old Red), the younger being of much less depth. An example is the Middle Old Red of Caithness, which lies up to 3,000 feet thick. Other phenomenal events were in train at this time – the Moine Thrust, volcanic eruptions, and the Great Glen fault movement.

The Moine Thrust plane, whose visible phenomena have given

fame to the Moine schists on a 100-mile line between Skye's Sleat Peninsula and Loch Eriboll, was caused by horizontal pressure from east-south-east generated by the Caledonian orogeny. This huge body of schist was thrust forward to override all rocks whether older or younger than itself to westward – the gneiss, sandstone, and Cambrian quartzite-limestone. The gneiss has even been prised up in places, pushed forward, and the rock strata been turned completely upside down. The edge of a limestone plateau that has been thus carried forward can be seen in the pass through Assynt near Loch Awe. It lines the east side of the road. Several springs gush from its base through green grass. The plateau is topped by two 1500-foot hills, Beinn an Fhuarain (Springs Hill) and Beinn nan Cnaimseag (Bearberry Hill), which are ploughed-up rock lifted on to the back of the advancing mass. On either side of Glencoul, south-east of Kylesku, there are splendid examples of displacement where slices of gneiss 1,500 feet thick have been carried over Cambrian quartzite that rests on undisturbed gneiss. These Cambrian strata of shiny quartzite and dark blue or pale limestone, marble, and dolomite, crop out along the whole line of thrust in a band one to eight miles wide between Loch Carron and Loch Eriboll. The quartzite gives a poor and barren soil, most noticeably where it rises to mountain height on the Sutherland range of Foinaven and Arcuil, but where limestone appears in the glens the scene is suddenly brightened by emerald grass or fertile ground. It is not clear whether the Moine Thrust, which had early and late phases, mainly occurred in a succession of rapid movements or was long dispersed. But during the 130 million years of the orogeny the Moine rocks shared in the succession of fold movements that laid down the north-east to south-west grain of the Highlands.

Among the crustal movements that followed the folding, none was more extraordinary than the development of the Great Glen fault between Loch Linnhe and the Moray Firth. The Hercynian orogeny was starting in Europe, America, North Africa, and Siberia. A mountain chain was rising from Ireland through Germany to Russia. The crustal pressures generated caused a wrench-tear in the Great Glen. One suggestion is that over a period of perhaps 100 million years extending into the late Carboniferous, the northern block of Scotland drifted south-west for a distance of 65 miles – an estimate from the correlation of granite at Foyers with that of Strontian. Other geologists argue for a much more complex history. The

1. Red deer hind and fawn.

2. Iron Age broch, Glenelg.

3. Granite slabs, A' Chir ridge, Isle of Arran.

4. South peak of the Cobbler.

Hercynian tear not only split Scotland in two but caused such deep cleavage of the rocks that the crust to this day has remained unstable and subject to earth tremors.

The last phases of igneous activity during the Caledonian earth-movements took place during the Lower Old Red Sandstone period. Volcanoes poured molten lavas over the land. Together with intrusive granite they built the rock formations that now appear (by erosion) as the Pentland Hills, the Ochils, the Sidlaw Hills, the Cheviots, the Lorn plateau, and the mountains of Glen Coe and Ben Nevis.

The Glencoe and Nevis volcanoes were a special kind of peculiar interest, named cauldron subsidence. After the lavas had poured across the land and piled up sheet upon sheet to great thickness, a circular column foundered like a loose-fitting piston in a cylinder block of Dalradian schist. Molten magma welled up through the gap between piston and cylinder-wall and crystallized as granite. Volcanoes round the rim poured lava into the cauldron.

In Glen Coe the cylinder took an oblong form nine miles by five and the column within subsided 4–5,000 feet. The lavas inside were thus protected from the full forces of erosion that have completely stripped them off surrounding country. No sign of this cauldron now persists as a recognizable feature. Its circular fault line runs from Dalness in Glen Etive up Gleann Fhaolinn of Bidean nam Bian to An-t-Sron, down to Loch Achtriochtan in Glen Coe, up to Meall Dearg on the Aonach Eagach, then in an eastward curve through Stob Mhic Mhartuin to Meall a' Bhuiridh. Between there and Dalness the cauldron was later invaded to a depth of five miles by Cruachan granite, which builds Clachlet and its neighbour Beinn Mhic Chasgaig and cuts the lavas of Buachaille Etive Mor. The cauldron fault is narrow and its granite intrusions, compared to those of Ben Nevis, form only a thin vertical shell. They widen out and are best seen on An-t-Sron and Meall Dearg. The mountains of Glen Coe are relics of the deep-sunk lava plug. Their varieties of igneous rock like rhyolite, andesite, or granite, are simply magma which has crystallized differently in response to different rates of cooling or to changes of heat, stress, and pressure. The rhyolites that form Buachaille Etive Mor are the most imposing cliff-scene of their kind in Britain.

The Ben Nevis lavas too were erupted in successive flows over a land surface of schists. At the same time, but far below the surface, a circular fissure was forming in the crust. It widened to five miles in diameter while it was successively intruded by magma in four phases.

THE BEN NEVIS CAULDRON SUBSIDENCE

0   1   2 MILES

0   1   2   3 KM.

N

OUTER GRANITE

Distillery

MARGINAL INTRUSION

MARGINAL INTRUSION

Allt na Coillich

Allt Daim

Allt a' Mhuilinn

INNER GRANITE

Fort William

Achintee

Lochan

▲ Aonach Mor

Carn Mor Dearg ▲

LAVA

▲ Ben Nevis

Aonach Beag ▲

Glen Nevis

INNER GRANITE

Polldubh

River Nevis

GRANITE

Steall

The first three, now called marginal intrusions, crystallized as fine, medium, and coarse-grained granite. A fourth and much broader inner ring was then intruded, which crystallized as porphyritic granite, now called the Outer Granite (in relation to the ring's centre). These four rings were injected rapidly enough to merge into each other before hardening.

The final phase was now at hand. It too occurred subterraneously. The centre of the ring subsided as a cauldron three miles in diameter. Its roof of schist topped by lava then foundered into the magma that filled the cauldron. While it sank, the roof's circumference bent up to shape a basin, giving the rock an inward dip. Since the roof had been relatively cold it chilled the magma to produce round its margin a fine-grained granite, which is well seen on the ridge joining Ben Nevis to Carn Mor Dearg. At the same time the central core of lava was thoroughly baked to produce an andesite resistant to erosion. This core now forms the summit cap, one mile in diameter and 2,000 feet thick, while all the surrounding lava beds have been eroded away to expose the once deeply subterraneous intrusions of pink granite, which form the lower slopes of Ben Nevis and build the surrounding mountains of Carn Dearg, 3348 feet (upper Glen Nevis), Carn Mor Dearg, 4012 feet, Carn Dearg Meadhonach, Aonach Mor, 3999 feet, and Meall an t-Suidhe. The two latter were part of the shell of outer granite, which having more dark minerals than inner granite appears grey against the other's pink.

The cliffs under the summit of Ben Nevis form an arc almost two miles long facing north-east. They still rest on their base of schist 2,000 feet above sea-level, with granite farther below and their mass of andesite lava rising 2,000 feet above. The cliffs have intervening beds of agglomerate, where blocks and boulders of pale quartzite, red felsite, and andesite, exploded by the volcano, have been gathered and consolidated. Everywhere the rocks dip towards the centre, so that ledges and holds usually (but not invariably) slope inwards. The rock mass is exceptionally sound, being hard baked and completely free of dykes, therefore reliable for climbers.

It is important to remember that these rocks, both granites and lavas, lay deep below the land surface, and were exposed only by subsequent denudation.

The Highland period of crustal folding and its volcanic aftermath had lasted 150 million years. There now followed a dormant period nearly twice as long. Dormant is here a relative term. Farther south, volcanoes erupted the lavas of the Campsie Hills and Arthur's Seat (near the future sites of Glasgow and Edinburgh). During this Carboniferous period, tropical jungles flourished and the coal seams of the future were laid down in the Lowlands. The whole land was reduced to an undulating plain, but in the Highland area, down-warpings were developing, which allowed warm shallow seas to cover much of the western area, and to deposit sedimentary rocks (Triassic, Jurassic, and Cretaceous), which outcrop today on Mull, Eigg, Raasay, and Skye. Between the Carboniferous and Jurassic rocks, New Red sandstone accumulated in great quantity, best seen now in Arran, where it covers the south half of the island. The deposits were made by water flow and flash floods. Smaller relics of New Red appear in Skye north of Loch Slapin, and in Ross-shire at Applecross Bay and the Gruinard peninsula. All this while the climate was tropical. The North Pole, which had been centred on the North Pacific in the Cambrian period, had since been 'moving' north-west, while the crustal drift had been shifting Scotland to a point 20 degrees north of the equator. Scotland arrived there in the Permian period and still lay there (approximately) at the time of the Triassic deposits. The climate till then was hot and dry, but began cooling to subtropical before the Tertiary era.

In the first or Eocene period of the Tertiary era, Greenland separated from Norway, with which Scotland remained linked. This drift has been dated to 60 million years ago. There broke out about then in west Scotland the most prolonged volcanic action of Britain's history. Six volcanoes on Arran, Mull, Ardnamurchan, Rum, Skye, and St Kilda poured out lavas in successive flows, some of them 50 feet thick, a few 100 feet, and these over many millions of years spread far across the land, piling up to a high tableland. There were two main phases of eruption. The first built the great lava plateau, which must have been fed from numerous other volcanic centres, some now drowned under the widening sea, for the igneous province extended from Greenland across Iceland to northern Ireland. The flows have been radiometrically dated to 60–50 million years ago. The soil and clay, the plant fossils sandwiched between them, and the scarcity of ash, show that eruptions were not the most violent kind, were intermittent, and shifted from centre to centre, allowing time for normal conditions of growth between outbreaks. Clear trace of the craters has been mostly removed by erosion and the rise of plutonic rocks (granite and gabbro) from below. One crater clearly

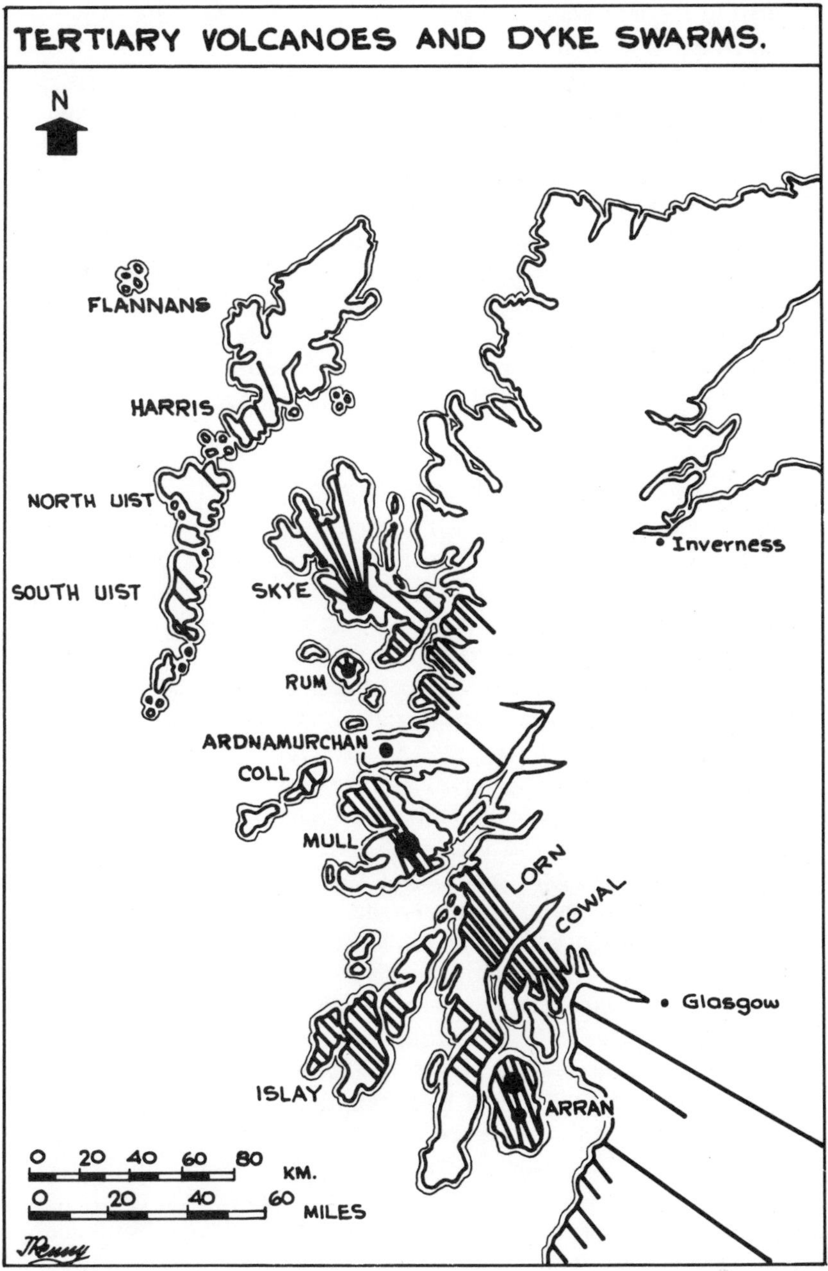

TERTIARY VOLCANOES AND DYKE SWARMS.

N

FLANNANS

HARRIS

NORTH UIST

SOUTH UIST

SKYE

RUM

ARDNAMURCHAN

COLL

MULL

LORN

COWAL

ISLAY

ARRAN

Inverness

Glasgow

0 20 40 60 80 KM.

0   20   40   60 MILES

JRenny

dated to the lava plateau phase is that of Mull, seven miles east of Ben More. It is six miles wide.

The second phase was the rise of magma under enormous pressure but crystallizing subterraneously to form dome-shaped intrusions. These plutonic rocks by deep burial cooked long and cooled slowly to form coarsely crystalline gabbros and granites. Both during and after these intrusions, magma exploded vents through the upper rocks, while linear dykes emplaced along parallel crustal fissures swarmed out as far as north England. These were possibly tension cracks along the continental margin following drift. Their fissure-eruptions came too late to act as feeders for the lava plateau. All take a north-west to south-east course, and swarm thickest through Skye–Glenelg, Knoydart–Morar, Mull–Lorn–Cowal, and Arran–Knapdale–Islay.

The basalt plateau, topped by numerous volcanic cones, formed a huge territory, taller than all surrounding country. The lavas today stand 3,000 feet high on Mull, but then were several thousand feet thicker. Less than 30 million years later, long before the Tertiary era had ended, all, or nearly all, had yet again been reduced to sea-level. So thorough was the dissection and denudation that the roots of the old volcanoes were laid bare even down to the plutonic rocks, once so deeply buried. They appear as St Kilda's cluster of islands – on Hirta, where the granite of Conachair is Scotland's highest sea-cliff (1,397 feet), and on the gabbro stacks and islands standing close by. On Rum, granite builds the Orval hills and gabbro the Cullin ridge. On Arran, granite mountains are thrust up through Dalradian schist and Old Red sandstone. On Skye, granite forms the Red Cuillin and gabbro and basalt the Black. Since all have been exposed by the stripping of less resistant basalt, it is worth noting that much of the Black Cuillin is still basalt because the plutonic rocks were intruded by sheets and dykes of lava, which given such cover had become tougher than the slaggier plateau basalt. But swarms of more brittle dyke-lavas pierced the gabbro and these weathered to gullies and notches leaving pointed peaks and free-standing towers, whereas the Red Cuillin kept more rounded shape.

The Inner Hebrides are relics of that once great plateau. Mull and Skye are the more substantial fragments, clearly displaying the lava flows on terraced hill-slopes, best seen along Mull's west coast, and on truncated faces, which are the sea-cliffs. Only on Mull does plateau-basalt lift to mountain height.

In the latter half of the Tertiary era new crustal movements raised the Alps. At much the same time a prolonged series of upward pulses lasting from 30 to 20 million years ago raised Scotland (as part of Scandinavia) with a shore line west of St Kilda. The land which had been reduced to a near sea-level plain, now rose as a solid block without folding but rose in steps, for the uplifts came in succession off-centre to the west. The new rivers, flowing approximately south-east and west were thus able to cut down through the tableland until they were in time intercepted by rivers running at right-angles along the weaker rocks of faults in the Caledonian structure (as described in the last chapter). The two between them broke up the land, carved the glens, and isolated long mountain ridges, while the normal work of denudation by weather proceeded. Even the hard Moine and Dalradian schists which had been stripped sufficiently during the later Old Red Sandstone period to expose the plutonic granites under the Caledonian mountains, were eroded in places to form valleys 2,500 feet or more deep. In the Northern Highlands, the Torridonian was naturally more completely stripped than the metamorphic Moine, which remains the most extensive rock formation of the Highlands. It forms a band nearly 40 miles wide between the north coast and Morvern (where it passes under the island of Mull), and constitutes the Monadh Liath and much of the Gaick and Atholl forests. The ancient gneiss of the North-West, which had been successively covered by Old Red sandstone and Mesozoic deposits, was now exposed in part.

About 10 or 15 million years ago the landscape was coming a little closer towards the shape of today's, when two major events made Scotland as we know it now recognizable as a land-form and in detail of relief.

The first was the gradual downwarping of Europe's Atlantic margin. The North Sea basin and the Minch were flooded. The second, after a further 10 million years, was the Ice Age. Continental drift had brought the poles to their present position. The hot dry climate of Mesozoic times had been cooling for 100 million years or more, and the apparent consequence was four great glacial advances, the first of which began approximately 600,000 years ago. Each was followed by interglacial periods of warmth, in one of which we now are. In Scotland, no record has been left of the three earlier glaciations – the fourth swept away all deposits.

The last ice-age began 70,000 years ago with a slowly cooling

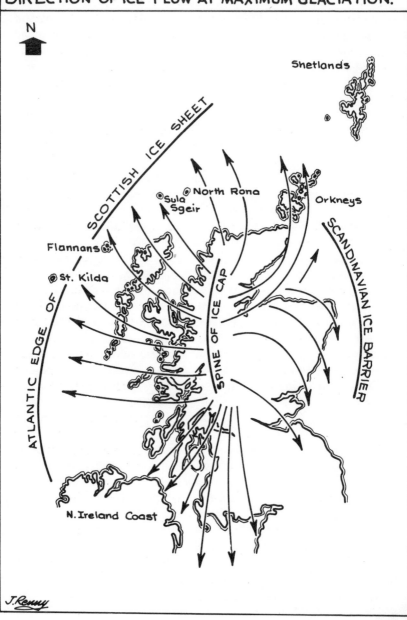

DIRECTION OF ICE FLOW AT MAXIMUM GLACIATION.

N

Shetlands

SCOTTISH ICE SHEET

North Rona

Sula Sgeir

Orkneys

Flannans

St. Kilda

SCANDINAVIAN ICE BARRIER

ATLANTIC EDGE OF

SPINE OF ICE CAP

N. Ireland Coast

J. Renny

climate that reached two maxima of glaciation, the first 55,000 BP (before present), and the second 20,000–12,000 BP (radio-carbon date).

At the earlier glaciation Scotland and Scandinavia bore an ice-cap 5,000 feet thick. It thinned at the edges, where it streamed south into Germany, France, and England. Its western edge, which fell short of St Kilda by only a few miles, ran 2,000 miles from Norway's North Cape to the south of Ireland. The entire Hebrides were buried except for one nunatak where the top of Clisham projected. The Highlands under a cap so thick were not much sculpted by glaciers, for the direction of surface flow at maximum glaciation was not necessarily that of the deep slower-moving and less erosive ice beneath. At a later stage their scourings had notable effects. The eastern flow, deflected south by a big Scandinavian ice-barrier, filled the North Sea down to London, depositing 600 feet of detritus on the bed. The southern flow down the Firth of Clyde filled the Irish Sea to a depth of 1,800 feet, carried sea-shells to the top of Welsh hills, and left Ailsa Craig granite in the English Midlands.

A recession occurred. Temperatures rose and the ice-cap and its glaciers shrank sufficiently to allow a brief return of arctic mammals. Their number included hairy mammoth, woolly rhinoceros, giant deer, elk, reindeer, bear, lemming, and lynx, which were able to move in both from England and direct from Scandinavia across the North Sea basin, for that had again become dry forested land by withdrawal of water locked in polar ice. They were present at least until 27,500 BP (carbon date for woolly rhinoceros in Glasgow). Two thousand years later the second phase had begun. This time Scotland had two glacial centres, on the west coast and Grampian spines. At the maximum glaciation (20,000–17,000 BP), the ice-cap at Rannoch moor was 3,600 feet thick near Glen Coe and 3,000 feet at Schichallion. It maintained this latter depth southward where it crossed the Highland Line, and over the North Highlands rose again to 3,500 feet. East and west it fell to 2,850 feet on the Cairngorms and 1,600 feet on the Hebrides. On the Atlantic edge it fell away over North Rona forty miles out from Cape Wrath. From these figures it is clear that a host of nunataks thrust out from the ice-sheet, notably the tops of Ben Nevis and the Cairngorms, and very many other Munros. It is clear too that western precipitation was much heavier than eastern – as now in rainfall, so then in snowfall. The heavier weight in snow gave a more powerful and prolonged and faster ice action; therefore a much more vigorous dissection of the western hills, with deepening of glens and sea-channels, than occurred eastward. For example, where the westward flowing glaciers were deflected by the Tertiary volcanic mountains in Skye and Mull and Arran, they so deepened the channels that Arran was severed from Kintyre, and Skye and Mull became islands after the later rise in sea-levels. The Loch Alsh and Loch Carron glaciers cut the Sound of Raasay to depths of more than 1,000 feet. (Such deepening of sea-lochs has recently made them attractive to the oil industry for construction of production platforms, where these require deep water for towing to the North Sea.) The eastern hills kept better their smooth pre-glacial topography.

The steeper and faster glaciers on the west coast made other, emphatic landscape shapings. When they gouged the floors of the sea-lochs they shifted forward stone and gravel, which were often deposited as an outer lip or shallows, creating thus an over-deepened inner loch separated by narrows from a broader outer loch, like Loch Nevis. Some of these glacier-lips finally divorced lochs from the sea, like Loch Lomond, Loch Eck, Loch Awe, Loch Shiel, and others. Smaller scale examples are seen in the mountain corries, where the previously down-sloping hollows were gouged out as bowls, raising outer lips that often retained lochans, while the peaks or ridges behind were thinned or made sharper by the plucking action of ice on the rocks under them. Most Highland hills can show examples, the most impressive being the Coruisk basin of the Cuillin, circled by its nine-mile horse-shore of peaks.

The close of the ice age was marked by warmer summers, which brought on a dissolution not steadily progressive, for the ice made two great readvances around 15,000 and 11–10,000 BP, neither of which regained the ground initially lost by the break-up of the two main ice-sheds into numerous independent glacial centres. Retreat lasted longer in the west, for the line of permanent snow rose across the country from west to east; for example, when it had risen in the Cairngorms to 2,000 feet it remained as low as 750 feet on the Outer Hebrides.

There were two distinct phases in retreat: first the reduction of ice-caps to confluent glaciers, thick enough to flow across the ridges between glens and find outlet in several directions; second, the reduction of these to single valley glaciers. The signs of the confluent phase are moraines left on ridges and saddles, and lateral moraines high on the mountain flanks, where they formed terraces.

The high ridges or summits exposed to intense frosts began to disintegrate. The glens had their walls widened and straightened, their ravines ground from V-shape to U-shape, their floors over-deepened, and their lateral spurs truncated to leave hanging valleys – often with later waterfalls. A spectacular example in Glen Nevis is the Steall waterfall, which plunges 350 feet down the lower cliff of Sgurr a' Mhaim. All these scourings were continued into the valley glacier stage. Ice flows were then entirely directed by the walls of the glens, where the rock was striated and exposed. Older moraines on the upper slopes were largely removed and new lateral and terminal moraines left in the glens.

The eastern glaciers died away first. Like the rivers of today, many had long lines of communication to western sources, and advanced into an ever drier climate, hence they retreated west rapidly and died in their tracks. The shorter, better-fed western glaciers persisted much longer to sea terminals where they died so fast that surface stone was left unmarshalled. Thus the moors on the north side of the Cuillin are hummocked by drift where the huge Sligachan glacier wasted away. In the Cairngorms, such deposition of drift occurred on a greater scale. On their north side, for example, nearly all solid rock of the low ground (the Moine schists) became deeply buried under the gravel, sand, and clay left behind in mounds by the Glen More glacier (a branch of the Spey glacier), which flowed north through the Ryvoan pass, hence its deposits are all schists, not granite from the Cairngorms. It left moraines across the glen when retreating, one of which pounded An Lochain Uaine, and another Loch Morlich, the latter also occupying a 'kettle-hole' or depression where a great block of stagnant glacier melted. Not all deposits are morainic. For example, the big terraces in Glen Einich and the entrance to the Lairig Ghru are deposits left by running water, because the Glen More glacier had dammed the valleys to form temporary lochs. The Rothiemurchus and Abernethy forests owe their excellent growth to the soil given by thick glacial drift.

Most of the best or most easily seen exhibits of glacial action on rock are to be found in the Cuillin; the broad and striated gabbro sill between Loch Coruisk and Loch Scavaig; the immense gabbro slabs of Coire a' Ghrunnda, smoothed to boiler-plates; the scooping of rock bowls under splintered peaks, and of Loch Coruisk's huge basin to 100 feet below sea-level, and many others. Similar effects can be observed in every part of the Highlands by anyone who uses his eyes.

The two great readvances of Scottish ice are named the Aberdeen–Lammermuir and the Lomond Readvances. The latter (11–10,000 BP) was named from the southward growth of the Loch Lomond glacier, but intense cold was general. Lochaber was refilled by confluent glaciers, which dammed the wide mouth of Glen Spean so that mountain waters flowing in behind the ice-barrier formed huge lochs, not only in Glen Spean and the side-valley of Glen Roy, but also in Glen Gloy, which opens off the Great Glen three miles north. The beaches formed well-marked terraces on both sides of all three glens. They are now famous as the Parallel Roads, most clearly seen in Glen Roy, which opens north off Glen Spean at Roy Bridge. As the dams were reduced or breached, the lochs formed beaches at successively lower levels, which in Glen Roy appear at approximately 1,149 feet, 1,068 feet, and 857 feet. The only level seen in Glen Gloy is 1,165 feet, and in Glen Spean 855 feet.

The start of the post-glacial period for Scotland, called the Holocene, began c. 10,300 BP when the Lomond Readvance ended. The general retreat then became faster, because much ice had vanished from the land during the warmer (subarctic) centuries. The last phase was the withdrawal of valley glaciers to the upper glens, then to higher corries, and finally to the farthest mountain recesses such as the Garrachory of Braeriach, Coire Leis on Ben Nevis, the north corrie of Ben More Assynt, Coire a' Ghrunnda in Skye, and many others like them, where they slowly dwindled, lingering to a late period. All these had probably gone by 10,000 BP or soon after.

The ice age had two important aftermaths: rises in land and sea levels. The Highlands, depressed into the earth's mantle for thousands of years by the enormous load of ice on top, now lifted up in several movements of isostatic recovery. Rannoch Moor, which had carried the greatest weight, was the centre of an oval ring of uplift that included the Inner Hebrides. Each rise was followed by a period of rest long enough for coastal beaches to become established. These Raised Beaches appear round the coast – and also in the middle of the Great Glen – at heights between 25 and 100 feet above present sea-level. The real rises were nearly double these figures, for they have been masked by an almost equal post-glacial rise in sea-level caused by polar ice-melt in the years 8,500–5,500 BP. The world sea had begun rising after 17,000 BP, when it was 225 feet below present level. Sometime after 14,000 BP the rising sea flooded over the broad land-bridge between Lorn and Ireland, which had included the hill-groups of Islay, Jura, and Colonsay; had filled the glens between Mull and Morvern, Skye and Glenelg, Arran and Kintyre; and had split the Outer Hebrides into its numerous component parts.

The Highlands and Islands were thus created as we know them: crustal movements had forged and elevated the rocks; water had carved them, washing away thousands of feet of solid rock to shape the rough forms we can recognize today; and ice had sculpted these more finely, adding features and removing bulk, sweeping the landscape clean. No finishing touch had been given, for to landscape change there is no end. Life too had been swept away. Two thousand years were to pass before the Highlands were fully ready to receive man. Meantime, the colonization by plant and animal life had begun.

3   Colonization by Plant and Animal Life

Throughout the Ice Age, Britain remained a European peninsula and no ground south of the Thames had been glaciated. As soon as temperatures rose above 6°C (43°F), which in southern England may have been 20,000 years ago, the first colonizing plants were able to start moving north. These were mosses, lichens, sedges, dwarf birch and willow, mountain dryas, and juniper, which are today found on Scotland's hilltops. The Scottish post-glacial period opened around 10,300 BP (before present), but 4,000 years earlier the Lowland tundra carried enough plant life to feed hairy mammoths. Their tusks have been carbon-dated to 13,700 BP, after the first readvance of valley glaciers. A thousand years later, before the final Lomond readvance, the Highland spine of Ross-shire at Loch Droma was growing a general plant-cover of crowberry heath type with occasional birch-copses. Lower ground would have a longer growing season and a richer arctic vegetation. One advantage of an early post-glacial period is that soils are made fertile by minerals ground off the rocks; plants thrive on these and spread rapidly, tenaciously holding their ground despite subarctic cold. The tundra was well established with heather and crowberry in 12,000 BP, when temperatures in south Scotland rose to 10°C (50°F) in summer (the same as Iceland's today), and minus 7°C (19°F) in winter. Then came the Lomond readvance and for 1,700 years little or no pollen is found in deposits.

From 10,000 BP onwards there were five pronounced climatic changes, which have been dated by radio-carbon test and analysis of pollen:

10,000 BP	Pre-boreal	sub-arctic
10–7,000 BP	Boreal	dry and warmer
7–5,000 BP	Atlantic	warm and wet
4–3,000 BP	Sub-boreal	warm and dry
2,500 BP	Sub-atlantic	wet and cool, continuing

10,000 BP. After 10,000 BP, when the last permanent ice had melted off the Highlands, the tundra was invaded by juniper and then by sparse forests of birch, pine, and hazel. Long before that time, birds that could tolerate sub-arctic weather, like ptarmigan, willow grouse, snow buntings, golden plovers, red-necked phalaropes, black- and red-throated divers, and dotterels, would closely follow the retreating snow. Arctic birds then breeding and resident would probably include gyr falcons, king eiders, and ivory gulls. Birds flying north from the temperate countries to breed in Scotland in summer would be whooper swans, greylag, barnacle, and white-fronted geese; from warmer countries came knots, bar-tailed godwits, little auks, and pomarine and long-tailed skuas. Many other birds would be present only as summer migrants to the Isles and seaboard from breeding stations far to the south, like the cormorants, auks, and petrels.

The mammals too had long since been arriving. Among the first were hairy mammoths, but evidence of these disappears from 13,500 BP. After them came reindeer, elk, Irish elk that stood 6 feet and bore 90 lb antlers, red deer of much greater bulk than now, northern lynx, lemming, beaver, horse, goat, wolf, wild ox that stood 6 feet at the shoulder and carried horns of 4-foot span from tip to tip, fox, wild cat, stoat, otter, badger, blue hare, brown bear, and many others. When the first mammals were entering the Highlands the sea-channels in winter were solid with pack ice, so that most were able to reach the Hebrides. All were able to swim. Polar bears were probably early visitors.

10–7,000 BP. The Boreal period opened with growing warmth and dry weather that lasted 3,000 years, yet not so warm or dry as to inhibit peat formation, which began around 9,500 BP. The mainland, excluding the North Highlands, grew a forest of birch and Scots pine that was sufficiently open to allow such increase of hazel scrub that the three formed a closed canopy to the exclusion of heath. Where the ground was favourable, oak and elm spread well. This change from open pasture, which had grown a rich arctic vegetation, caused the extinction of the giant Irish elk. It was too bulky to survive; whereas red deer, formerly a much heavier animal than now, was able to adapt by reducing body-weight. The birds arriving at this time probably included the osprey, capercaillie, crested tit (now found mainly in Strathspey and Strathnairn), and crossbill. Among the songbirds coming in were the willow warbler, hedge sparrow, wren, and coal tit.

Around 8,000 BP the rising sea and subsidence of the North Sea

47

basin caused the opening of the Dover Strait. Only the flora that had already dispersed into Britain is thereafter called native. Although the spread of plants by natural means (air and sea currents and bird excreta) continued, many flowering plants, slower-moving than others, were stopped at the Channel, as also warmth-loving mammals. Thus Britain received only two-thirds of the mammal species that were able to reach Scandinavia. The most important new immigrants were men, whose charcoal found in a hearth in Fife has been dated to 6,100 BC (8,000 BP).

7–5,000 BP. The Atlantic period opened with a remarkable rise in mean annual temperature of 2°C (3·6°F) higher than today's. It came with a heavier rainfall, to which the Highlands responded by raising the forest tree-line to 2,000 feet. In the West, the deciduous forest became dense, while the North Highlands had a spread of birch and hazel that attained its greatest extent around 5,000 BP. The Lowlands were invaded by alder, which failed to gain ground northward, because the Highlands after suffering too prolonged rain were developing a wide spread of peat bog. Sphagnum moss choked out the scrub hazel, while pine and birch were robbed of opportunity for regeneration by the peat deposits. Ling heather spread fast over leached ground and up on the hills the tree line was cut back. Two animals only were unable to adapt to the change of climate (the lemming and the northern rat vole) – henceforth, man was to become the destroyer.

4–3,000 BP. Two thousand years of wet weather ended around 4,500 BP, to be followed by a nearly equal sum of warm dry during the Sub-boreal period. The basic pattern of woodland had been established in the Atlantic phase, and now this was hugely extended. The Highland forest mounted to 3,300 feet (today's upper limit is 2,000). Much peat bog was won over to woodland; oak, elm, rowan, and pine became widespread through the Highlands, with oak predominating in the West, pine and birch with oak in the Central and East Highlands, and birch in Sutherland and Caithness. Birch–hazel scrub clothed even St Kilda. One consequence was that bird life achieved a density never known before or since (oakwoods carry more birds than any other natural habitat), although when tree-cover was finally lost great numbers of woodland birds still held to the cleared ground. Forest clearance for cattle grazing began in Scotland around 3,000 BP, but not in the Highlands until a thousand years later, when the Picts were resisting Roman invasion.

5. The Cobbler, Loch Long and Firth of Clyde.   *Dalradian schist*

6. The Cobbler
Corrie.

7. Ben Cruachan, summit ridge.

8. The Blackmount. Corrie Ba and Stob Ghabhar.

2,500 BP. The last major change in climate occurred around 500 BC, when the Celtic tribes were moving north through Britain. The dry and sunny weather was succeeded by the wet cold climate of the Sub-atlantic period, which has ever since enveloped the British Isles. Temperatures fell 2°C (3·6°F). Moorland birds spread, for the effect on vegetation was recession of the tree-line, resumption of peat development, and the advance of heather on high ground.

In the story of Scottish vegetation, the Highlands' mountain plants hold a unique place by reason of their descent from pre-glacial times, their biological adaptations, and beauties of form and colour. There is interpolated here a brief account of them, written by Dr Hilary H. Birks and Dr H. J. B. Birks of Cambridge University, two of the country's authorities.

SCOTTISH MOUNTAIN PLANTS

When walking or climbing in the Scottish mountains you may have noticed that the vegetation changes with altitude, and that many of the plants in the vegetation are different from those of the bogs, moors, and grasslands of the lower slopes. These differences become more marked the higher you go, until on the highest ground you find plants which are virtually restricted to summit areas.

In a quiet moment resting on the summit of a mountain, you may wonder why the mountain plants up there are different, and how they came to be growing there, often many miles from their nearest neighbours on another mountain.

Scottish mountain plants are often termed 'arctic-alpine' plants for the reason that they also grow in the Alps and/or the Pyrenees of mainland Europe and in the tundras of Arctic Scandinavia. Within the Scottish flora there are in addition several so-called 'arctic-subarctic' plants that are otherwise restricted to Arctic Europe (for example the arctic mouse-ear chickweed *Cerastium arcticum*). There are also a few purely 'alpine' plants, such as mossy cyphel (*Cherleria sedoides*) whose Scottish localities are the northernmost in Europe. The Scottish mountains thus form a small but very important part of the total European distribution of the arctic, alpine, and arctic-alpine plants.

In considering the history of the Scottish mountain flora we must realize that during the last Ice Age all plant and animal life retreated southwards from the ice, although it is possible that a few hardy species may have survived on nunataks in Scotland, just as they do today in parts of Greenland.

During the last glaciation, the area of Britain south of the ice supported a tundra-like vegetation consisting of plants which could tolerate the open, unstable conditions and the rigorous climate, including many of our Scottish mountain plants. Evidence for the presence of these plants in lowland England at this time is provided by plant remains preserved in peats, muds, and silts deposited in waterlogged situations between about 30,000 and 15,000 years ago (as determined by radiocarbon dating). The results of analysing the fossil pollen and seed remains give us a good idea of what the vegetation was like at that time and how the vegetation has changed since the end of the Ice Age about 10,000 years ago. The vegetation of Britain at this time was treeless and mountain plants were common everywhere. However, with the warming of the climate and the development of soil on the glacial deposits, other plants could colonize the landscape. Juniper was one of the first and it formed extensive thickets throughout Britain at the beginning of the post-glacial period. Birch and hazel soon followed and as the post-glacial progressed deciduous forests occupied most of England, Wales, and southern Scotland, and pine became abundant in the central Highlands. In the north and on the islands, birch and hazel, possibly with some oak in the west, were the only common trees able to grow.

The plants of the Ice-Age tundra cannot grow in the shade and competition of trees, with the result that they were rapidly eliminated from the lowlands and had to find refuge on the mountains above the tree-line. At present virtually all of lowland Scotland is deforested and you may wonder why the mountain plants do not spread down there again. There are several reasons. Many species are adapted to cold arctic or alpine conditions and are killed by the high temperatures of the lowlands. Many of them also require open base-rich soils. Over the last 10,000 years under the heavy Scottish rainfall, most of the soils have been leached and thoroughly acidified, and large areas have even turned into peat bog. There are, however, some exceptions. For example, soils on limestones and other basic rocks are still base-rich, and many screes, cliffs, and river gravels are sufficiently open and unstable to maintain a steady supply of soil nutrients. In such places mountain plants can often be found, frequently descending to sea-level, especially in the north-west where the summers are cool. An additional reason for the continued restriction of mountain plants is the almost universal grazing of our hills by sheep and deer. Many mountain plants cannot withstand grazing, and are thus restricted to inaccessible areas such as cliff ledges and steep gullies.

With increasing altitude up a mountain the vegetation gradually changes. The heather zone of the Eastern Highlands and the heather and bog zone of the west give way to bilberry (*Vaccinium myrtillus*) and crowberry (*Empetrum nigrum*) heaths and to grass heaths. Physical factors, particularly wind exposure and drainage, affect the vegetation quite markedly. There is often a dramatic vegetational change where there is some shelter and where snow can lie in the early summer. When the snow has melted these areas can be easily distinguished by the great abundance of mat grass (*Nardus stricta*), bilberry, and a variety of mosses and lichens. Mountain plants such as alpine lady's mantle (*Alchemilla alpina*), *Sibbaldia procumbens*, least willow (*Salix herbacea*), and least cudweed (*Gnaphalium supinum*) may occur here. In longer lasting snow-patches there is often a striking zonation, with a moss-dominated zone within the mat-grass zone and, in the centre where the snow lies longest, an area of small creeping liverworts and lichens.

In contrast exposed summit plateaux are often clothed with a continuous carpet of the grey woolly hair moss (*Rhacomitrium lanuginosum*), often appearing wave-like in response to the wind. Closer examination of this moss-heath reveals scattered plants of mountain sedge (*Carex bigelowii*), least willow, fir clubmoss (*Lycopodium selago*), and occasional dwarfed plants of moss campion (*Silene acaulis*), mossy cyphel, and viviparous bistort (*Polygonum viviparum*). In very exposed areas the ground may appear to be just stones, the so-called 'fell-field', but here many low-growing plants may be found such as the mountain azalea (*Loiseleuria procumbens*), black bearberry (*Arctous alpinus*), spiked woodrush (*Luzula spicata*), least willow, and mountain sedge. Such fell-fields are the habitats of some of our rarest mountain plants, such as *Artemisia norvegica* (restricted to a few remote hills in West Ross) and *Diapensia lapponica* (on a single hill near Glenfinnan). In wetter areas within open stony ground on the basalts of Skye and Mull grows the curious little annual, Iceland purslane (*Koenigia islandica*) along with the three-flowered rush (*Juncus triglumis*).

Mountain grassland covers much of the gentler slopes, the main grasses being bent-grass (*Agrostis tenuis*), fescue (*Festuca ovina*). wavy hair-grass (*Deschampsia flexuosa*), and in damper, richer places, tufted hair-grass (*D. cespitosa*). The fir and alpine clubmosses (*Lycopodium selago* and *L. alpinum*) commonly grow in such grassland. Three-leaved rush (*Juncus trifidus*) is another common mountain plant, which, in the Cairngorms, covers many acres of summit plateau and is a fine sight in the autumn when the foliage is russet coloured.

Boulder fields and screes are another typical habitat for mountain plants. *Rhacomitrium* moss may clothe the more stable boulders, and the crevices in between are good places to look for ferns such as parsley fern (*Cryptogramma crispa*) and alpine lady-fern (*Athyrium alpestre*). Amongst basic rocks you may chance upon the handsome but rare holly fern (*Polystichum lonchitis*).

To find a large variety of mountain plants you must look on cliffs and broken ground where there are open conditions with less competition from the dominant species of the main vegetation types, where there is protection from grazing, and where the soils are richer because of the general instability.

The Cairngorms contain some of the finest cliffs in the Highlands, but the rock, mainly granite, is acid and is superficially rather dull to the botanist. Although the variety of plants is not large, there are several rarities virtually restricted to the Cairngorm corries by virtue of the high altitude and cold climate. Amongst these are the brook saxifrage (*Saxifraga rivularis*) growing in high wet gullies, the tall blue sow-thistle (*Cicerbita alpina*) restricted to large inaccessible cliff-ledges, the highland cudweed (*Gnaphalium norvegicum*) on stony gullies in cliffs, the tufted saxifrage (*S. cespitosa*) on high-level mildly basic rocks in one or two remote corries, alpine speedwell (*Veronica alpina*) flowering in damp clefts, and curved woodrush (*Luzula arcuata*) with its drooping heads growing insignificantly in open gravel in stone shoots and gullies. Otherwise the acid cliffs are rather unrewarding for the botanist, for he will find only a few species, such as bilberry, starry saxifrage (*S. stellaris*), and least willow brightened up by the occasional yellow splash of an alpine hawkweed (*Hieracium* spp.).

Cliffs composed of more basic rocks are easily recognized by their greener more fertile appearance and by the luxuriant grassy slopes below favoured by sheep. The commonest, and some of the most attractive, mountain plants are to be found on such crags. You have to be early in the year to see purple saxifrage (*S. oppositifolia*) at its most handsome, but later on you will be rewarded by the magnificent hanging gardens of lush herbs such as globe flower (*Trollius europaeus*), red campion (*Silene dioica*), sorrel (*Rumex acetosa*), alpine mouse-ear chickweed (*Cerastium alpinum*), rose root (*Sedum rosea*), wood cranesbill (*Geranium sylvaticum*), alpine saw wort (*Saussurea alpina*), stone bramble (*Rubus saxatilis*), and mountain sorrel (*Oxyria digyna*). Occasionally the handsome mountain willows such as *Salix lapponum*, *S. myrsinites*, and, more rarely, *S. lanata* grow with the herbs on the more inaccessible ledges. Festoons of the yellow mountain saxifrage (*Saxifraga aizoides*) mixed with purple saxifrage, alpine meadow-rue (*Thalictrum alpinum*), and alpine meadow-grass (*Poa alpina*) occur on dripping basic cliffs and in gullies. On drier basic rocks you may be lucky and find the elegant white mountain avens (*Dryas octopetala*) with leaves like miniature shiny oak leaves, growing with alpine cinquefoil (*Potentilla crantzii*), black sedge (*Carex atrata*), hair sedge (*C. capillaris*), reticulate willow (*Salix reticulata*), holly fern, and the rather elusive alpine saxifrage (*Saxifraga nivalis*). You will have to go to special localities to see the rarer cliff plants, such as the Cuillin of Skye for alpine rock-cress (*Arabis alpina*). The Breadalbane range (including Ben Lawers) and the Caenlochan–Clova hills to the south of the Cairngorms contain the greatest concentrations of rare mountain plants by virtue of their soft basic rocks and their high altitude. Notable rarities include alpine forget-me-not (*Myosotis alpestris*), alpine milk-vetch (*Astragalus alpinus*), snow gentian (*Gentiana nivalis*), mountain bladder-fern (*Cystopteris montana*), yellow oxytropis (*O. campestris*) boreal fleabane (*Erigeron borealis*), drooping saxifrage (*Saxifraga cernua*), and rock speedwell (*Veronica fruticans*). However, some of these and other rarities have now been discovered in other, more remote areas, such as the Ben Alder range, the Nevis hills, the Beinn Dearg–Seana Bhraigh hills in West Ross, and the Glen Feshie area west of the Cairngorms, so there is still the possibility of the great thrill of discovering a rarity in a new locality in a botanically unexplored range of mountains.

Now that you have an idea of the history of our mountain flora and the great difficulties under which these plants survive today in Scotland, you will be able to appreciate them for their beauty as individual living plants and for their toughness and tenacity against the harsh natural environment, coupled with additional man-made hazards such as the creation of sheep walks, deer forests, and grouse moors. Since the last century, botanists have been the greatest threat to the rarer plants through their urge to collect them. There are now more dried-up specimens of some of our rarest plants in herbaria than there are growing on the hills today. There are documented extinctions as a result of collectors, and even within the last ten years rarities such as the alpine woodsia fern (*Woodsia alpina*) have decreased in Scotland due to collecting. Perhaps the most pleasing way now of preserving the beauty of a mountain plant and the rich memories it evokes is by plant photography but this requires patience, skill, and determination to produce an attractive picture. Rock climbers also owe it to our flora to take care when clearing vegetation from ledges that rarities are not destroyed. They have the unique opportunity of exploring parts of cliffs inaccessible to the average botanist and they could well make some exciting discoveries if they were to notice the plant life around them for its intrinsic interest, rather than simply as a nuisance on the climb.

Hilary H. Birks and H. J. B. Birks

BOG

While the mountain plants hold pride of place in the history of vegetation, the Highlands are hardly less well known for their moorland bog and its untold wealth in peat. Peat-formation is caused by an annual deposit of withered vegetation, which fails to decay when the action of micro-organisms is stopped by cold, wet, or acid ground. It then piles up year by year as a thickening mat, which over the last 9,000 years has buried 700,000 acres under layers from 2 to 20 feet deep. Much peat-covered land (nearly 50,000 acres) has in the last 20 years been reclaimed for agriculture by fertilization and re-seeding; but deep peat-banks have given the Highlanders a valuable fuel resource over the last few thousand years. Peat is still much burned in crofters' houses along the north and west coasts and in the Hebrides. The smell of peat-reek in the evening air has long welcomed the tired walker or climber on his way down from the hills.

The plant communities that give rise to peat-bog and thrive on it are classified as blanket bog, basin bog, and raised bog, according to the kind of ground they occupy and manner of growth. *Blanket bog*, unlike the others, does not depend on the accumulation of local drainage water but on constant rain or humidity, and granted that it spreads across the land as a continuous cover (except on rock outcrops and steep slopes), and there will continue to build itself up year by year indefinitely. It depends on an oceanic climate and is not well developed anywhere else in Europe except the Norwegian seaboard and west Ireland. *Basin bog* forms in hollows where water gathers and stagnates after draining off acid rocks. It depends not on high rainfall but bad drainage – glacier-scooped gneiss is ideal. The bog then produced is confined to the wet basin, where sphagnum becomes the dominant plant. *Raised bog* can then be formed as a secondary growth on top of the basin bog, building up until it fills the basin and flows over, sometimes rising above the outside moor. The upper growth is no longer watered from its parent basin, and to maintain growth it now requires the rain and humid air essential to blanket bog. The distinction between raised and blanket bog can often be uncertain.

There has been little or no change in bog vegetation since the Boreal period. The common plants are ling heather, bog myrtle, cross-leaved heath, purple moor grass, deer-grass, cotton-grass, bog asphodel, sundew, and sphagnum in the wettest areas. The species vary widely according to ground, climate, and altitude, and more markedly from east to west. The typical eastern plants on the blanket bog are the dwarf shrubs like ling and bell heather, bearberry, cowberry, and hummocked mosses, whereas the west is dominated by purple moor grass and sedges like deer-grass and cotton-grass. The eastern plants are all present in the west, but restricted in area by the heavier rainfall. On the other hand, rain appears to encourage in the west plants that beyond Scotland grow in richer conditions, such as bog rush, bog myrtle, long-leafed sundew, mud sedge, cow wheat, and several liverworts that thrive in the north-west.

The plants of the blanket bog vary too from north to south and by height above sea-level. Low ground tends to be grassy and sedgy rather than heathery. The high-level bog of the Grampians is characterized by its stronger element of arctic-alpine flora. Above 1,750 feet, where the peat ends, the common plants are sheep's fescues, bent grasses, mat grass (changing to soft rush in wet places), and wavy hair grass, growing amid a sparse cover of heather, blaeberry, crowberry, wild thyme, and perhaps creeping azalea. The plants mentioned are only the barest indication of the many others that may be present at all levels of bog country, and without reference to the arctic-alpine flowering species.

MAMMALS

Mammals came into the Highlands as permanent residents earlier than birds, and before the glacial readvances, through which some would be able to persist. It is unlikely that any, except introduced species like the rabbit, arrived in the Highlands after the Atlantic period. That may seem a short time for any evolutionary change to be seen, yet several Highland species have differentiated from European and British, and several Hebridean from Highland. No mammal has evolved as a separate species. As might be expected, most that have differentiated are island-bound, cut off from mating with mainland relatives. They are the stoat of Islay and Jura, smaller than the mainland breed and akin to the Scandinavian; the Hebridean field mouse, with shorter ears, longer feet, greater weight, and bigger; the St Kilda field mouse, of still bigger size, which is believed to be the only mammal of Scotland to survive the Ice Age – St Kilda lay beyond the ice-cap; the Rum field mouse; the short-tailed vole of all islands except Lewis, with other sub-species on Muck, Eigg, Gigha, and Lewis; the bank voles of Mull and Raasay; and the common shrew of Islay. The blue hare, native only to the Highlands (and introduced later to other parts of Britain) has evolved there as a smaller sub-species with a coat never entirely white. Thus it is apparent that mammal sub-species have been thrown up mainly by the rodents and insectivores. But the best-known of Highland sub-species is the wild cat, *Felix silvestris grampia*, which is usually 3 feet long from nose to tail with a body-weight of 15 lb. Its colour is darker than the European race with blacker markings on the legs and black rings round the bushy tail. Its distribution covers the entire Highland area except Kintyre, the Hebrides, and the eastern counties. It does not normally go above 1,500 feet and has not ventured south of the Highland Line. A kitten was caught swimming from Glenelg to Skye, so that a return to the Isles is not beyond possibility (wild cat bones dated to the Iron Age have been found in Lewis).

Fourteen wild mammals have become extinct in the Highlands and Islands in post-glacial times. They are, in order of extinction:

1. Giant Irish elk: Unable to adapt to forest growth and climate of Boreal period.
2. Lemming: Small rodent, unable to meet climatic change of Atlantic period.
3. Northern rat vole: Unable to meet climatic change, Atlantic period.
4. Northern lynx: Killed out by Neolithic man.

5. Brown bear: Killed out in 10th century by hunting and destruction of forest.
6. Reindeer: Killed out in 12th century by hunting and destruction of forest. Reintroduced in 1954.
7. Elk: Killed out in 14th century by hunting and destruction of forest.
8. Ox (aurochs): Killed out in 14th century by hunting and forest clearance.
9. Beaver: Killed out in early 16th century by hunting for its fur.
10. Boar: Killed out in early 17th century by hunting and forest destruction.
11. Horse.
12. Wolf: Killed out by man mid-18th century and by forest destruction.
13. Harvest mouse: Last recorded in Outer Hebrides, 1903.
14. Black rat: Last recorded in Outer Hebrides, 1903.

At the present day there are 38 wild land mammals inhabiting the Highlands and Islands, excluding sub-species, and domestic animals gone wild like the sheep of Soay. Introduced species are marked with an asterisk.

Red deer
Fallow deer*
Sika deer*
Reindeer*
Roe deer

Goat*

Fox
Badger
Wildcat
Otter
Polecat
Pine marten
Stoat
Weasel
Mink*

Red squirrel
Grey squirrel*
Bank vole
Short-tailed vole
Water vole
Musk rat*
Brown rat
Long-tailed field mouse
House mouse

Hedgehog
Common shrew
Pygmy shrew
Water shrew
Mole

Daubenton's bat
Pipistrelle bat
Long-eared bat

Brown hare   Natterer's bat (Loch Fyne)
Blue hare   Whiskered bat (Kinlochrannoch)
Rabbit*   Noctule bat (Moray)

The red deer of Europe is a woodland animal, nearly double the weight of the Scottish red deer, which has adapted to bare moorland and mountain territory. A stag's antlers rarely grow to more than 12 points in the Highlands, whereas in Germany they may grow to 24. This difference marks the harder living conditions in Scotland, yet the red deer there do not seek woodland when available, except for temporary shelter in winter storms. They forage on all wild ground, in the Highlands and Islands only, from sea-level to the mountain tops, but do so on a seasonal basis – in summer they keep high in the corries and on upper slopes, and in winter come down to the moors, glens, and more sheltered ground. They are gregarious, moving in herds each with a distinct although overlapping grazing territory. The stags and hinds keep apart for most of the year, and come together for the rut, which starts in mid-September and lasts about six weeks. The hinds calve in June.

The only other deer native to Scotland is the roe. It stands only 2 feet at the shoulder (half the height of a red deer) and is definitely a woodland animal. At dusk it will go up to the bare hill slopes to graze, but by day keeps to close cover low down, especially birch and oak scrub when available. Like red deer they have their own territories, but unlike the red the sexes do not segregate; they move in family parties (buck, doe, and fawns) rather than herds. The fawns are born in May or early June.

Reindeer were introduced to the Cairngorms from Scandinavia in 1954 as a kept herd. They now number 100 of Highland birth.

The fox is common throughout the whole Highland area, but its island presence is reduced to Skye alone. They range from the moors right over the mountain tops, where their spoor is a common sight on the snow. Their diet is principally deer and sheep carrion, and the remainder hares, shrews, voles, and rabbits when available – much the same as the eagles'. There is no hunting to hounds on the hills. The fox is shot, but maintains its numbers.

Badgers are plentiful in some Highland areas, scarce in others, and absent from the Hebrides. They excavate ramifying burrows or sets, either in woodland from sea-level upwards, or on open but lower hill-slopes where fallen crags give shelter. They are omnivorous, and will eat most animals from slugs and worms and beetles to rabbits and hedgehogs, and vegetables like bluebell bulbs, roots, acorns, grain, and much else.

Otters like badgers have been much persecuted in the past – the badgers for allegedly preying on farm-stock, and the otters for their fishing skill. Otters are usually sea-fishers, but also eat birds, rats, mice, and frogs. They haunt burns, lochs and woods throughout the Highlands.

The stoat, weasel, polecat, and pine marten may be difficult to tell apart at a distance, all being small animals with brown backs and lighter underparts. The stoat and weasel are red-brown, the other two rich or dark brown. The pine marten and polecat are very much the larger of the four, and weigh 2–3 lb against the weasel's 2–4 ounces or the stoat's 4–11 ounces. The stoat turns white in winter but has a black tail-tip at all times. The pine marten has the longest tail, about 12 inches, at least four times longer than the weasel's and more than double the stoat's. Polecats have a large creamy patch between the ears and eyes. The stoat, weasel, and polecat all make dens in holes, such as old rabbit burrows or the crannies in dry-stone dykes or tumbled rocks. The pine marten (like the wild cat) prefers holes at tree-roots or between rocks and boulders, but will often nest on tree-tops using a deserted drey or the nest of a large bird. A woodland animal by nature, it is expert at catching birds and squirrels. When it came close to extinction around 1900, through destruction of forests and gamekeepers' persistent use of gin-traps to catch rabbits or birds of prey, a few managed to adapt by retreating to the screes of Reay Forest, Assynt, and the Fannaichs. From there they have gradually spread south again to Wester Ross and the Great Glen, and east more sparsely to the Monadh Liath and Cairngorms. In 1972 one was reported from Raasay after a century's absence from the Hebrides. All four of these carnivores prey on rabbits, the smaller mammals, and birds, and take eggs, insects, and amphibians. The true polecat is rare in Scotland. Nearly all alleged sightings prove to be of feral ferrets, which are albino in the domesticated variety but produce a brown crossbreed after mating with polecats.

Amphibians. The amphibians of the Highlands are all three newts (webbed, crested, and common), toads on the lower moors, and frogs up to 2,000 feet. Frogs sometimes go higher. I have seen the spawn in a lochan at 3,000 feet on Clachlet. They have been recorded at 3,400 feet in the Cairngorms.

Reptiles. The reptiles are slow worms (8 inches) near sea-level, not often seen, common lizards (5 inches) up to 2,000 feet, rarely above unless in favoured places like the east corrie of Beinn Laoigh, where I have seen them basking at 2,500 feet, and adders (20–30 inches). The diamond pattern down the adder's brown back conceals it well on moorland. It is rarely seen in the South Highlands, but seems to thrive in the Cairngorms and north of the Great Glen, for example in Glen Affric, where I have seen more lizards than anywhere else in the Highlands. Reptiles can swim, therefore all are present on the Inner Hebrides and Arran, but only the slow worm has reached the Outer Hebrides. Since the Inner Isles also have all amphibians, which cannot endure salt water, these were probably introduced as tadpoles.

Insects. The Highland insects, and also the spiders and allied animals (arachnids) are so numerous that I make no account. The *lepidoptera* alone would overtax space, and I refer the reader to the two books, *Butterflies* and *Moths* written by E. B. Ford. The ants, bees, beetles, dragon-flies, and spiders are in particular absorbing studies, although ticks and midges, which have always had intimate relations with mountaineers, have bulked larger in literature since dining for four months on Prince Charles Edward Stewart. The midge plague falls across the entire Highland area in summer. Research work to find a way of reducing them to tolerable proportions has failed. They thrive in damp warmth, and are therefore at their worst in the West Highlands during July and August, but are tolerable in early June before they prodigiously multiply, and in September which is cooler and sometimes drier. Butterflies and moths are more numerous in the hills than elsewhere, and the Highlands have a large number of sub-species. Three arctic butterflies are of great interest, for they must have entered Scotland before the end of the Ice Age. These are the mountain ringlet, seen only south of the Great Glen above 1,500 feet on the western Grampians; the Scots argus, widely distributed north to south, but not extending west beyond Skye; and the large heath, which is present even in the Outer Hebrides. All are brown butterflies. The large heath is paler than the others, with barely discernible eye-spots, but the Scots argus, as the name implies, has prominently marked red eye-spots with metallic blue centres.

BIRDS

It is questionable whether any of the present birds have been longer than 12,000 years in the Highlands, except as summer visitors. They are so much more mobile than mammals that it is surprising to find that five island birds have differentiated within their species in so short a time. Changes are mostly in feather pigments. They occur in stone-chats, rock pipits, song-thrushes, hedge-sparrows, and (most famous of all) the St Kilda wren, which has also a different song. On the mainland, other differences have appeared. The crossbills in Strathspey have developed heavier bills than the English birds, and red grouse have evolved from the willow grouse (*Lagopus lagopus*) of Scandinavia, northern Eurasia, northern Canada, and Alaska. Red grouse have long been regarded as a separate Scottish species (*Lagopus scoticus*), but this is no longer accepted. The two are identical anatomically, but the willow grouse turns white in winter, while the red no longer does so. Their food, habits, and voice are not the same, and in summer the willow grouse is lighter with white wing-quills. The red grouse has become a sub-species with title *Lagopus lagopus scoticus*.

The Highland birds fall naturally into three groups: those of the lochs and burns, the forests, and the moorlands and mountains. Nearly all range more widely than any group classification would imply. The oystercatcher, for example, a seabird once confined to the shores, began nesting inland and is now often seen far up the glens. Swifts too, which breed mainly in roofs and walls, will fly on a summer day over the mountain tops to hawk flies. Buzzards range from woods to sea-cliffs and mountains. And so on.

Lochs and burns

The osprey is king. It lives on surface-swimming fish, which it grasps in its talons after a plunge from height. It was killed-out by 1916 for its alleged intake of trout. In the middle fifties a pair returned to Loch Garten, Strathspey. They successfully nested on a pine-top, and due to the close guard set up by the Royal Society for the Protection of Birds they spread in 20 years until 14 pairs were nesting in 1974. The Loch Garten sanctuary is still protected by the RSPB, who have an observation post from which visitors may watch the birds through a telescope.

The other water birds are principally ducks, waders, divers, and gulls. Mallard are found everywhere up to 2,000 feet. Pochard are common in winter but only small numbers stay to breed in summer. Widgeon are common, descending in winter to estuaries where they are joined by migrants from Iceland. Gadwall are rare and their presence as breeding birds appears to be a natural spread from Scandinavia and Iceland. Teal are rare in the west although common on eastern lochans. Goldeneyes are winter visitors from Scandinavia, but small numbers visit the lochs in summer. They do not breed but can be seen courting. Scoters breed in the northern counties and Perthshire. During this century, tufted ducks have colonized most of the central and southern Highland lochs. The coot has a wide distribution in shallow waters and loch-shores, but moorhens keep more to the central and east Grampians. Water rail tend to be east Highland birds and are always difficult to see. The little grebe (dab-chick) breeds in nearly all the counties; black-necked grebe and great crested grebe prefer Angus and Perthshire, and Slavonian grebe, Inverness-shire. Whooper swans are likely to be seen as winter migrants in any of the lochs up to 1,000 feet, including the Moor of Rannoch.

Black- and red-throated divers breed from Argyll to Sutherland and west to the Hebrides, but not eastward. The black-throats prefer the large lochs, where they feed, although they are frequent visitors to smaller ones, like Loch Achtriochtan in Glen Coe. They winter at the coast or at sea. Red-throats will breed on small lochans, and fly many miles to the sea to win some of their food. In courting displays they race across the water, bodies half under, or flit low across the surface, wailing and crying with wings beating the water. Herons are most numerous on the sheltered coasts of Argyll, but everywhere some go inland to fish the lochs. They prefer to nest in trees, but will accept many sites including reeds and sea-cliffs. Sandpipers are one of the more ubiquitous lochside birds. They fly in from the south in April and leave in early October. Common and arctic terns arrive in mid April (the latter from the Antarctic); although seabirds, some breed inland, the common tern up to 1,000 feet on shingle.

The greylag goose is a native breeding bird, from which the farm-yard goose descends. Numerous in the Hebrides, it remains rare in the Highlands, where it breeds only on the loch-studded moors of the northmost counties and in Wester Ross. At the opposite end of the size-scale, the red-necked phalarope is the smallest swimmer and much rarer bird. It breeds only on a few Hebridean and northern isles, but may occasionally appear on Highland lochs, bobbing its head and spinning in circles to stir up water insects.

The river birds start with the dippers, which inhabit most burns, sometimes close to 2,000 feet. Head down, they will occasionally walk upstream on the river-bottom against a current. The red-breasted merganser, while the most common of West Highland sea-ducks, goes far inland up the bigger rivers. Goosanders too are river rather than loch birds, although they do appear on many lochs, for example, Loch Morlich. Saw-toothed like the merganser, their fishing efficiency has led to persecution, but they still breed widely across the Highlands. The grey wagtail with bright yellow breast has marked preference for the rocky banks of mountain burns, where it darts from boulder to boulder, flicking its long tail.

Woodland

The main body of woodland birds are the willow- and wood-warblers, white throats (not common), tits, chaffinches, tree-creepers, siskins more especially among the east Highland conifers, bramblings, redstarts, wood pigeons, woodcock, jays especially in the south and east Highlands, pied flycatchers in the south and east Highlands and on Loch Lomond since 1974, spotted flycatchers, which are most numerous in the pine forests around the Cairngorms, and goldcrests (Britain's smallest bird). Crossbills are confined to the pine forests, where they feed on the cone seed and tend to move annually from one forest to another in search of the best crop. They will also take spruce and larch seed. The capercaillie (grouse family) is the largest Scottish gamebird and can weigh 17 lb. In appearance it is not unlike a giant black grouse, with the same red eyebrow but a fan tail instead of a lyre tail. Its breeding grounds are coniferous woods of the north and east Highlands, where it feeds mainly on shoots, buds, and berries. Its cry is weird – a resounding rattle changing to a long-drawn gurgle, followed by a crash of wing-feathers on the ground. The black grouse is more a bird of the birch scrub, where it feeds on catkins and buds, but it takes conifer buds too and is commoner in the east than the west.

The great spotted woodpeckers nest locally throughout the Highlands in well-wooded country, whether coniferous or broad-leaved. Last century they became extinct in Scotland, deserting the woods around 1850 as a consequence of excessive felling. Reafforestation seems to have encouraged their return. Since they feed mainly on insect larvae, new coniferous plantations must give a sparser diet than the old mixed woods. The crested tit is found only in Scotland, and although not rare (there are several hundred breeding pairs) is confined to the north-east Highlands. Its main colony is Strathspey, with several outposts in the wooded hills of Banff, Moray, and Nairn. A recent spread has taken it to east Sutherland and the Aberdeen border. Like the goldcrest and other tiny birds, its numbers suffer severely in hard winters, but seem to recover two years later.

The birds of prey are the owls (tawny owls common, the long-eared uncommon) which feed mainly on mice, rats, insects, and small birds; the buzzard; and the sparrow-hawk. During the last 30 years buzzards have largely increased in the west following the growth of forest plantations, which harbour voles and other rodents. This latter increase has offset the dearth of rabbits following myxomatosis in 1953, so that buzzards remain the most common large birds of prey. The rarer rough-legged buzzard is an annual winter visitor to the north Highlands from Scandinavia. Sparrowhawks have become rare by persecution, for they feed mainly on birds, including the young of gamebirds. They were given the protection of law in 1966 but have probably suffered from farmers' pesticides and are apparently not increasing.

Moor and mountain

The small birds of the moorland and mountain grasslands are first and foremost the meadow pipits, then skylarks, twites, stonechats, wheatears, wrens, pied wagtails, and reed buntings. All are widespread, and even the wren, which is often thought of as a hedgerow bird, inhabits ground up to 1,700 feet if heathery or craggy and steep. Cuckoos penetrate far up the glens and lay eggs in the meadow pipits' nests, while peewits go as high as 2,500 feet on grassy hills.

The mountain blackbird or ring ouzel, which has a white crescent on its neck, can hardly be called common, but has a wide distribution on the high moors. It winters in the Atlas mountains and Mediterranean hills. Snipe are to be seen in bog-country, and heard most often in spring (even during the night) when the males' outer tail feathers make a loud humming sound as it makes short dives, usually while courting. Their numbers are greatly increased in autumn by winter migrants from north Europe. Greenshank appear on the desolate moors of the upper Spey and the north-west, and elsewhere like Rannoch Moor less frequently. Jackdaws nest on rock-outcrops of low hills, and curlew cry along the moors. Curlews are Scotland's largest waders. They breed on open country from moors to sand-dunes, and in winter move to the coast. Golden plovers are distributed across all Scotland. Their cry on the moorland where they breed is as melancholy as the curlew's. They belong to the moors rather than the high hills but have been known to nest up to 4,000 feet on stony ridges. The large eggs, pear-shaped and blotched in dark brown, are laid in a shallow hollow usually beside a large stone. Golden plovers are occasionally attended on the moors by dunlin.

The high mountain birds are dotterels, snow buntings, and ptarmigans. The dotterel is a plover, midway in size between the golden and ringed, distinctively marked by white stripes on eye, throat, and breast above a lower chestnut breast. Dotterels are surprisingly tame for their rarity (only some 80 pairs) and breed on the Cairngorms, Monadh Liath, and neighbouring mountains, where they nest from near 3,000 feet to above 4,000. The eggs, usually three, are hatched by the male in a scrape lined with lichen on a hollow in fringe-moss. Snow buntings are one of the rarest breeding birds in Scotland – perhaps five pairs all in the Cairngorms, although not more than three pairs (with several unmated cocks) have been seen. Only once in the last 60 years have a pair been known to nest elsewhere, on Ben Nevis in 1954. Migrant flocks from the Arctic are seen along the east coast in winter, or in small parties inland. Their winter plumage is pale brown on the back and the rest mostly white. The male in summer wears strongly contrasted black and white. Nests are often placed far in among loose boulders near the tops up to 4,000 feet.

The ptarmigan is the only Highland bird that changes colour from pale brown in summer through autumn grey to winter white. Like others of the grouse family it has a prominent red wattle over the eye. Unlike them, it is a bird specifically of the bare mountain tops, rarely seen below 2,000 feet except on the exposed ground of the northern Highlands. On the Cairngorms it breeds between 2,500 and 4,000 feet. Only in blizzards does it move down to lower slopes, where its food is heather shoots; higher up it feeds also on the berries, shoots, and leaves of arctic-alpine plants.

Red grouse are moorland, not mountain-top birds, yet rival ptarmigan for their endurance of bitter weather. In heavy snowfall they tread the snow down with their feet to avoid getting buried, and will stay high in blizzard provided the wind is violent enough to drift the snow and blow it off the heather. Heather shoots are their staple diet, or their seeds in autumn, and the shoots, leaves and fruits of the berry-bearing plants. The hens lay in April and May, and wait till all the 4 to 9 eggs are on the nest before sitting. Thus the eggs often get badly frosted yet rarely fail to hatch. The high birth-rate is offset by a short life-span of one and a half years. Grouse are likely to be found on all heathery mountains north of the Highland Line, but the most numerous populations are where the best heather grows, on the east Highland moors.

The scavengers of the hills are ravens, hooded crows, and black-backed gulls. Ravens occupy the entire Highland area, more numerously west than east. Their hoarse croak is familiar to all mountaineers, for they particularly like crags and enjoy acrobatic displays. They give valuable service in sheep country by scavenging carrion, thus keeping blow-flies in check. The hooded crow, named from its grey body, has similar use, but is too abundant in the north and west Highlands. Its numbers are in need of reduction: it is a persistent menace to other birds, searching out their nests and eating the eggs and young. The black-backed gull is equally rapacious on hills round the coast, where it notoriously kills new-born lambs. Like the raven and hooded crow it will eat any carrion.

The birds of prey on moor and mountain are eagles, peregrine falcons, hen-harriers, merlins, kestrels, and short-eared owls.

The golden eagle is by far the most splendid bird of the Highlands, and not only for its great size – nearly 3 feet long with a $6\frac{1}{2}$-foot wingspan. Its movements whether soaring or stooping have a majestic sweep, for its telescopic eyes allow it to scan the ground for prey when soaring at great height, and then to stoop at 90 mph. Its prey is blue hare, rabbit, ptarmigan, grouse, numerous small animals, including fox cubs, and carrion. It will occasionally take a weak lamb. The hunting territory needed by a pair of eagles varies from 10 to 20,000 acres, but they poach each other's ground, and I have seen four together over Sgurr Alasdair in the Cuillin – they were being harried by gulls and ravens. Eagles pair for life. The eyries are usually set between 1,000 and 2,000 feet on craggy ground, but they also use pine trees and sea-cliffs. Each pair has several eyries (3 to 10), which they use in annual rotation. They share equally the duty of sitting on the two eggs. It is rare for two eaglets to survive, for the stronger takes all it wants, and the weaker dies unless the parents provide a surplus. Their only enemies are man: egg-collectors, farmers, and owners and keepers of grouse moors. Eagles were much more numerous until last century, when sheep came and grouse were conserved for sport. Legal protection has helped survival, as also the ban on toxic chemicals used in sheep-dip.

The peregrine is little more than half the size of an eagle, but can stoop at twice the speed – up to 180 mph. It is also more ruthless and will sometimes kill birds in the air, leaving them to fall while it speeds on. It breeds on craggy ground and is likely to be seen anywhere, although as something of a rarity, for its numbers have been decimated since the 1950s by crop pesticides, ingested by the birds and mammals on which it preys. The hen-harrier, which is much the same size (16–20 inches long), is the only bird of prey definitely increasing, although its numbers are still very small in the Highlands. It breeds on heather moors and feeds on ground animals, but will occasionally take a small bird on the wing. The merlin, not a common bird, is pre-eminently a prey-chaser, not a pouncer. It outflies small birds by persistently tailing them at high speed, following every turn and twist. Its territory is all hill country between shore and mountain. It nests on the ground or on pine tops. The kestrel, on the other hand, is the commonest of all birds of prey, for it feeds mainly on rats, mice, voles, and insects, and so is welcome wherever it goes – and it goes everywhere from central London to the Highland moors. It builds no nest, but lays on the ledges of a cliff or a tall building, or on a deserted nest in a tree. The kestrel is a constant hoverer, and can be readily detected by this trait. Other birds hover only occasionally.

The short-eared owl is the only owl to inhabit moorland or hill-slopes. The nest is set on the ground among sedge or heather, but no proper nest is made. It takes its food by day (almost entirely field-voles) and can soar, wheel, and hover like a buzzard. It can be distinguished at dusk from the tawny owl by its much longer wings. The spread of conifers in the west has boosted the vole population and led to an increase in owls as well as buzzards. Snowy owls are winter visitors, seen occasionally north of the Great Glen, and recently in the Cairngorms. They have bred in Shetland since 1967.

Six birds have become extinct in the Highlands and Islands since the improvement of fire-arms. They are the crane and bittern (18th century), and the great auk (1840), all hunted out for food and feathers; the white-tailed sea-eagle (1890), and the kite and goshawk

(1960). In 1975 two pairs of sea-eagles were reintroduced to Rum from Norway by the Nature Conservancy.

I have made no mention of seabirds, nor of sparrows, thrushes, starlings, blackbirds, rooks, and others commonly seen that either reside and breed in the Highlands or appear (like the rare nightjar) only as summer breeders or winter visitors. Abundant as the principal Highland birds may be, their numbers are a large reduction from the early Middle Ages, when a Caledonian forest stretched across the land from Loch Tay to the borders of Ross, and from the Atlantic coast to Balmoral. Still earlier, when man first came to Scotland, he found it covered by continuous primeval forest to a height of 3,000 feet. And such would have been the land's condition today, wooded to a slightly lesser altitude, had it not been for man's intervention. The wide moorlands and treeless deer forests that now typify the Highlands are not the land's natural condition.

4   Man in the Highlands

In the course of the Ice Age, during the warm and long-lasting interglacials, Scotland may possibly have been inhabited by small numbers of men as England was after 400,000 BP. But if so, all trace was wiped out by the last glaciation. The first evidence of man in Scotland was a dug-out canoe found in the Tay valley near Perth. The alluvial clay deposited on top of it has been carbon-dated 6,400 BC. A second date for charcoal found in a hearth in Fife was 6,100 BC, plus or minus 255 years, for carbon dates are not closely accurate.

Such mesolithic men coming in during the next 2,000 years and more were nomadic hunters and fishermen. A hundred site deposits have been found: stone and bone tools, a few arrowheads, and midden debris of shellfish, sea-birds, fish and mammals. It has become evident from the sites that although the immigrants were widely dispersed up the east and west coasts, their number could not have exceeded a few score. They lived in coastal caves, on beaches, and a few among the trees and brushwood. They were too few and poorly equipped to alter the natural environment.

The first record of neolithic man in Scotland is approximately 4000 BC from the island of Arran. That is a calendar date, computed from a carbon date of charcoal found at a chambered cairn at Monamore west of Lamlash Bay. These New Stone Age men had arrived in south Britain 200 years earlier. They came through Ireland and England, probably originating near the Caspian Sea and spreading along the Mediterranean shore to Spain, and up the Danube to north Europe. Their skeletons show them to be short in body and long-headed. They were farmers, the first to breed domestic animals in Scotland, to grow crops of barley and wheat, to spin and weave, and to make thick, earthenware pottery. Before 2000 BC they were using saddle querns for grinding the corn. By that time their numbers in Scotland have been estimated at 10,000. There was land for everyone and no wars. The principal hunting weapon was the bow and arrow, the latter tipped with leaf-shaped flint and used for taking horses, red deer, and birds among much else. Their stone tools show a great advance on those of mesolithic compatriots. Picks, knives, and sickles were ground to work wood or reap. Axe-heads were ground and polished to give an efficient edge for tree-felling. Land could now be cleared for pasture and sowing. The men began to specialize in trades. The first neolithic axe factory in Scotland has been found north of Killin under Craig na Caillich, 2990 feet, which is one of the tops of the Tarmachan ridge. Axes from this site have been discovered in Aberdeenshire, and axes from a Langdale factory were imported to south Argyll. Trade was sea-borne, for the neolithic people were expert seamen, using the skin-covered coracle to colonize the Hebrides and west coast from Ireland, and the east by way of the North Sea. It has been shown that a 32-foot coracle would ferry a 3-ton cargo, including a 9-man crew, and bigger boats may well have been built.

Megaliths

The most obvious memorial left on the ground by neolithic man from 3000 BC is the earliest megaliths – many hundreds of chambered cairns standing 6 to 10 feet high. These were burial tombs of two basic types: galley graves and passage graves. The galley type are rectangular chambers covered by a cairn of stones and 60 feet long on average. The passage type are round chambers entered by a low passage and covered by a round cairn usually 50 feet in diameter. Every modification of these is found, with round cairns predominating. Cairns much larger than average are often seen, for example, in Mull at Port Donain, 5 miles south of Craignure, where the cairn measures 100 feet by 50. One of the largest is the south cairn at Nether Largie in west Argyll, 5 miles north of Crinan. Its diameter is 134 feet with a sepulchral chamber 19 feet long, roofed by slabs.

Chambered cairns are absent from the central Highlands but widely spread around them. Their design and distribution show them to be the work of people from Spain and south France moving up the west coast and through the Great Glen to the north and east Highlands. Kilmartin in west Argyll, a few miles south of Loch Awe, has a considerable collection: the Stone, Bronze, and Iron Age settlements there were large ones, for the site gave access both to the Clyde lochs and Atlantic passages. Many appear in Skye. One convenient to walkers in the Cuillin lies $3\frac{1}{4}$ miles south-south-west of Glen Brittle House, on the north shore of Loch na h-Airde. The cairn is 65 feet in diameter, its height 11 feet, and the chamber in good state. North of the Great Glen there are few on the west coast – Assynt has a dozen – but there are 350 in the north-east Highlands, Caithness, and Orkney and Shetland. The most famous is the Clova group, which includes 30 cairns in Strathnairn and the Monadh Liath up to 1,000 feet, 10 in Strath Spey, and another 30 between Loch Ness and the Black Isle. The eastern Cairngorms have 60 between the Dee and upper Deveron, and the Kincardine hills a dozen more. In Caithness and Sutherland there are nearly 80 between Thurso and Bonarbridge. Everywhere, most of them have been stripped of stone in historic times for local building and road metal. At least one has been used to harbour an illicit still. The original spiritual rites were those of burial and cremation, continued over many centuries and accompanied by the deposit of pottery and ornaments, with burial of animals beside the human bodies, all clearly showing a belief in life after death.

From 2000 BC onwards, new immigrants slowly moved into Scotland and spread gradually through the Highlands and Islands bringing new arts and crafts and the use of metal. Megalith building was developed in the erection of standing stones, stone circles, and henges, often with astronomical alignments. They appear to have served a double purpose as centres for religious rites and observation of the stars. They are most numerous throughout the Hebrides, and along the west Highland coast. Henges were confined to the mainland. These were named from horizontal slabs bridging tall standing stones (seen now only at Stonehenge in England). In Scotland, their surviving feature is the circling earthwork bank about 300 feet in diameter and ditched on the inner side. Examples can be seen in Aberdeenshire, 1 mile south of Inverurie, or in Argyll at Balmeanoch, $1\frac{1}{2}$ miles south of Kilmartin.

Bronze Age

The use and manufacture of bronze in Scotland began around 1700 BC. Ireland was rich in copper and gold, and Ayrshire had big copper deposits at Kaim. Tin was imported from Cornwall and bronze from Ireland. Copper ore, bronze ingots, and the implements made from them, like dagger-axes, copper hatchets, spearheads, and Irish gold ornaments, were traded from the Lowlands and Clyde with north-east Scotland by way of the Great Glen. Amber, jet, and copper goods came from the Baltic and Spain, probably with grain, salt, hides, and flax direct to Ireland by barter for metal. This trade percolated up the Scottish west coast to Loch Linnhe.

Picts and Celts

During the last millennium BC the Celts began arriving in Scotland. The important landscape changes made by man were theirs. The Celts (pronounced Kelts) were a confederacy of nomadic and pastoral tribes sharing a similar tongue. Their origin appears to have been in the mountainous region south of the Caspian Sea. During the Stone and Bronze Ages they spread across Europe and developed the use of iron from 900 BC. They revolutionized life in a forested Britain by introducing iron axes and ploughs to clear land by felling and to break it open, the pottery wheel, minted coins, and a form of clan organization that later came to flourish in the Highlands and Islands.

The Celts by Roman description were tall men with red or fair hair, which the Caledonian Picts wore flowing over the shoulder, and blue or grey eyes. It is not known how early in the Bronze Age they moved into Scotland, but their decisive overrunning of the country began between 700 and 500 BC, and continued during the last century BC when the Romans attacked West Gaul. In AD 79 the Romans invaded Scotland and named the principal tribe of the central Highlands *Caledonii* (perhaps from the Gaelic *Caile-daoine*, a spearman). From AD 297 they named all Highland tribes *Picti* or *Pictones*. It seems clear from the evidence that the Picts were not a distinct race, but mixed stock of Bronze Age peoples including early Celts, together with the late Celtic immigrants of 500 BC onwards. Their law and speech were Celtic, the Pictish tongue being later superseded by Scots Gaelic.

Strongholds

The Celtic immigrants brought the first need of walled strongholds to Scotland. These were of three kinds, built in drystone: (1) hill forts, (2) small forts called duns and brochs, and (3) stone houses, and earth houses or souterrains.

Hill forts were natural strong points around which defensive walls were built to close the gaps between crags, and to protect wooden round-houses or lean-to huts inside. The simplest kind can be seen at the summit of the Scuir of Eigg, which is ringed by crags except on the west side, where an 80-foot gap is closed by a wall 10 feet thick. More elaborate forts had walls from 8 to 40 feet thick. The greatest hill fort of the Highlands and Islands was Digh Mhor on south Islay, enclosing nearly 3 acres behind triple-terraced walls.

9. Beinn Achaladair from Crannach Wood.

10. Approaching storm on Buachaille Etive Mor, Glencoe.

11. Crowberry Ridge and Crowberry Gully, Buachaille Etive Mor.

13. Ben Nevis. Coire Leis. North-East Buttress (left), Tower Ridge (right).

14. Loch Leven and Beinn a' Bheithir.

15. The Ben Nevis plateau.

16. Glen Nevis and the Mamore Ridge.

The best-known mainland fort, famous as the capital fort of the first Scots kingdom, is Dunadd, east of Crinan, Argyll. This was a multiple structure of several small forts on one hill. The walls elsewhere were often built around a timber frame. In 70 such forts the walls have been vitrified, that is, the stones have been fused by heat. The question whether this was deliberate, or caused accidentally by attackers firing the framework, has not been resolved to the satisfaction of all archaeologists. The two principal vitrified forts, which may once have been the seats of Pictish kings, are Craig Phadrig at Inverness, where the walls are continuous, double, and concentric around the top edges of steep slopes (which make accidental firing improbable), and Dun Mhic Uisneachain in Benderloch, which is a multiple structure like Dunadd. Vitrified forts are most numerous on the west coast (25) and the north end of the Great Glen (15). They have been carbon-dated to 590 BC at Dun Lagaidh on Loch Broom, and to 490 BC at Finavon in Angus. They belong to the late Bronze Age. Between the seventh and sixth centuries several hundred homesteads were built both in stone and timber in the Southern Uplands and Lowlands. Many of these were walled settlements, or pallisaded sites, or ringed by hill-top earthworks enclosing up to 10 acres with 15 round-houses. They were the first villages, and their inhabitants felled the forests of south Scotland.

During the 400 years ended AD 200, many hundreds of duns (Gaelic, pronounced doons) were built along the west coast, mostly on rocky points or commanding sites. They were circular or oblong, with an internal diameter of 10 to 60 feet between walls 10 to 20 feet thick. Most were too small to stand siege; their siting suggests that they were manned as watch-posts, or as emergency shelter in short raids. There is evidence that the larger were permanently occupied, probably by the local chief. Some had internal galleries, like Dun Liath in north-west Skye, which measures 150 feet by 80. When these had a second gallery above ground-level they were named semi-brochs, for they were the precursors of brochs proper.

The brochs were built during the first century BC and display an immense advance in masonry skills. They were round towers built 30 to 50 feet high from a base 50 to 60 feet in diameter. The walls were built double to a thickness of 15 feet or more with four to six internal galleries floored with stone slabs set into the two walls. Short stairs linked each to the one above. The wall stones were cut square and laid so close with such skill that where they were not pulled down a few have lasted unbroken for 2,000 years. The outer wall, unpierced by windows, was sloped slightly inwards up to the vertical top half. The tower was left unroofed. Windows in the inner wall lit the galleries and gave command of the courtyard. The brochs had only one entrance – a narrow passage 5 feet high closed by a massive wooden door that swung on a stone pivot and was barred by a beam. A small guard chamber was set in the wall to one side.

There are 500 brochs in Scotland (none in England), nearly all concentrated in the north. Sutherland and Caithness have 220, the Shetland and Orkney Islands 179, the Inner Hebrides 40, and the West Highlands 3, all in Glenelg. The east Highlands have one near Beauly and the rest are in the Outer Hebrides and Lowlands. The design and distribution, the relics and carbon dates, suggest that brochs were constructed by professional builders for the native Pictish communities and accepted immigrants, as protection either from the late Celtic immigrants then moving north in search of land, or else from Scandinavian sea-raiders engaged in the slave trade, which was then lucrative. Slaves formed the basis of nearly all Iron Age societies in Europe and Britain. Unless taken by surprise, brochs were impregnable, and their purpose was clearly temporary refuge. The best surviving examples are Mousa in the Shetlands, and Carloway in Lewis. The best in the Highlands is Dun Telve, 2 miles up Gleann Beag in Glenelg. Only a third of the wall's circumference rises to 33 feet, the rest having been taken down for local building, but the galleries coursing the walls are well exposed to view.

Stone buildings in the Highlands were almost exclusively for defence. The Highlanders' houses were wood and wattle huts roofed with tree-branches and thatched with heather and turf. Timber construction continued into the twelfth century, when domestic housing in stone became widespread – but the wood and wattle style could be found in remoter areas until the late eighteenth century. One early exception to the timber rule was the earth-house, built in small numbers by Picts from the early Iron Age and used far into historic times. Its plan was a subterranean passage nearly 6 feet high and driven to lengths of up to 78 feet, ending in a chamber. On the Hebrides they went up to 90 feet but with less head-room. All were roofed and walled in stone. The main concentrations were in Aberdeenshire at the heart of Pictland, where 50 lie within 2 square miles on the moor of Clova. The passages take a sharp bend before the terminal bulge. In the Hebrides they are most numerous in Skye, where they are tunnelled into hillsides. A good example is at Vatten, near Dunvegan, which has offsets from the main corridor.

Crannogs, artificial islands usually framed by timber, were built on at least a hundred freshwater lochs, and the wooden round-houses set on top were occupied from Iron Age times to the Middle Ages. Crannogs were made of stone and rubble, or logs and brushwood, or both, either built up from shallows or contained between wooden piles driven into the loch's bottom. All were linked to land by a submerged, zig-zag causeway. Some had a dock for canoes, and some houses had balconies projecting over the water on piles. Perhaps the best specimen of a stone-built crannog is on Mull at Loch Sguabain in Glen More. It can easily be seen from the roadside. A nearer site for most people is on Loch Lomond, $2\frac{1}{2}$ miles north-west of Balmaha near Strathcashell point, where an Iron Age crannog lies 30 yards from the shore. Its flat back, 70 feet in diameter and marked by a lone tree, breaks surface when the water level is normal. If you wade out to a 3-foot depth from the sloping rim, the big containing timbers can still be seen.

Romans

Although the times were troubled by immigration, the tribes flourished and grouped themselves in petty kingdoms that gradually amalgamated. By AD 79, when Agricola invaded Scotland, the people had formed themselves in two groups: Britons south of the Forth–Clyde line and Picts to its north. Agricola made only a brief incursion into the Highlands in AD 84, when he made his way up the east coast to a point north of the Tay named by Tacitus *Mons Graupius*. The name Grampian derives from the old Gaelic *Gruaimpeinnean*, meaning grim or dark mountains, and this most probably was the name that Tacitus heard. The Picts rose and were defeated. Thereafter they fought guerilla warfare so successfully that for 300 years they held the Romans to the Lowlands at one or other of their two walls – Hadrian's between the Tyne and Solway and the Antonine between the Forth and Clyde.

The Scots clans

The Picts in the third century were helped by an Irish tribe, the Scots of Dalriada in Ulster. The Scots were Goidelic Celts who had already begun to colonize Kintyre and the islands of Argyll. Around

75

AD 220 the colony came under the rule of Cairbre Riada, the son of the High King of Erin. Since he held the small settlements as part of his home country, they too were named Dalriada (the portion of Riada). The north boundary was Glen More in Mull, marked by cairns that still appeared in Blaeu's map of 1608.

It was said of Cairbre Riada by the Roman Julius Solinus that 'The King of the Hebudae was not allowed to possess anything of his own lest avarice should divert him from truth and justice'. His remark penetrates to the original democratic principle of the clan system. The Gaelic *clann*, meaning children, was a large family tribe. It allowed no private property in land, which was held communally, and that rule applied to the elected chief. The chief represented the people's common ancestry, therefore his office was hereditary, but not to his person, only to his particular family from whom successors were chosen by the people. The point was safeguarded by the Celtic law of Tanistry, which excluded succession by primogeniture. The chief would appoint his successor (*Tanistear*, or second person) from the oldest or most able men only after getting his clan's consent. The chief on inauguration was granted land, cattle, and grain to maintain his office and family on the understanding that he held all property in trust for his people. His job was to manage the clan's land for the good of all, to lead his people, and maintain their safety and dignity. He governed to this end by dividing the land among his near relatives, each according to his rank, and they in turn worked the land through sub-tenants – the Highlanders for whom chief and chieftains were trustees. No formal leases were given. Rents even as late as the fifteenth century were nominal and paid in kind. The chief had no need of rents. He had real need of well-fed fighting men, and that meant also cattle and crops. The task of his relatives was to make sure that he had them all. A chief could be deposed if found wanting, but till then was given obedience and the right of jurisdiction. There were points of high merit in the clan system. Although aristocratic, it had no element of feudalism. The full members were virtually classless, following their chief by choice, enjoying his respect, and able to say what they thought without question of disloyalty.

Union of the Kingdoms

The Romans abandoned Britain early in the fifth century. The Lowlands were then held by Britons and Angles, and by the close of the century the Scots had begun colonizing Argyll in formidable numbers. By the middle of the sixth century, the Scots population of Dalriada had grown to around 8,000, and their territory stretched from the Firth of Clyde to Ardnamurchan. They were now at war with the Picts. Pictland was an organized kingdom divided into seven provinces ruled by mormaers, and strong enough to hold the Scots in check.

The Pictish religion was Druidism; the Scots were Christian. In 563 St Columba, who was a scion of the House of Dalriada, settled on the island of Iona with twelve monks to convert the northern Picts. The conversion of the southern Picts had begun nearly 300 years earlier, been continued by Ninian and others in the fifth century, and penetrated far into the Highlands long before Columba's arrival. He and other Irish missionaries working at the same time completed the success of their predecessors, and made possible the union of the several divisions of Celtic rule and civilization in Alban – a Gaelic plural word meaning Mountains, used from the fifth century BC to distinguish Highland Britain from south.

The Picts with skill, courage, and good organization had contained the invasions of the Romans, Anglo-Saxons, Britons, and Scots, for the tribes had been united by the need to defend their land and liberty. They now held Pictland as an independent nation. But a still further union of Celtic lands and people was soon to become essential in order to forge a viable nation in face of new threats from Norway. In the summer of 794 the Viking longships made their first recorded descent on Britain. All coasts were ravaged, and for the next eighty years the raids on Alban and Erin continued with seasonal regularity. The twofold cause was Norway's division into twenty-nine kingdoms to which only one male of each ruling family could succeed and draw maintenance, and an economic crisis produced by a population explosion. Seaborne expeditions, ably planned by surplus men of leadership quality, were thus devised to win a living by piracy, slave-trading, and land-raiding. They were launched on a national scale. The first phase was seizure of the northern isles, the Hebrides, the Irish isles, and the Isle of Man, as summer bases for mainland plunder. The second phase, which had different cause and effect, opened when Harold Haarfager became king of all Norway in 872. He imposed a feudal system on his country, which many landowners refused to accept. They settled on the Hebrides, Shetland and Orkney, and Caithness, from which they attacked the Norwegian coast. Harold had to gather a fleet and take the islands, which for the next four centuries were ruled by jarls, acting as viceroys. At the height of their power they ruled not only the Hebrides but almost all of Argyll and the whole of north Scotland down to Inverness.

Meantime, the Picts and Scots drew close by virtue of a shared Christianity, inter-marriage between their royal houses, Celtic tongues not greatly dissimilar, and the common Norse affliction. The Picts were unable to repel the Norse as they had earlier invaders. They had many ships, but none to match Norse longships. Their independence weakened and the Scots grew dominant, until in 843 Kenneth MacAlpin, King of Scots and a prince of the Pictish royal house on his mother's side, united the two kingdoms. He asserted paramountcy over the Lothian Angles and made alliance with the Britons of Strathclyde. Gradually the names Pictland and Alban disappeared. Scotland became the sole nation north of the Cheviot Hills. Its Highland people were thus largely Celtic Picts and Scots with an admixture of the aboriginal peoples (also classed as Picts), Britons, and Norsemen.

Divorce of the Highlands

The young Celtic kingdom had made a good start. Two most important elements of strength were first, that Gaelic became the language of all Scotland except in the Norse colony and along the English border, and second, the application of clan tanistry to the throne. This law, by not recognizing the right of succession by primogeniture, ensured that there were no interregnums, or minority rules, and that kingship went to men of most experience or ability. Its abandonment after 1057 had a most disastrous effect on the unity of the nation. Malcolm III (Canmore) married the English princess Margaret, under whose influence he allowed English to supplant Gaelic as the court language, and the Roman Church the Celtic. The interests of the people were neglected. When his son David succeeded in 1124 after a twenty years' absence in England, he brought in a thousand Anglo-Normans to whom he gave estates on the feudal principle. Gaelic fell into disuse in the Lowlands. The consequence was a racial, linguistic, and political cleavage between the Lowlands and the Highlands. Each thought the other's tongue and culture barbarous. Mutual trade became minimal. The Gaels loathed the feudal society's stratification into classes, but later kings from Robert the Bruce onwards forced the chiefs to accept charters for their clans' lands, which they no longer held in trust for the clans but in their own names. Thus even in the Highlands primogeniture came to supplant tanistry in chief-selection. The result was mis-government, national and local. The whole nation was weakened. In the Highlands and Islands the democratic clan system, now under-mined, degenerated until feuds and clan wars became a way of life in the sixteenth century. The end-result was to be the collapse of Gaelic society and culture in the eighteenth century.

Paradoxically, the first great division of the kingdom gave it strength against Norway. This was Somerled's founding of the kingship of the Isles, and of Clan Donald (his grandson's name). Somerled's mother was Norse, but his father Gillebride, the rightful king of Argyll whom the Norse had dispossessed. Around 1130 Somerled drove the Norse out of mainland Argyll, and to oust them from the Isles built in secret a fleet of 60 warships. In January 1156 he defeated the Norse battle fleet off Islay, and took the Argyll islands including Bute and Arran. His successors held rank as kings of the Isles. They formed a most convenient buffer state when, in 1196, the king of Scots seized North Scotland from the Orkney jarldom. The Norse still held Skye and the Outer Hebrides. By systematic attacks on Skye, the Scots goaded Hakon of Norway into his fatal expedition of 1263. He sailed with 120 ships to the Clyde. Landing at Largs in a westerly gale, his men were defeated by lack of supplies and reinforcement, while many of the ships were wrecked. Norway ceded the Hebrides after an occupation of 400 years. The place-names of Lewis are still eighty per cent Norse, and in Skye sixty-six per cent. The principal effect on the natural environment was devastation of woodland, which Magnus Barfod and others deliberately fired while punishing Hebridean compatriots. The island trees suffered a set-back from which they were unable to recover before population mounted and the weather worsened to the 'Little Ice Age' of 1430–1850.

Lordship of the Isles

The Clan Donald Kingship of the Isles, centred on Islay, gave invaluable aid to the king of Scots after the seizure of the crown by Edward of England in 1296. When the War of Independence broke out ten years later, Clan Donald sheltered Robert the Bruce in adversity on their island and mainland castles, harried the English warships at sea, and captured the fleet's base on the Isle of Man. These were important contributions to the victory at Bannockburn, where they fielded 1,800 men from Islay. Thereafter the Islay fleet supported the Scottish invasions of north England. These and other acts won territorial rewards from the crown, hugely augmented by wise marriages. By the fourteenth century the kingship of the Isles (now called the lordship) extended from Assynt to the Mull of Kintyre, and from the Great Glen to Rockall. MacDonald, Lord of the Isles, was acknowledged by all as head of the Gaelic race. His Atlantic principality had become the greatest of the Scottish kingdom, his power on land rivalled that of the king, and his power at sea greatly excelled it. The temptation to take all was great. The ninth prince, John II, succumbed to it when James III, King of Scots, was a minor. John made a treaty of 1462 with Edward IV of England to dismember Scotland, John to take the Highlands. Scotland was long plagued by such products of feudal power and royal primogeniture. In all parts of Scotland the too powerful barons jockeyed for position against the crown or each other – troubles earned by the kings through foisting feudalism on their people – and this in turn brought down on the clansmen's heads a misfortune that was to last 300 years.

Their chiefs, controlled no longer by the democratic principle essential to the working of the clan system, became infected by unbridled militarism. This had been effectively suppressed under the firm rule of the Lords of the Isles up to John II. The Lowland parliament then discovered his plot. Thrice they raised armies, which were thrice defeated by John's son Angus – yet they emerged victorious in the end: for John favoured submission, Angus did not, and the Clan Donald loyalties were divided. Father and son fought at sea off Mull. Angus won but was assassinated. James IV, King of Scots, gained manhood and found the strength to abolish the Lordship of the Isles in 1493. The Highlands and Islands no longer had a common head. While the clan chiefs respected James, his death at Flodden left them with no other object of loyalty. James V was one year old, Scotland in turmoil, and the division between the English speaking Lowlands and the Gaelic Highlands became complete.

The fiery cross (charred sticks dipped in goat's blood and crossed) soon sped through the glens, passes, and sea-lanes. The clansmen were called to fight their chiefs' battles. The sixteenth century opened with three full-scale rebellions and six clan feuds. The pace eased after mid-century. Highland life at its worst was tolerable for half of the year, when spring sowing, autumn harvest, and winter brought relief, but during the rest of the year the townships of the glens and shores had to suffer at uncertain intervals burned homes, destroyed crops, fired forests, theft of livestock, or massacre. Clan wars ended in the seventeenth century, but the chiefs were always involved in the national risings, or wars of succession. The Highlanders continued well-practised in the use of arms. Against that hazardous background they lived a life that should have brought no profound changes to the Highland environment, had they been granted peace.

The Clan Settlements

The Highland and Island townships were and are quite different from Lowland villages. A township means a group of houses whose tenants win livelihood from the land on which the houses stand. According to the lie of the land, their pattern might be lineal or clustered, and their size vary from four families (the smallest practicable for teamwork in clearing woodland, reclaiming moorland, or providing a boat's crew) to a population of several hundred. The Scots were cattlemen. Since the land was their clan's, and no person could own land, the township people held the hill and moorland pasture in common, and divided the arable land by lot. The allotments were runrig, meaning that the strips for which each household was responsible adjoined each other, and were changed by lot annually.

The tools used for tillage were the *cas-dhireach* (straight foot), a spade 6 feet long with a single step; the *cas-chrom* (crooked foot), a kind of foot-plough made from a 6-foot shaft of oak or ash, which had the bottom end bent to a wide angle and shod with iron; primitive ploughs of Norwegian design; and light harrows. The *cas-chrom* was used mainly in the north-west Highlands and Hebrides, where it proved more efficient than plough or spade. Twelve men could dig an acre a day. The *cas-dhireach* was most effective for digging lazybeds, required where drainage or soil were insufficient. This English name is from ley, meaning untilled ground; the Gaelic name was *feannagan*, from *feann*, to scarify. Narrow beds, not under 3 feet wide or more than 8, were made by digging parallel trenches and throwing the earth to centre. Moorland and hill-slopes were made fertile, and when fed with seaweed or cattle-dung yielded large crops of oats and barley. Lazybedding has almost died out on the mainland, but is still extensively used in the Outer Hebrides.

The amount of land held by the common run of township varied between 600 and 1,000 acres, of which little more than a fifth would be arable. Oats and barley were the main crops, with smaller fields under flax or linseed, hemp and rye. Grinding was a daily chore. If the corn was dry, the women prepared it for milling by switching it from the ear with a stick, winnowing, and parching it over the fire in a pot; if the corn was damp, they dried the whole or the cut-off ears in a kiln, then set fire to the straw on the floor, and winnowed the blackened grain. The latter method was called *graddan* (*grad* = quick); its more popular form in the Hebrides, because it gave more palatable bread, was to fire a sheaf of oat-ears, and at the moment the husk burned, beat off the grain with a stick. The grain after parching was ground in querns. It is recorded that corn for a day's food would be graddened, winnowed, parched, ground, baked into bread, and eaten within two hours of reaping.

From the earliest Celtic times to the nineteenth century, cattle-farming was the universal occupation of the Highlands and Islands, and the main form of man's wealth. His close secondary occupation after the fifteenth century was cattle rieving, pursued by men of high and low rank in every part of the country from Northumberland and Cumberland to Caithness. Although the main emphasis was on cattle until late in the seventeenth century, the Scots kept sheep in considerable numbers. The neolithic breed had been small and dark-haired, like the Soay sheep of St Kilda, and seem to have changed little by historic times. Their weight was 25–30 lb. Some were four-horned, all had a meagre fleece weighing only 20–30 ounces, but the wool was a fine short down mixed with long hair. By the fourteenth century $1\frac{1}{2}$ million fleeces were being exported annually, of which a great proportion came from the Southern Uplands and Borders. Sheep stocks in the Highlands were limited by the need to fold them at night for protection against wolves, and by the belief that unless sheep were folded throughout the winter they could not survive snow-storms and icy winds. In consequence, they failed to grow a thick fleece.

The black cattle, by which wealth was reckoned, were the aboriginal Highland breed, shaggy beasts that varied in colour from black to reddish brown. They weighed around 400 lb. Lively and vigorous, they could live on the mountain grazings at all seasons. They were known as kyloes, and throve on the coarsest pasture. In the North Highlands the only export market in the sixteenth century was the royal burgh of Inverness, but in the West, Central, and South Highlands droving to the Lowlands and England had already begun.

Argyll cattle were sold at Dumbarton, and the rest went to other trysts (like Killin and Crieff) in the south and east Highlands. The prevalence of clan feuds made droving hazardous and fighter escort was necessary, still more so following the Reformation of 1560, when the Covenanting wars and Royalist campaigns in support of the Stewarts were waged through much of the seventeenth century by Montrose, Dundee, and others, causing the glens and woods to fill with travelling armed bands on the seasonal break-up or assembly of armies. Drovers were despoiled of whole herds, yet despite all handicaps, 18,000 black cattle were passing through Carlisle alone in mid-century, and the annual value of exports in 1614 was nearly £750,000 Scots.

Celtic feudalism

By 1578 the chiefships of clans had mostly become hereditary. By 1600 the chiefs had abolished the brieveships (judges and courts appointed under the ancient Celtic laws) and taken to themselves the powers of heritable jurisdiction, which extended to life and death over all followers. As a general rule, they took advice and administered quick justice impartially. Their rental had hitherto been their fighting men, but the growing boom in cattle was increasing the value of land, which between 1600 and mid-century multiplied forty times. In short, as more money circulated they increased their rents, which were paid in kind (grain, butter, cheese, cows, sheep, and poultry) and shipped to the Lowlands for sale. Goods went by boat wherever possible. There were no roads in Scotland that could take wheeled vehicles outside the large towns. The chiefs' relatives, the gentlemen of the clan, now became tacksmen, that is, they received their land at a rent or tack. They sublet the farms to their tenants on a 'steelbow' tenure, under which the stock carried was usually the tacksman's and leased with the land. On the rest of their land they settled large numbers of cottars, each with a house and sufficient ground to sow a few bushels of oats and graze a few cows. From all such tenants the tacksmen exacted rent in kind and feudal services. The chiefs' sense of trusteeship still persisted, but overriding that came the realities of this new Celtic feudalism; the land was no longer the clans'; the people's freedom was lost. The patriarchal character of the chiefs made this not too hard to accept for another century, especially as clan warfare had died away by 1650. Cattle raiding continued, but the chiefs were settling personal disputes by litigation. Their government became orderly and relations between chief and clansmen remained intimate. That this was so had been largely due to the influence of Andrew Knox, the Bishop of the Isles, who in 1609 had persuaded the great chiefs of the Highlands and Hebrides to sign the Statutes of Iona, promising to maintain the Church and clergy, cut down their huge household staffs, relieve their tenants of burdens, encourage education at Lowland schools, and discourage militarism. A later, most harmful edict by the Privy Council, banned the use of Gaelic in schools.

Houses

Housing throughout the Highlands varied widely according to the building material and natural shelter available. Beehive construction in stone dates from neolithic times, and a few such houses – internal diameter 6 to 14 feet – were built by the Scots on the west coast before the ninth century, when they first began to build stone chapels and churches. Stone replaced wood for housing in the twelfth century, but only by degrees and regions. Building in turf began too early for dating, and like stone beehives the turf houses continued in use in the Hebrides until the twentieth century. In the north-west Highlands and Hebrides, houses built of turf blocks were given double walls for strength against weather. Sometimes only the outer wall was turf, and the inner stone. Many were roofed with turf and looked like green hillocks in summer. A few, built against a crag or bank, were grazed over the roof by sheep, goats, and hens. After the Viking era, drystone building became general.

Stone houses were single-walled and thatched, but the Hebrides and North Highlands developed double-walled long-houses with the roof set on the inner wall. The wall-space was packed with peat or rubble. These were named *tigh-dubh* or dark houses (anglicized as 'black houses'), to distinguish them from *tigh-geal* or white houses, which having cemented walls looked lighter. The interior measurement of a black house could be 60 or 70 feet by 12 feet. The floor was beaten earth. Roof and floor sloped from one end to the other, for the low end was the cow's byre. Many had a barn built on to the back wall with access from the living room. The interior was at first lit only from the central door; later, tiny windows were set deep in the thatch close to the wall-top, where they were blocked in bad weather by divots or straw bags. The hearth was central, without chimney, smoke finding its way through a roof-vent. In time, many hearths were given a free-standing stone back. The peat fire burned day and night, always topped by a black pot or kettle which hung by a chain from a beam. The houses were lit at night by small iron lamps called cruisies. These had an open bowl of oil with a wick of bullrush pith. Many had no light. The *tigh-geal* were occupied by chiefs and tacksmen. They burned tallow candles and had their houses partitioned. The greater chiefs had their castles, but the lesser were housed little better than their clansmen and went about their farms barelegged. Beds were springy heather spread on the floor, or failing heather, straw. Blankets and pillows were neither used nor wanted, and when given these when travelling in low countries, the Highlanders cast them aside and used only their plaids.

Highland dress

The tartan plaid worn kilted became male outdoor dress of nearly all Scotland, including the Lowlands and Borders, after the conquest of Lothian in 1018. During the Roman occupation, the Celts including the Picts had worn the sagum, which could be a sheepskin but was more commonly a striped woollen cloak or blanket woven in several colours. It was thrown across the shoulders and fastened by a wooden pin. Under the cloak, the Scots wore a tunic shirt of less than knee-length and close-fitting, therefore left open at front or side. *Truis* or breeches closely fitting the lower leg were also worn, but usually the legs were bare. Untanned skins were tied to the feet with thongs. Women wore the same tunic shirts but without sleeves and with low-cut breast. In Ireland and the Highland and Islands, the striped cloak was woven in patterns peculiar to districts, and these became traditional – the women to remember the sett or pattern marked a bit of wood with the number of threads to the stripe. The result was that a man's home region could be told by the tartan. The name tartan derives from the Irish–Scots Gaelic *Tuar*, colour, and *Tan*, district. Not till the seventeenth century did it come to mean clan colour. The Irish record *Senchus Mor* (AD 438) refers to tartans of the BC period. There is no record of the date when the tartan cloak developed into the kilted plaid, except that it was probably thus worn by Scots in the tenth century, and certainly by the eleventh, when Magnus Barfod introduced it to Norway from Scotland. The Scots still wore a sleeved tunic shirt of saffron linen, which was now reaching below the knees and belted at the waist. This was replaced early in the sixteenth century by short shirts of

85

wool or linen. Many men preferred tartan *truis* for travel on horseback. Whatever the garb, the kilted plaid was worn on top out of doors, and from the sixteenth century became the national dress of the Highlands and Islands.

The Highland plaid – *am breacan feilidh*, the chequered covering – was a sheet of woollen cloth 18 feet by 6 feet. In old Irish the word *ceilt* (hard c) meant screening, but the word kilt came to mean 'tucked in pleats'. The kilted plaid was male garb only. The man on dressing laid his plaid on the ground on top of his broad leather belt, folded one end in narrow pleats, then lay on top and belted the plaid to his waist. He wore the kilt shorter than is now fashionable, and drew the upper plaid over his back and across the left shoulder, where he fastened it with a bone pin or a big silver brooch. The later *feilidh beag*, or little covering, became common between 1715 and 1745, and was so named because it was made in two parts, a shortened plaid and a separate kilt from waist to knee. Highland dress bore little likeness to its modern imitations. Shoes and stockings were not much worn in summer except by gentry. Stockings were not knitted, they were of cloth from the web of the plaid. The sporran if worn was a simple pouch of goatskin. No neck-cloth was worn. Hide shoes were not cut to the shape of the feet till the seventeenth century. Round bonnets and hair flowing to the shoulder were worn from the days of the ancient Caledonians. Until banned by government, the kilted plaid lasted eight centuries because it was the most practical dress for Highland life and territory. Although it required much more material than *truis*, it was simpler to make, for no one had to cut it to shape, and of much more practical value. The lightness and stretch of the kilt allowed freer use of the legs on rough, roadless ground, in fording burns, and crossing wet heather. On campaigns it allowed armies greater mobility, for two or three men sharing plaids and warmth could sleep out in any weather, including snowfall, when others were crippled by exposure. Tents were not wanted. During the '45 Rising, the clansmen refused to use those provided.

Women when in full dress wore a scarlet bodice with wide sleeves rimmed with lace at narrow wrists. They wore on top a white plaid called an *Arisaid*, thinly striped in black, blue, and red. This fell to the feet, was plaited all round, and exposed the red sleeves of the bodice. Above the waist, it was secured by a high leather belt inlaid with engraved silver, on which coloured stones were set, and secured at the breast by a brooch of brass or silver, often as big as a saucer, engraved round the rim with animal and symbolic figures, and bearing at centre a big crystal ringed with small stones.

Health and food

The people as a whole were well clothed and fed until the eighteenth century. The population of all Scotland in 1250 was around 600,000 and took 500 years to double. In the Highlands especially, population was held in check by infant mortality, smallpox, and occasional outbreaks of typhus or cholera that would sweep away a whole township. But the general level of health was high and longevity the rule for those who escaped unhappy accidents. Credit for that must go to pure air and frugal diet. Despite the great store of cattle and sheep, the clansmen were largely vegetarian. Only men of rank ate meat daily, although beef and mutton were only $\frac{1}{2}$p a pound (1640–1725), and hens 1p a dozen. The Highlanders ate two meals a day in ample quantity. Their staple food was oatmeal, eaten as bread and *brochan* – the bread baked as a flat bannock, and the brochan made by moistening the meal with boiling water and butter. To these were added cheese, eggs, milk, fish, butter, and barley bread. Potatoes were widely grown, but only in small crops before 1750. Pure water was drunk with meals – tea and coffee were unknown. The townships distilled their own whisky (*uisge*, water, *beatha*, life) usually from oats and not generally from barley until around 1750. Ale was brewed from malted grain and heather-tops. Claret and brandy were imported from France in large quantities.

The Highlanders' way of life in their own settlements had not greatly altered their natural environment, not even seriously diminished the Caledonian forest except by local clearance for tillage and pasture. The Lowland forest had long since gone, but the Highland remained, if not intact, still of vast extent in the Middle Ages.

Caledonian Forest

The old forest was predominantly pine, oak, and birch. The Scots pine (the only native pine) was a splendid tree growing 70 to 100 feet or more, its gnarled red boughs contrasting with its bottle-green top. It mounted to the highest level on the hills, dwindling in size to a mere bush. The lower ground was largely taken by oak, together with hazel, alder, willow, and holly. Birch and rowan spread everywhere. The destruction of the North Highland forest began around AD 800, when it was burned by the Vikings, perhaps to rout out the

Picts, but more likely as punitive vandalism on overrunning the country, for that was the treatment they gave to their own people in the Hebrides. They felled much timber for boat- and house-building in four centuries. A halt was called to indiscriminate felling and burning under the Donald Lordship of the Isles, but when that fell in 1493, destruction was resumed. During the political chaos of the sixteenth century, and the Restoration wars of the seventeenth, the woods gave shelter to outlaws and rebels, brigands, large armed bands either fugitive from war or deliberately bent on plunder like those of the clan raiders, or the Wolf of Badenoch (Robert II's son), and lastly to *Canis Lupus*, the common wolf, which plagued townships and their stock, frightened travellers, caused the folding of sheep at night, and in many districts forced the burial of the dead on islands. There is no record of attack by wolf packs on man, but the wolf made more than a nuisance of itself. For these varied reasons, the forests were fired by kings, generals, barons, clan chiefs, and the men of the townships, who from time to time resolved to tolerate the occupants no longer.

To these incendiaries was added a far worse, because more efficient and persistent, destroyer – the first developers with a profit motive. Queen Elizabeth had taken alarm at the destruction of English woodland by iron-smelters, when oak was needed for ship-building. She banned felling in 1584 and the iron-smelters moved to the Highlands. Lowland Scots joined in this profitable mission, which continued through the seventeenth century despite prohibition by the Scots parliament, which penalized fellers only by fine. The fellings increased in scale after the Jacobite rising of 1715, for English companies bought forfeited estates to exploit the timber. Both before and after the second rising of 1745, clan chiefs who had adopted the Sassenach (Lowland) way of life following the union of crowns and parliaments (1603 and 1707), needed money to spend in Edinburgh and London. Other great landowners, like the Duke of Gordon, had similar need. They sold huge forest areas to the smelters, from whom they drew annual profits of up to £20,000. The work continued into the nineteenth century. The great pine forests of Strathspey, and the oakwoods of Lorn in Argyll and of Loch Maree in Wester Ross, were either decimated or entirely cleared. All over the Highlands exploitation had followed similar lines on lesser scale. Not even the Hebrides escaped. The Inner Islands like Skye, Mull, Lismore, and others had been well wooded in oak and birch in the seventeenth century, but some, Mull especially, were now stripped to make charcoal for England's furnaces.

The charcoal was not all exported. In the West and Central Highlands several bloomeries (furnaces) were built where bog-iron and plentiful timber existed side by side. The local ore was then augmented by imports from Cumberland. One such bloomery at Taynuilt in Argyll is now preserved as an industrial monument. Bog ore was found where the deeply buried forest peat of past eras had changed to coal under a top layer of silt. The burns then often brought down iron in solution with other sediments, which were deposited as ironstone with a twenty-five per cent iron content. An ore of this kind recently worked in Raasay (1959) formed a deposit of 10 million tons in a band 8 feet thick.

The Highland industry ended around 1813, when coke replaced charcoal. The great forest had now been fragmented, spread through with much desolate moorland. Six wild mammals, deprived of their woodland habitat, had been hunted to extinction in the process (brown bear, reindeer, elk, ox, boar, and wolf), but the forests were granted no respite for regeneration. More thorough destroyers had arrived – the sheep and their flockmasters' fires. The way for the sheep had been made plain by a series of political, social, and economic events.

Military roads

The first of these events were the Jacobite attempts to replace the Stewarts on the throne. Although they failed, the long-term effects profoundly altered Gaelic society and Highland environment. On the sudden death of Queen Anne in 1714, the Highland chiefs and clansmen were no more happy over the succession of George of Hanover than they had been with that of William of Orange twenty-five years earlier. The rising of 1715 had to be organized too hastily and collapsed. General George Wade was appointed commander in Scotland. In the twelve years from 1724 he built the Highlands' first cross-country roads, all between the Great Glen and the High-land Line. Until then there was none, other than foot-tracks of man and beast. He made five roads of 16-foot width totalling 250 miles: (1) Inverness to Dunkeld over the Drumochter pass; (2) Glen Garry to Crieff by Tummel Bridge; (3) Inverness to Fort William; (4) Fort Augustus to Dalwhinnie over the Corrieyairack pass, with a branch to Ruthven near Kingussie; and (5) Glen Roy (not proven). By an irony of fate these roads were of great aid to Prince Charlie in the Forty-five Rising. After the Highland army's defeat at Culloden in 1746, 1,000 miles of new roads were added under a succession of army commanders, most notably General Caulfeild, until 1790. The more famous additions to Wade's were (1) 1746–8, Dumbarton to Inveraray over the Rest-and-Be-Thankful pass; (2) 1750, Blairgowrie to Poolewe by way of Braemar, Fort George, Contin, and Strath Bran, (3) 1750, Stirling to Fort William by Lochearnhead, Tyndrum, the Black Mount, Glen Coe, and Kinlochleven. In 1722 before Wade's appointment, a road had been built from Fort Augustus to Glenelg. And all this work, which cost £300,000, was wasted as an aid to wheeled traffic, for no thought had been given to maintenance in a Highland climate of blizzard, frost, heavy rainfall, and flash-floods. The roads were in ruin within a decade. When the countess of Seafield in 1799 tried to get from Contin to Poolewe, her coach was a wreck within 15 miles. A coach that made the journey from Inverness to Edinburgh in 1740 took eleven days and broke three axles. The roads, however, helped to speed the immigration of sheep and the emigration of clansmen. Over a shorter period, they helped the cattle-drovers.

End of the clan system

Culloden was the last military battle fought in Britain. The chiefs were shorn of their feudal powers, and the clans thus freed of a parasitic growth could have been reinvigorated, at least after the duke of Cumberland had done harassing them. The chiefs chose otherwise. They still held the clans' lands in their own names. They clung to them until the time came to sell out to Lowland and English sheep-farmers, or to clear the land of people for sheep of their own. To this latter rule there were several exceptions, like Campbell of Argyll, MacLeod of Dunvegan, Murray of Atholl, and a few others. The clan system ended between 1763 and 1775. In that short period, 20,000 Highlanders and Islanders emigrated. This first great emigration was caused by rack-renting, not yet by the Coming of the Sheep, which had only begun. The Highland landowners at first made no effort to expand sheep-farming, for the black cattle trade was reaching its peak of prosperity.

Cattle droving

A temporary cattle shortage had been caused by Cumberland's men, who had driven off 20,000 head from the North-East Highlands alone. Scarcity, and cattle-disease in England, trebled the price. By 1766, droving on a large scale from all the cattle districts to the Falkirk tryst was in full swing. Until 1760 the Crieff tryst had been the principal market, for Crieff was at one of the main gateways to the Highlands and trade was mostly in Scottish hands. But in 1760 Crieff was superseded by Falkirk (first opened 1707) for that site was more convenient to English dealers, who came in ever larger numbers as the times grew peaceful. Scotland was covered by a network of several hundred trysts and drove roads, all integrated as gathering points and routes for the main drive south in autumn, when the beasts were in best condition. The cattle flowed like rivers down these drove roads, travelling ten miles a day. The two main streams from the north took source in Caithness and the Hebrides, each being swollen by bellowing tributaries from all the hill-regions en route to Falkirk. The Caithness and Sutherland herds went for sale first to Muir of Ord, where they were joined by all beasts from Wester Ross between Loch Broom and Loch Alsh, which came by Strath Bran, Glen Cannich, and Glen Affric. They then went on to Kingussie and through the Drumochter pass, or else down the Great Glen where they were joined by the Skye and Outer Hebridean droves for the crossing of the Corrieyairack pass to Upper Spey and Drumochter. The Skye droves crossed Kyle Rhea to Glenelg, and reached the Great Glen either by Glen Shiel to Invermoriston or else by Glen Loyne to Invergarry. In the North-East Highlands all the great passes between the Spey and the Dee – Lairig an Laoigh, Lairig Ghru, Feshie-Geldie – were used to supply Braemar and numerous other trysts along the length of the Dee to Banchory and Aberdeen. From the Dee in turn, all southward passes to Strathmore and Strath Tay were busy with traffic, notably the Cairnwell pass from Braemar to Glen Shee, the Capel Mounth from Ballater to Glen Clova, and the Cairn o' Mount south from Banchory. All these routes and many more were blocked for days on end by immense herds, sometimes stretching up to 10 miles where routes converged. In 1772, 24,000 head were sold at Falkirk; by 1812, 50,000 cattle and 40,000 sheep; and the figures rose year by year until 150,000 cattle were sold annually around 1840. After 1850, the development of steamer services and railways steadily reduced droving traffic. By the 1890s all had ended.

Sheep

The Coming of the Sheep greatly changed the face of the High-lands, stripping it of men, grass, and trees. After 1750 a demand for Scottish wool sprang up in Europe and England. The flockmasters of the Southern Uplands started by exploiting the grasslands of Cowal in Argyll, and of Glen Falloch, Glen Dochart, Loch Earn, and Callander in Perthshire, where they could be sure of a good return to pay high rents. Their sheep were blackfaced Lintons, which henceforth ousted the smaller indigenous sheep. The American and Napoleonic wars and rising population intensified demand for wool and beef grown at home. As prices rose, more sheep were bred, but when it was discovered that sheep throve without night shelter, and that heavier Cheviot sheep could withstand the Highland winter, the landowners began to amalgamate small farms, to cut down beef and dairy stock, and to breed sheep in ever increasing numbers. Farms that employed 20 servants in 1770 required only one or two shepherds in 1810. In the West Highlands and Islands, the surplus cottars at first found employment in the booming kelp industry.

Kelp

Kelp was an alkaline ash obtained from the burning of seaweed, and needed in large quantities for the manufacture of soap, glass, and linen. Prior to 1750, the need had been supplied from barilla imported from the Mediterranean, but the supplies were cut off by wars with France and America. The price of kelp rose from £1 a ton to a maximum of £22. From chief to cottar, the people reaped a rich harvest for 66 years. Men were now needed in the west. A gold-rush situation developed. Population rose while farming and fishing were neglected. This was made possible by the potato supplanting oats and barley as the staple food, while the winter gap between crops was covered by whisky distilling.

Whisky

The potato, first produced as a main crop in Uist in 1743, had released for distilling much barley formerly needed as food. The growth of the whisky trade came as a response to rack-renting, and then to government prohibition, which aimed at conserving grain in time of war. In the Highlands and Islands, illicit distilling and smuggling of the product to Lowland cities prospered as never before. It grew to a township industry of economic importance. Prohibition having failed for half a century, the government in 1822 (when whisky was 6p a bottle) reduced the licence fee to £10. This modest sum induced distillers to register. The birth of the Scotch whisky industry dates from 1823.

The death of the cottage industry coincided with the bursting of the kelp bubble. The Napoleonic wars ended and new sources were found for soda. Ruin faced everyone. The Hebridean and West Highland chiefs either sold their land to Lowlanders or turned for salvation to the sheep. The landowners now had too many men on their estates, supported only by the potato crop, and by cattle which they wished to run down in number. They conceived three possible solutions: clearance of the Highland people, fisheries, and the distribution of land as crofts.

Fisheries

Fisheries were tried first. In 1786 a British Fisheries Society had been established with stations on Skye, Mull, the Outer Hebrides, and mainland coast at Ullapool, where the Society built houses, stores, and quays. They hoped to create a reserve of men for the navy. The project failed in the Isles because the price of salt for curing became exorbitant. It did prosper at Ullapool and Stornoway, and this inspired MacDonald of Skye, MacLeod of Dunvegan, and Mackenzie of Gairloch, to spend much money building fishing boats and piers. They found that Skyemen would not take to commercial fisheries; the landowners' efforts there were wasted.

Crofting

In 1811 MacLeod and many other landowners tried to help their people by giving them crofts. Under the runrig system, a township's land, arable and pasture, was held in common, with annual re-allotment of the arable strips to give all a fair share. Under the new system, the arable was permanently divided between tenants as separate crofts, on the principle of one man to one holding, the pasture as before remaining common. The immediate gain was the incentive given to each holder to improve his lot. He still had no lease, and so could be evicted at will. When the kelp failed, and cattle farms were amalgamated as sheep farms, the crofts became congested with displaced men and their families, for the crofters could not allow friends and relatives to wander homeless. The crofts thus had to feed twice the number of people for which they could naturally provide. Intensive cultivation of potatoes and oats without enough land for rotation of crops impoverished the soil. The yield dropped as the population mounted.

The Clearances

The third solution, clearance of the people by eviction, had begun as early as 1785 in the lands of MacDonell of Glengarry, which stretched from the Great Glen to Knoydart. His wife evicted 600 tenants from Loch Quoichside to make way for sheep. Similar evictions followed during the next three years, and continued off-and-on for seventy more. In 1801 Strath Glass between Beauly and Loch Affric was cleared by William Chisholm, and again long continued. Nearly all these people emigrated to Canada, 20,000 it is said from the MacDonell country alone. Lesser lairds aped the greater. Despicable as they were in betraying their people, and motivated at that time only by self-interest – to get money to spend in town – these early evictions were not accompanied by the violent cruelties that were soon to make the Sutherland clearances notorious. Elizabeth, the Countess of Sutherland (Anglo-Norman descent) had married George Granville Levenson-Gower, the Marquess of Stafford. This man was of Yorkshire family. His marriage to Elizabeth made him the greatest landowner in Britain. In 1807 he decided to 'improve' his land for sheep, and achieved this in the course of 13 years by evicting 15,000 men, women, and children, burning their homes, barns, crops, clothes, and furniture, destroying livestock, and leaving the helpless people to wander to the coast. All were left shelterless. Some were given tiny, infertile allotments on the shore; others walked if they were able to the emigrant ships at Wick and Thurso. The army, police, law-officers, and clergy were all used to suppress resistance. The Church disrupted when the evil effects of patronage were seen. The Free Church of Scotland was established in 1843. But the king created his subjects' oppressor the first duke of Sutherland.

Caithness, Ross, and Inverness were likewise cleared. Most of the Hebrides were sold to Lowlanders and Englishmen, but one or two islands remained in the hands of clan chiefs, who were revolted by the Leveson-Gower Improvement. Rum was the first island to be cleared. MacLean in 1828 shipped 443 of his crofters and cottars to North America, without violence, and brought in 8,000 sheep.

A series of natural disasters was in train. Around 1830 the herring shoals vanished from the sea-lochs of both the Inner Hebrides and mainland. The grain harvest failed in 1836 throughout Scotland and brought famine to the Highlands and Hebrides. MacLean impoverished himself buying food for his 1,500 people of Coll, and MacDonald spent large sums to help a thousand Skyemen to emigrate to Australia and Canada. The land could not support them any longer. At least two-thirds of the Highland and Island people had become dependent on the potato when blight struck the crop in 1846. The effect was immediate destitution, rapidly escalating to famine. The blight struck again in 1847, 1848, and 1850. The people not only starved, they no longer possessed a change of clothes, were wearing meal bags for under garments and outer, and went barefoot. Young and old died. In this national emergency the Free Church and the best of the landowners appealed in vain to the London government for aid. The government refused funds, and although the granaries of the southern ports were full, they allowed no distribution of grain or other food, nor would they direct the Scottish east coast farmers, who had plentiful wheat crops for export to London where prices were higher, to divert grain to the Highlands. In short, since the Highland and Island crofters had no vote, their fate was a matter of indifference to ministers of the crown. In this situation, MacLeod of Dunvegan and MacDonald chose ruin rather than stand by and watch their people die. They paid out in relief all money they possessed. When they went bankrupt, their estate trustees appointed factors as ruthless as any in the land. MacLeod founded relief committees in Edinburgh and Glasgow, which raised £209,000 and administered the fund through two Destitution Boards. No productive industry could be established, so that much of the money was spent on road-making to give employment.

A more drastic solution had to be found. The landowners appealed to government for a grant of £120,000 to ship 40,000 Highlanders to Canada at a freight of £3 a head. Government refused. But the prime minister, Lord John Russell, was now wanting to be rid of this nuisance, and when Fraser, a lawyer in Skye, set up a local Emigration Society, this was suddenly seen to be respectable, given Treasury backing, and reconstituted in London. Queen Victoria gave it £300 and money flowed in. Transport ships were made available to relieved landowners, who now evicted their people in great numbers. Where persuasion failed they put them aboard by force. All was done on the Sutherland model, with burning of townships, confiscation of property, the free use of troops and police, but now with government money too. The *Quebec Times* (1851–2) recorded that many of these ship-loads of Highlanders were dumped as a worthless cargo on the Canadian coast and left to starve or beg.

The new clearance lasted thirty years. The Improvers' defence was that sheep were no longer bringing large profits, while under the Poor Law Act the landowners had to contribute money to support the poor in the parishes. Profits had dropped for two reasons. First, peace with the USA coinciding with the Industrial Revolution was causing the mass production of cheap cotton cloth and a fall in wool prices. Second, sheep did not, like cattle, enrich the land with dung or give life to fine grass by cropping the coarse; instead they impoverished the land by nibbling too close, and by causing huge areas of hitherto fertile land to be covered in bracken, the seed of which they carried far and wide in their fleeces. Former grass moors were invaded by heather. The ground would no longer carry its former stock, and in winter large flocks had to be grazed in the Lowlands at high rent. The landowners' answer was not to balance their farming by bringing back cattle and men, but to go on clearing the people to extend the sheep ranges.

Large-scale emigration, of the kind called The Clearances, ended before 1870, but the clearance of ground to extend sheep and deer ranges continued for another 20 years. Deer forests and grouse moors were earning large rents after 1850. They had become immense-ly more valuable as new roads allowed new English industrialists to penetrate the Highlands to find there a fashionable recreation in shooting the wildlife – henceforth conserved for the purpose at the expense of natural predators. These new roads were the work of the Parliamentary Commissioners, and their engineer Thomas Telford.

The Telford roads

The old military roads had lost their bridges and fallen into chronic disrepair before Telford started work in 1803. He was given a triple commission, to cut the Caledonian Canal through the Great Glen, to build new roads and bridges, and to rebuild the more important military roads. The Great Glen was the heart of his work, which lasted 25 years, and most of his new roads radiated from there: Loch Linnhe to Moidart; Fort William to Arisaig, and to Speyside by Laggan; Invergarry to Loch Hourn; Invermoriston to Kyle of Lochalsh and Glenelg, with a link from Cluanie to Glengarry;

17.
Glen Feshie,
the Cairngorms.

18. Cairn Gorm. Edge of Coire an t-Sneachda.

19. The Lairig Ghru from Sron na Lairig.

20. Cairn Toul from Braeriach, with Lochan Uaine below Angel's Peak

Inverness to Aviemore and north to Tongue and Wick; and Dingwall to Kyle of Lochalsh by Glen Carron. In addition, he made the main roads through Skye, and elsewhere a dozen shorter ones, like the Hell's Glen road from Loch Fyne to Loch Goil. The military roads rebuilt included Tyndrum-Glencoe, which he took to Ballachulish instead of Kinlochleven. Hardly less important for its long-term effect was the road he built from Carlisle to Glasgow. His aim was to help the trade of the country, and therefore, so far as he could, he made much use of the old drove roads, and surfaced them for use by cattle (which none the less had to be shod in iron) rather than wheeled traffic. Most were 15 feet wide. He laid down first a close-set cobble of big stone, then a heavy layer of smaller stone, and surfaced the whole with a foot of gravel. The work was of high quality with good drainage, thorough turfing or walling of the cuts to stop erosion, and strong, stone-built bridges of adequate span. Until Telford came, Highland bridges were almost non-existent; bigger rivers had to be crossed by ferry – not even the Tay and Spey were bridged in their lower parts. Telford built 1,117 bridges and nearly 1,000 miles of road. His labourers earned 1/6d (7½p) a day. Modern Highland roads still follow his original lines.

His work had far-reaching beneficial effects on the deteriorating quality of Highland life. All products went faster to market; trade and new enterprise were stimulated; stage coaches could be used and tourist traffic began. He gave the base for a full development of communications, so that by 1860 the social and economic life of the Highlands had changed out of all recognition. A wider spread of schools and higher education swiftly followed. The canal, on the other hand, proved a commercial failure. It opened in 1822, but steamers were now rapidly replacing sailing ships, and the canal was not deep enough to take the American and Baltic trade. The first steamships serving the Inner Hebrides sailed in 1830, and so multiplied that by 1890 a dozen steamers a week were entering West Highland ports as remote as Loch Dunvegan in Skye. In 1863 the Highland Railway was completed from Inverness to Perth, and numerous other lines were laid.

Crofters' revolt

Behind this splendid front, the oppression of the crofters by landowners proceeded. Their holdings were continually diminished without reduction of rent to extend the owners' farms, deer forests, and sheep runs. Dispossessed tenants were settled on other crofts against the crofter's will; appalling congestion once again exhausted the ground. The lairds would not allow crofters to protect their grazings and crops from deer, and the gamekeepers shot the guard dogs. On some estates the crofters were unable to renew the thatch on their roofs, because the lairds would not allow heather and rushes to be taken from the hills, lest grouse be disturbed. The list of tyrannies grew long. The most effective revolt was in Skye. In 1882, at the battle of the Braes (south-east of Portree), the crofters fought 60 policemen brought from Glasgow to evict them. The government took alarm and sent in warships and marines, but Gladstone – puzzled to know what was amiss – appointed a royal commission under Lord Napier. Within the year, Napier reported to Parliament 'a state of misery, of wrong-doing, and of patient long-suffering, without parallel in the history of our country'. The result was the Crofters Holding Act 1884, which gave tenants secure tenure and established a Crofters' Commission to take from the landowners the management of all crofting estates with power to fix fair rents. The most serious evil of Highland life was removed.

Emigration

When emigration was renewed at the opening of the twentieth century, it was this time by men and women acting on their own initiative, seeking job opportunities commensurate with higher education, or attracted by higher standards of living now brought within easier reach by mechanical transport services – or, as always, a simple lack of local employment. Some 18,000 crofts survive to the present day because the communal system despite all faults is the only one that can hold people to land so intractable. Without crofts, the Highland counties would be still further emptied. The products of the croft are worth several million pounds annually. Yet crofting is mainly a subsistence husbandry, and to pay for his imports the crofter has to take part-time work in ancillary industries, like the building trade, road-making, fishing, weaving, seafaring, transport services, forestry, and tourism. There is a strict limit to Highland employments, therefore emigration of the young is inevitable. Crofters' children, who could get local work, have had to wait until parents died to acquire a house, for the law has not allowed more than one house to be built on croftland. Until that law is amended, an event expected in 1976, the native people cannot repeople their land.

In 1965 the Highlands and Islands Development Board was formed to improve the Highlander's lot by encouraging appropriate industries. Much of its good work has been undermined because freight charges by land or sea are so high that price levels are much above those of the Lowlands, while average incomes are lower. The young Highlander, hoping to buy a house, cannot compete with the holiday-homer from town, either on the house-market or for land on which to build. This again is causing a new clearance, made worse by property speculators, and by the freight handicap on small or prospective industries. Inequitable law and lack of government control still tend, as they have since the nineteenth century, to the dispossession of the native race. The oil industry, and the coastal construction of its production platforms, has been the reverse of helpful: it has withdrawn labour, skilled and unskilled, from the inland communities.

The natural resources of the Highlands are by no means all of the land. Sea fishing has prospered on the west coast, and never more so than during the early 1970s, when the HIDB's help to the industry met spectacular success. Nearly 1,000 boats were in action and Mallaig became a principal herring port of Europe. Other ports with big landings are Campbeltown, Oban, Uig in Skye, Lochinver, Ullapool, and Kinlochbervie. The annual export of salmon and venison has fluctuated between £1m and £2m for each – figures that pale before the whisky export, valued in 1975 at nearly £300m. Highland whisky, like electricity, is a product, not a resource but the production of both depends one on the quality of Highland water and the other on its quantity, which must be reckoned a resource of peculiar importance.

Hydro-electric power

The first power stations in the Highlands were opened by the British Aluminium Company, at Foyers, in 1896, and Kinlochleven in 1909, for its own use. Although the Highlands' potential water power was immense, further development was opposed by the coal industry until national demand caused Parliament to establish the North of Scotland Hydro-Electric Board in 1943. During the next 30 years the Board constructed power stations great and small throughout all Highland districts. The greater schemes were made by damming glen-lochs, to which additional water was fed from ramifying tunnel systems, which tapped wide catchment areas among the surrounding mountains. Examples of these catchment systems are Loch Sloy–Glen Shira, between upper Loch Lomond and Loch Awe; Breadalbane, between Loch Earn and Loch Lyon; the Tummel Valley north to Drumochter; Glen Garry and Glen Moriston; Glen Affric and Glen Cannich; Strath Farrar; the Conon valley from the river Orrin to Strath Vaich (including the Fannaichs); and Loch Shin. Such huge and complex constructions ended in the sixties, and further development has meantime been restricted to pumped storage stations, which store electric power generated elsewhere by nuclear fission. The first of these was built on Ben Cruachan and opened in 1965. There is no way of storing electricity in large amount except by rebuilding a potential water-power. Thus the Hunterston power station in Ayrshire, which uses nuclear fuel and cannot be halted when demand falls at night or at week-ends, now feeds electric power to the Cruachan power house at Loch Awe, where the turbines are reversed to drive water back up the mountain to the reservoir at 1,200 feet in the south corrie. The dam there is 1,000 feet long and 150 feet high, but the real engineering marvels are hidden below, where a vast machine hall has been cut out of the mountain's granite core. The Board has recently made surveys for a similar scheme above the east side of Loch Lomond.

The most remote areas of the Highlands have thus been supplied with power, except for some isolated crofts and islands, and the uneconomic cost of distribution has been met by exporting surplus power to the Lowlands. A heavy additional cost has been impairment of the natural scene, exacerbated by government refusal to spend money on undergrounding cables even in the most sensitive areas.

Minerals

Scotland's wealth in coal and iron is all Lowland. The Highlands have these and many other minerals of no great economic importance. Gold occurs in river alluvium in Sutherland, where a minor gold rush occurred in 1868–9 – 400 men were at work in the Strath of Kildonan. Lead mines were at first worked for their silver, but for lead alone at Strontian, Ardgour, from 1722 intermittently until the start of this century, and at Tyndrum, Arygll, from 1741 to 1920. At Strontian, the mines were reopened in 1963. They lie on the hillside above the Strontian burn. Here the mineral strontianite (named from the place) was first found in 1764 and later proven to be a distinct mineral. (The element strontian was isolated in 1808 by Davy as a yellow metal, which burns with a brilliant red flame and is used in fireworks.) At Tyndrum, some of the lead veins were 20 feet thick. Work was brisk there until 1815, thereafter spasmodic. In 1955 amateur prospectors at Tyndrum found the two radioactive minerals uranite and kasolite. These were first-recorded discoveries in Scotland, but amounts were not big enough to work.

Haematite ores were worked for their iron at Tomintoul from 1730 to 1737, and 1840 to 1845. Magnetite, also valuable for its iron, occurs in Skye near Broadford, but is not yet worked. Sedimentary ironstone was mined in Raasay during the first world war and briefly in 1959 when a steel manufacturing company investigated but made no public report. The second world war led to the opening of a sandstone mine at Loch Aline in Morvern, where a cretaceous band 110 feet thick, and 99·7% silica, had been discovered by the Geological Survey. The mine became Britain's only source of optical glass in wartime. The annual extraction is still 60–70,000 tons from nearly 30 miles of tunnels.

Numerous other minerals have economic value: building stone, quartz (including Cairngorm stones), diatomite, marble, serpentine, gravels, limestone, slates, copper, nickel – these and many more were either worked off and on through the years, or became locally important industries that have since died. The slate quarries of Easdale in Lorn employed several hundred men for two centuries until 1965, when soaring freight charges and cheaper roofing materials killed the industry. The same tale can be told of the Ballachulish slate quarries, which opened in 1694 (only two years after the Glen Coe massacre). Cairngorm crystals have been widely quarried from quartz veins on the Cairngorm hills, notably Ben Avon, where the workings can still be seen on the south slopes at Allt an Eas Mhoir. The colour is brown, but blue crystals have been found. Men were able to earn a living last century by searching the gravel in burns or digging with a hammer. Very large specimens may be seen on the altar of St Andrew's Church at Fort William. Ugly scars have been left by the slate quarriers, lead miners, aggregate extractors, and sand miners; neither the developers nor local and central government have made any effort to restore the scene.

Future

Man required a thousand years thoroughly to strip the Highlands of its ancient forest. A hundred more sufficed to strip away the bulk of the native people and their Gaelic culture. 'Improvement' now goes faster. Motor-cars, tractors, electric power, telephones, wireless, television, fast ferries and air services, have brought benefits that few men now living in the Highlands would be willing to do without, but also problems that no one has mastered. Hydro-electric dams scar with their concrete mass the best Highland glens, which are festooned with pylons and wires. Hillside pipes have been left unburied. The motor-car, as an aid to the fuller life, brings in to the Highlands a multitude of townsmen, who by sheer weight of number destroy the thing they seek – a natural environment. Their litter fouls the land from the hedgerows to the summit of Ben Nevis. Livestock and wildlife die of it. The efforts by government or by landowners to provide facilities for the public enjoyment of the Highlands, or made by developers for their own profit, institutional-ize the natural scene by addition of car-parks, lavatories, picnic sites, information bureaux, signposts, big litter bins, small shops, tearooms, ski-tows, chairlifts, sno-cats, snowbikes, and more besides. Scotsmen find it hard to appreciate the truth that the Highlands are a natural asset, which they have been too ready to expend. Intrusive structures, whether dams or construction yards for oil production platforms, or factory buildings, are essential to the nation. There is no need to do without them, for they could invariably be sited elsewhere than the regions of outstanding landscape quality; sometimes at a greater cost in money, which civilized man should be prepared to pay. To find a wholly wild scene, unmarked by man's building, one has to go ever farther into the hills. The mountaineer is fortunate that his goal is mainly there. But even the wilderness is shrinking fast. Deer forest owners, who formerly used foot-tracks to get access for stalking, and ponies to bring down the carcases, have bulldozed more than 1,000 miles of wide tracks to get access by Landrovers. Some of these bulldozed roads in the Cairngorms go right over the main ridges and mountain tops. In Glen Feshie, the most beautiful of the region's right-of-way paths has been partially wrecked. Until 1960, the Cairngorm plateau was reckoned to be the most extensive area of high ground remote from roads, but these have so proliferated that little ground is more than a mile from any road.

The huge if short-term demand for timber during two world wars continued the destruction of forest during this century. Annual heather burning in spring to give new growth for sheep or deer, prevents the regeneration of trees. Reafforestation has come largely through the Forestry Commission, established in 1919 under immediate post-war conditions to produce a timber reserve against national emergencies. These earlier pressures have relaxed, allowing a more liberal policy on landscape effects and recreation. Good work has been done. New forests have clothed bare hill slopes and moors to advantage, and old forests like the Black Wood of Rannoch and upper Glen Affric might have died of neglect and deer had the Commission not taken the property. They now manage almost two million acres, but much of their planting has diminished the quality of the landscape and restricted access without need. This is seen in the clearance of native oakwood and birch to excessive degree, and the substitution of a sitka-spruce monoculture, so that the former variety and relief given by broad-leaved trees is being replaced in the West Highlands by a coniferous monotony. This involves a diminishment of wildlife, for commercial spruce, close-packed and regimented, stifles ground plants. The interiors of such forests are dead places. Larch, whose bright spring green gives needed relief, is no longer planted commercially.

Public pressure on the Highland environment has assumed such magnitude that a national conservation policy is an urgent need. Resolute attempts to respond constructively to the problems arising have been made by the National Trust for Scotland, who have been pioneers in this field, by local and central governments, by the Nature Conservancy who have nearly forty nature reserves, and by the Countryside Commission for Scotland – but all this on a piece-meal basis. The Highlands are afflicted, as the towns were before them, by haphazard development. Nothing less than a clear national policy, given effect under national rather than regional control, can save the better Highland landscape through positive land-management. An important move to meet this need was made in 1975 by the Countryside Commission for Scotland, who proposed to government that a park system be instituted. If this should be realized in the near future by new legislation, it could be successful only if management boards were given planning powers not as yet available to local planning authorities, and if central government were resolute in support – which they have never been in England under that country's park system. The tale of man's activity in the Highlands has been one of ruthless exploitation, in which, with some rare exceptions, he has taken all and given little. It will not be easy to stem the tide, and none who try must be chilled by the tempting analogy with King Canute.

THE HIGHLANDS – DISTRICT AREAS.

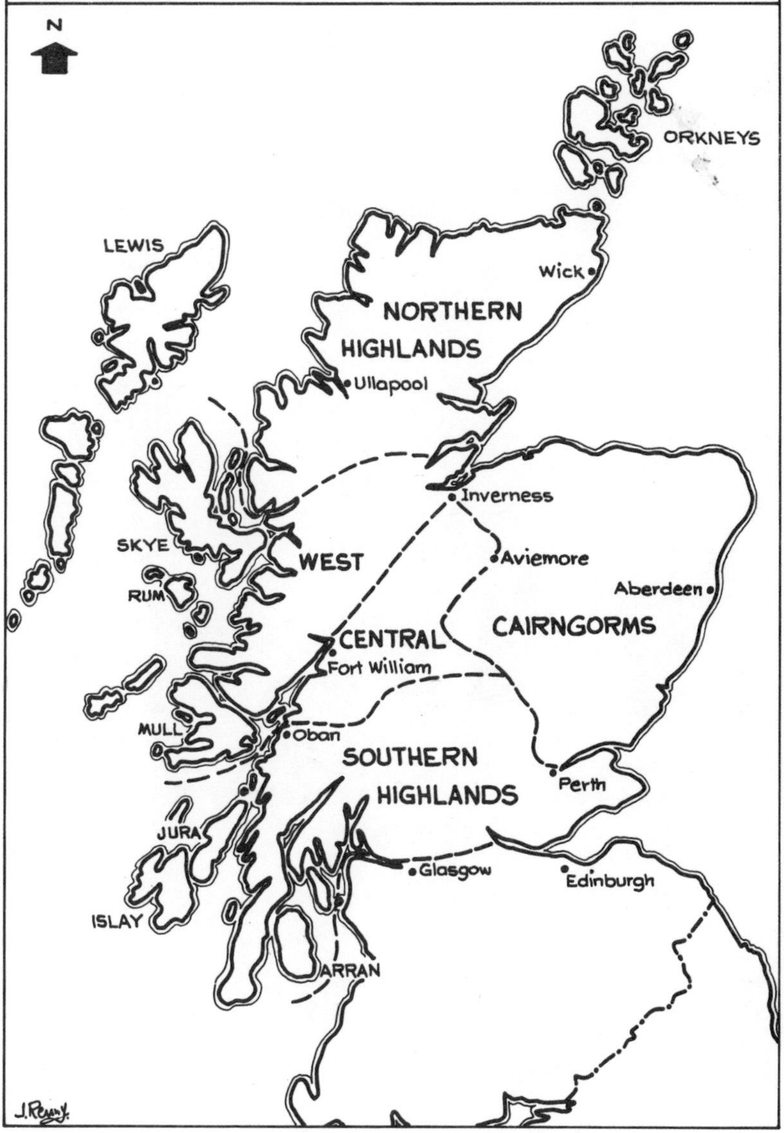

N

ORKNEYS

LEWIS

NORTHERN

HIGHLANDS

Wick

• Ullapool

• Inverness

SKYE

WEST

• Aviemore

Aberdeen •

RUM

CAIRNGORMS

CENTRAL

Fort William

MULL

• Oban

SOUTHERN

HIGHLANDS

Perth

JURA

• Glasgow

• Edinburgh

ISLAY

ARRAN

J. Perry.

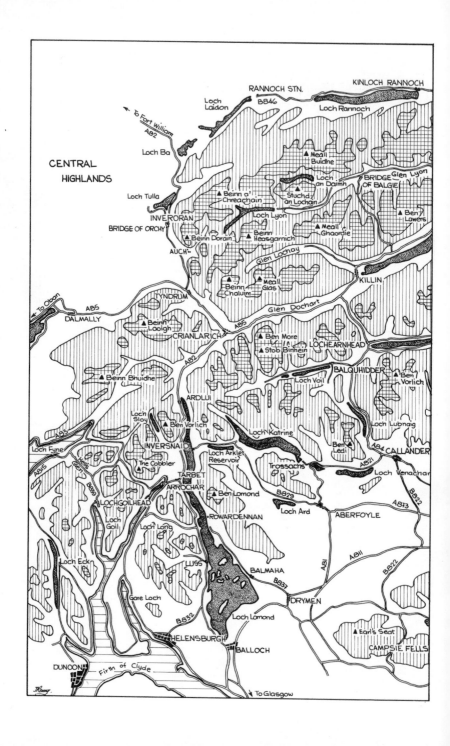

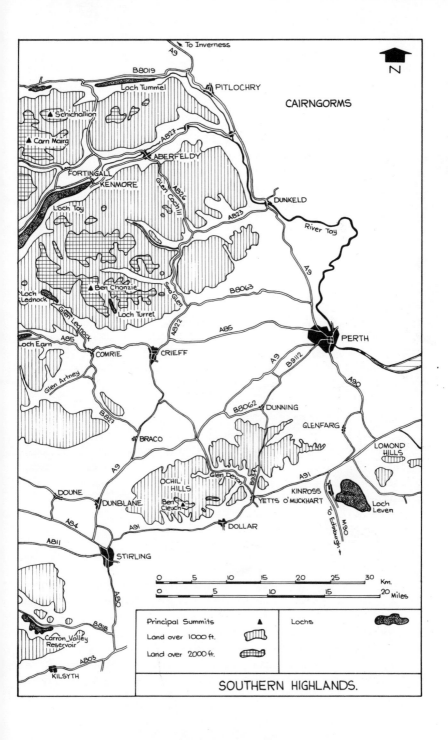

N

To Inverness

B8019
Loch Tummel
PITLOCHRY

CAIRNGORMS

▲ Schichallion

▲ Carn Mairg

A827
ABERFELDY

FORTINGALL
KENMORE

Glen Cochill

DUNKELD

Loch Tay

A826

A823

River Tay

A9

▲ Ben Chonzie

B8063

Loch Lednock

Loch Turret

A822

A85

Glen Lednock

PERTH

A85
Loch Earn

COMRIE

CRIEFF

A9

B9112

Glen Artney

A822

A90

B821

B8062
DUNNING

GLENFARG

BRACO

LOMOND HILLS

A9

OCHIL HILLS
Glen Devon

A91

DOUNE

Ben Cleuch ▲

KINROSS
YETTS O'MUCKHART

B934

Loch Leven

DUNBLANE

To Edinburgh

M90

A84

A91
✝ DOLLAR

A811

STIRLING

| 0 | 5 | 10 | 15 | 20 | 25 | 30 | Km. |

| 0 | 5 | 10 | 15 | 20 Miles |

A80

Carron Valley
Reservoir

B818

Principal Summits ▲	Lochs
Land over 1000 ft.	
Land over 2000 ft.	

A803

KILSYTH

SOUTHERN HIGHLANDS.

5   Southern Highlands

The Southern Highlands extend from the Highland Line to Loch Rannoch. Their west boundary is the Atlantic; their east, the road from Perth to Pitlochry; and the north, the road from Oban by Loch Awe and Glen Orchy to Bridge of Orchy, and from there straight across Rannoch Moor to Loch Rannoch. Arran is included, for the Highland Line crosses the island's centre. The mainland is divided by the sea and the glens into fourteen distinct mountain groups.

Access

The main gateways are Loch Lomondside and the Tay-Tummel valley from Dunkeld. Other lesser breaches go from Callander by the Pass of Leny to Loch Earn, and from Crieff either west to Loch Earn or north by the Sma' Glen. All these passes give access by road to the entire district. There are two railways: the West Highland line from Glasgow to Mallaig by way of Loch Long, with stops at Arrochar, Crianlarich, Tyndrum and Bridge of Orchy, and with a branch from Tyndrum to Oban; and the Perth–Inverness line through the Tay–Tummel valley. The West Highland line gives the more useful access, and the road system has bus services, but for all practical purposes of exploratory hill-walking and climbing a car is essential for access unless on a long holiday planned in advance.

Topography

The district's predominating rock, except on the Isle of Arran, is a laminated mica-schist greatly altered from an original sandy sediment by pressure, heat, and folding. The rock weathers unevenly according to its angle of lie and degree of hardness, to form rounded grassy hills often with craggy outcrops on the flanks, but without sizeable cliffs except on the Cobbler at Arrochar. Seventy tops rise above 3,000 feet, of which 46 are Munros. The seaboard is more deeply riven than any other part of Scotland. The great sea-lochs of Loch Long and Loch Fyne run 40 and 50 miles into the hills from

THE ISLAND OF ARRAN.

the open sea at Garroch Head on Bute. These with several other branches of the Firth of Clyde split south Argyll into a tattered fringe of peninsulas, of which the greatest are Cowal and Kintyre. The Kintyre–Knapdale peninsula stretches 55 miles from Crinan to within 12 of Ireland. These peninsulas, together with the low ground of Nether Lorn, Loch Lomond, and the Trossachs, show a scenic variety not found in the higher districts to the north, where the Southern Highlands roll towards Rannoch in waves of increasing height, which come close to 4,000 feet on Ben Lawers. The high country has more imposing mountains, but the southern area the more beautiful combination of woodland and water.

Arran

Arran is 20 miles long by 10 wide, sheltered from the west and given a mild climate by the huge protective arm of Kintyre. Nowhere else in Scotland is there such diversity of rock formation and therefore of soil, scene, and flora packed into 200 square miles. The variety, compactness, and shelter give Arran a character unique among Scottish islands. The Hebrides by comparison are stark. All around the Arran coast are whitewashed cottages whose gardens are crowded with fuchsia and honeysuckle. They lend the island a comfortable air rarely seen outside the Firth. The cornfields run in brightly coloured aprons to the shore, fringed by silver-barked hazels and rowans from which the high peaks rise behind.

Access is by daily car-ferry from Ardrossan to Brodick, or from Cloanaig in north Kintyre to Loch Ranza, the latter in summer only.

South of the Highland Line – the String road between Brodick and Blackwaterfoot – are heathery moors and sheep-runs of upland kind; to its north, a truly Highland scene of granite mountains with deep but fair glens. Their highest point is Goat Fell, 2866 feet, 3 miles north-west of Brodick Bay. While the northern half of the island is mountainous, the big hills lie in the eastern sector, where they form two horseshoes lying back to back. One faces north-east enclosing Glen Sannox; the other south, enclosing Glen Rosa with Goat Fell on its east wall. Sixteen peaks are linked by the high ridges, and so excellent is the walking on top that the dozen main summits can be traversed in a very long day from Brodick or Corrie (8,500 feet of ascent). The most enjoyable day of all is the traverse of the long west ridge from Beinn Nuis to Suidhe Fhearghas. Ben Nuis is best reached from Glen Rosa up the left bank of the Garbh Allt. The traverse over the top leads on to Beinn Tarsuinn, and so to Arran's thinnest ridge, A' Chir (the Comb). This stretches a mile to Cir Mhor and is formed by huge up-ended slabs that dip on the west to Glen Iorsa, while on the east they present a continuous cliff to Glen Rosa. The crest gives an exhilarating scramble, and the top of Cir Mhor is one of the sharpest in Scotland. At every turn of the long ridge over Caisteal Abhail (Ptarmigan's Castle) until the final descent from Suidhe Fhearghas to Sannox Bay, the walker enjoys vivid contrasts – the serrated crest and shelving cliffs, the company of gulls, the sweep of green glens below, the yellow sands of Brodick Bay, and the low far-off hills of Ayrshire.

An excellent introductory walk, and also a quick way to reconnoitre the hills, is to traverse Glens Rosa and Sannox from Brodick to Corrie. The route crosses the Saddle, 1413 feet, between Goat Fell and Cir Mhor. The Rosa track is wide to the Garbh Allt, where the glen swings north to disclose a memorable sight – the great spike of Cir Mhor at its head, the tip of the 'Castles' behind, and in the foreground the Rosa burn sparkling where it runs across granite into crystal pools. The Saddle is 2½ hours from Brodick, and the descent to Sannox village 1 hour more.

Goat Fell is most easily climbed from Brodick by the left bank of the Cnocan Burn on to the mountain's east ridge. There is a path all the way (2½ hours from Brodick to the top). Your reward is a panorama from the hills of Ireland far into the Highlands and Lowlands, and west across jagged ridges to the Hebrides lying on sunlit seas. The faster route of descent is down the south ridge. A usual continuation is on to North Goatfell by the Stacach ridge, then over Mullach Buidhe and around the rim of the Devil's Punch Bowl (Coire na Ciche). The descent from the last top, Cioch na h' Oighe (the Maiden's Pap), must be made west into Glen Sannox to avoid slabs.

There are nearly 100 rock-climbs in Arran, of which the best are on Cir Mhor, either on the north-east face from Glen Sannox, or better still the south face from the Rosa corrie (Fionn Choire), which is dominated by the Rosa Pinnacle. The granite there is coarsely crystalline. The south ridge of the pinnacle (855 feet) is one of the most enjoyable routes in Scotland. The north-east face has no first-class routes, for the rock is much broken by broad diagonal ledges, giving a series of inter-connected climbs, short but interesting. The feature of Arran granite is the cyclopean wall formation, caused by cracking of the rock when cooling, and its subsequent weathering into cubic blocks along the hair-lines. Overlapping slabs have formed where the blocks have dropped away. The granite was also intruded by lava-dykes, which by erosion now form the principal gullies. These give poor or dangerous climbing, like the notorious Ben Nuis chimney.

Cowal

The Cowal and Kintyre peninsulas are reached over the Rest-and-Be-Thankful pass (806 feet) at the head of Glen Croe between Loch Long and Loch Fyne. The principal Clyde resorts are spread along the south coasts of Cowal at Dunoon, Innellan, Tighnabruaich, Rothesay in Bute, and some others. In among them at Ardyne Point, at the entrance to the Kyles of Bute, and at Portavadie on Loch Fyne, construction yards for oil production platforms were built in 1974. The wounds to the peninsula are likely to form permanent scars. The interior is split north to south by several parallel folds containing Loch Goil, Loch Eck, Loch Striven, and Loch Riddon. The broad hill ridges between them rise in eastern Cowal to 30 tops over 2000 feet. They often give enjoyable bog-walking, although much ground is soft and the lower slopes usually forested.

The best walk in the southern part goes up Glen Massan from the head of the Holy Loch to the top of Beinn Mhor, 2433 feet. At the foot of the glen, the Younger Botanic Gardens should be seen in June, when the rhododendrons are in bloom. North-east Cowal is mostly a National Forest Park, with the result that access to the hills has become increasingly difficult, both through blanket-planting of hillsides formerly open, and by restriction of access to lanes, which tend by use to become quagmires (rainfall is 90 inches) or to close up as the trees grow. Much excellent walking has been lost during recent years. The only Munro in Cowal is Beinn an Lochain, 3021 feet, close by the Rest-and-Be-Thankful. The best route up is from Butterbridge in Glen Kinglas.

South of the Rest, the Ardgoil peninsula between Loch Goil and Loch Long is known as Argyll's Bowling Green – a corruption of its old name of the droving days, *Buaile na Greine*, the sunny cattle fold. A spine of mica-schist hills runs down its middle. They rise at the north end to 2774 feet on Ben Donich, and 2580 feet on the Brack. A right-of-way goes between the two from Glen Croe to Lochgoilhead. The Brack has some rock-climbing on its north face.

21. Scots pines, Glen Quoich, Cairngorms.

22. Cairngorms. Rising storm on Morven.

23. Glen Derry, Cairngorms.

24. Cliffs of Lochnagar. Left to right: Tough-Brown Ridge, Raeburn's Gully, Black Spout Pinnacle (centre), Black Spout, Black Spout Buttress.

Kintyre

Kintyre is farming country, and the best in Argyll. Since no high hills draw cloud, the rainfall drops to 40–55 inches. Rolling moors occupy the interior, nearly all of it less than 1,200 feet and above 400, uninhabited except in the south and along the coastal fringe. The hills are grassed to the tops and without much heather. The fishing ports on the east coast are Tarbert, Carradale, and Campbeltown. From West Loch Tarbert, ferries serve the islands of Islay, Jura, and Gigha. The three Paps of Jura are quartzite mountains, 2571 feet, especially worth climbing for their seaward views ranging from the Isle of Man to the Cuillin of Skye. The Paps' enormous scree-slopes can be turned by zig-zag strips of grass.

Knapdale, which is the northern part of the peninsula between the Tarbert and Crinan isthmuses, is congested with rough moorland hills. The lower flanks tend to be forested, especially in the north-west around Loch Coillie Bharr, where the Forestry Commission has a reception centre. The west coast is heavily indented by Loch Sween and Loch Caolisport. The village of Tayvallich on Loch Sween is the best centre (camp and caravan site) for exploring a coast of great scenic and archaeological interest. At Kilmory, near the Point of Knap, and at Keills where the road ends on the most westerly point, and again on Eilean Mor 2 miles off Kilmory, are three ancient chapels dating from the eleventh to fourteenth centuries, famous for their carved stones and crosses. Eilean Mor can be reached by canoe or by hiring a motor-boat at Crinan. By the shore of Loch Sween, 2½ miles north of Kilmory, stands Scotland's earliest castle of square Norman build. It was built by Somerled between 1125 and 1135, while driving the Vikings out of mainland Argyll. Its keep and round tower are thirteenth- and fourteenth-century additions. The castle rises from grassland beside a sandy beach, a once-splendid site now despoiled by a big caravan park.

Mid-Argyll

Northward across the Crinan isthmus, the districts of Mid-Argyll and Nether Lorn stretch 27 miles to Loch Etive. Loch Fyne bounds them on the east, and Loch Awe divides one from the other. The interior moorlands form a plateau nowhere rising to 2,000 feet except at the head of Loch Fyne, where Beinn Bhuidhe, 3106 feet, is the only Munro. Numerous lochs and rivers afford good fishing, but the plateau has never attracted hill-walkers. All excellence of scene lies below in the wooded glens and shores, and Lorn's islanded coast-line. Five towns or villages on the periphery give access.

Lochgilphead on a bay of Loch Fyne gives access north-west to Nether Lorn. Its near neighbour, Ardrishaig, is linked by 9 miles of Canal to Crinan, used by Clyde-based yachts and fishing boats bound for the Hebrides, to avoid an 80-mile detour round the Mull of Kintyre. Inveraray near the head of Loch Fyne gives access through Glen Aray to Loch Awe. The village with its white-harled houses was built by order of the third duke of Argyll from 1744 to 1794. His castle of blue-grey stone was built at the same time on the banks of the Aray, and richly decorated within. The Campbells' original castle was Innis Chonnail on Loch Awe. North Loch Awe may be approached through Dalmally in Glen Orchy, or from Connel on Loch Etive through the Pass of Brander. The chief town of Lorn is Oban on the Firth of Lorn, a shipping, fishing, and tourist port of great importance. Its piers offer ferry and steamer services to Mull, Colonsay, Coll, Tiree, South Uist, and Barra, and to Lismore and Morvern.

Mid-Argyll abounds in archaeological relics, historic and pre-historic. No one visiting the Crinan–Kilmartin district should omit climbing Dunadd, 176 feet, on the Moine Mhor (Great Moss). Only a few broken walls of that ancient fort now remain. Carved on rock slabs near the top are a wild boar, a basin for washing the feet, and the print of a human foot. On the inauguration of a chief, he set his foot in the print and took oath to walk in the steps of his forebears. On the low farmland at the north edge of the moss are numerous megaliths. There are several chambered cairns here, at Nether Largie, including the South Cairn (see p. 70). Nearby is the Templewood sun-circle surrounded by oak-trees. The central monolith is ringed by standing stones about 8 or 9 feet high, dating from 1,600 BC. Kilmartin churchyard, a mile to the north, has the most beautifully carved crucifixion to be found on any cross-shaft in the Highlands. This alone is worth travelling far to see.

Hill-walkers and anglers have ready access to the Lorn plateau and its scores of lochs from Kilmelfort on the west coast. A motorable side-road runs east from there over the moorland watershed to Loch Avich and down to Loch Awe (9 miles). From Loch Avich, another track, the String of Lorn, goes 4 miles north-west to Loch Scamadale, then 8 miles north-east to Loch Nant, before descending 3 miles to Glen Nant. Many other tracks lead up to the Braes of

Lorn by Glen Euchart, and by the rivers Oude and Nell. The western edge of the plateau gives panoramas across the islands of the Firth of Lorn.

Lorn's south-east frontier, Loch Awe, stretches 23 miles from Ford to Dalmally. It thus ranks with Loch Ness as the longest of Scotland's freshwater lochs, and with Loch Lomond and Loch Maree as one of the three most beautiful. Before the Ice Age it drained south to the Sound of Jura, but now north-west to Loch Etive through the Pass of Brander. Low conical hills enclose the south end, but the north head is pillowed by the big mountains of the Central Highlands – Ben Cruachan, 3695 feet, Beinn a' Chochuill, 3215 feet, Beinn Eunaich, 3242 feet, and Beinn Laoigh, 3708 feet – a barrier set spaciously back and split by the rivers Orchy, Strae, and Lochy. This wide north end of Loch Awe is graced by a dozen wooded islands, among them Inishail, bearing a thirteenth-century chapel, and Fraoch Eilean with a twelfth-century castle built by Dughall, the son of Somerled. Boats may be hired from Lochawe village. The best viewpoint over the loch is from the monument to Duncan Ban McIntyre (died 1812). It stands on a hill of 500 feet, 1½ miles south-west of Dalmally. Duncan Ban's one great poem, *In Praise of Beinn Dorain*, ranks high in Gaelic literature. He lived and died near Bridge of Orchy, where he was a gamekeeper. A prominent feature seen from his monument is Kilchurn Castle, built on a spit at the head of the loch by Sir Colin Campbell in 1446.

The head of Loch Fyne is less majestically crowned by hills. Beinn Bhuidhe may be climbed either by Glen Shira or Glen Fyne. Glen Shira has an 8-mile access road up the river's left bank to a Hydro-electric dam at 1,100 feet. The road is not always open to cars in its upper reaches, in which event permission may be granted by the Argyll Estate Office at Inveraray. If you choose to walk, take the old track up the right bank, which is free of traffic until three miles up it rejoins the new road on the left bank. It ends at Rob Roy's cottage 200 yards beyond the bridge over the Brannie burn. Beinn Bhuidhe can then be climbed in 3½ miles by its south-west ridge. Glen Fyne gives a quicker route if a car is driven 2½ miles up to the Lodge.

Trossachs

South of Ben Lomond, the Highland spine tails off down to the Lowlands. Eastward behind the tail lie the Trossachs. Foothills though they are, they are Highlands in miniature, with a combination of woodland, water, and craggy bluffs of the highest landscape quality.

The Trossachs form a compact group of more than 20 hills and 9 lochs centred around Strath Gartney, which runs 18 miles west from Callander towards the head of Loch Lomond. Most of its length is filled by Loch Vennachar, Loch Achray, and Loch Katrine. The north boundary is the Braes of Balquhidder above Loch Voil; the east, Strathyre and Loch Lubnaig; and the south, the Aberfoyle hills. The whole comprises 120 square miles at the very edge of the Lowland flats, where three-fifths of Scotland's people live. Hence year by year, in the absence of firm management, the Trossachs like Loch Lomondside have been deteriorating in quality.

The approach from Glasgow is usually made over the Duke's Pass, 796 feet, between Aberfoyle and Loch Achray. This gives the best view down to the heart of the Trossachs – the wooded Pass of Achray threaded by Achray Water, which flows east from Loch Katrine between Ben Venue and Ben A'n. Although Ben A'n is only 1520 feet, the spur of a bigger hill behind, the south face is rocky and stands boldly above an apron of birches that falls to the head of the loch, whose shores are fringed by reeds and rowans. The crags give a dozen short climbs traversed by heather ledges. The hill can be climbed to its east side by a path slanting between the woods and the grounds of the Trossachs Hotel. Ben Venue, 2393 feet, is seen to best advantage when the approach is made through Callander along the shores of Loch Vennachar. It too shows a craggy face to the pass, shadowed where Ben A'n is sunlit.

The Trossach's highest hill is Ben Ledi, 2873 feet. It stands in the angle between Loch Vennachar and Loch Lubnaig. The ascent is usually made by its long south-east ridge, but more interesting routes will be found from east and north by crossing the river Leny by a bridge above the Pass of Leny. You may then go either straight up, or better, follow the Stank Glen to nearly 1,000 feet, when you can strike south-west to the small corrie under the summit. Climb the corrie's north spur. The view from the top embraces 120 miles from Arran to the Cairngorms, and from Ben Nevis to Tinto Hill. The panorama from the Trossachs hills, especially Ben A'n and Ben Venue, is excellent out of all proportion to height.

The Trossachs are traversed by paths. They thread the Pass of Achray and go right round Loch Katrine, and each of the other lochs. All are fringed by oak, birch, hazel, and beech. There are many other tracks. Lochs Katrine and Arklet and their catchment areas belong to Glasgow Corporation. The raising of the water-level, the domestication of Loch Katrine's east end, from which a steamer plies in summer, and the inundation of the whole region by tourists, walkers, anglers, campers, climbers, and caravanners, have lost the Trossachs much of their natural enchantment. To see them at their best, visit in the quieter months of spring and autumn, when the trees are greening, or the leaves yellowing.

Ben Lomond

Loch Lomond is Britain's biggest sheet of inland water, although its 21-mile length is shorter than Loch Awe and Loch Ness by 2 miles. Its fame is entirely due to the mountainous setting of its woods and water, and certain peculiarities of these. The trees are broad-leaved, mainly oak, beech, chestnut, larch, and birch. Its shape, broad to the south where a dozen wooded islands give variety, narrows under Ben Lomond like a gimlet thrusting into the northern mountains. Ben Lomond is sited so well to take the eye that the loch is now named from it – prior to the thirteenth century it was called Loch Leven.

The principal West Highland road goes up the west side, which at summer week-ends is congested. The east bank has a motor road running 6½ miles from Balmaha to Rowardennan at the foot of the Ben's south ridge. A footpath continues from there to the head of the loch. This path is part of a Long Distance Route for walkers, projected by the Countryside Commission for Scotland and called The Highland Way. It starts at Milngavie near Glasgow and runs 89 miles by way of Drymen, Loch Lomond, Crianlarich, Bridge of Orchy, Glen Coe, then by Kinlochleven to Glen Nevis and Fort William. Rowardennan may be reached in summer by a ferry service from Inverbeg on the west bank. Ask at Inverbeg Hotel for sailing times, which change from summer to winter. Boats may be hired at Balmaha, where a ferry serves some of the islands. A steamer, *Maid of the Loch*, sails from Balloch to Inversnaid. On Saturdays and Sundays only it calls twice at Rowardennan, allowing 6½ hours and 5½ hours respectively for the ascent of the Ben. (Apply for times to Caledonian Steam Packet Company, the Pier, Gourock, or to Balloch Pier.)

Ben Lomond, 3192 feet, is visible from many parts of Glasgow and the Lowlands, but even from the foot of the loch at only 12 miles' range it does not impose itself, although its head lifts from massive shoulders without nearby rival. Its boldness of line and colour is tempered by gentleness. The most shapely of its several profiles is seen from the north-west near Tarbert, where its cone markedly sharpens. The summit in fact is a curved ridge half a mile long, from which cliffs drop to the north, and a gentle ridge falls to the south. It is climbed more often than any other mountain (not counting 'chairlift climbers' on Cairngorm), and the popular route is from Rowardennan by a footpath running 3½ miles up the south ridge: time 2½ hours. Snow climbing may be had in winter up some of the north gullies. The summit has an indicator, for it is the best vantage point in the Southern Highlands. Being close to the Highland Line, it gives views over the Lowland plain to the hills of Lanarkshire, Stirling, and the Forth estuary, and south-west across Bute and Kintyre to the Argyll islands. Northwards, Ben Nevis emerges like a whale from its Central Highland sea. Near at hand across Loch Lomond are the five Arrochar hills.

Arrochar

The Arrochar Alps, often so called, are five mountains in the angle between Loch Long and Glen Croe. Four are Munros, but the Cobbler, 2891 feet, is the chief of all. Maps by some purely literary convention still name it Ben Arthur, a name that never passes people's lips. For the last two centuries the people of the country have called it the Cobbler, and before that *An Greasaiche Crom*, the Crooked Cobbler. Loch Long runs to its very base; it lifts to its full height from the sea. Hence although not a Munro, it is esteemed as such by mountaineers. Its three tops are formed by mica-schist crags arching round a south-east corrie. The skyline is spectacular, and the rock-climbing good. The centre peak is the summit, but the north and south peaks have much more rock and look more formidable. The lower slopes have been planted by the Forestry Commission, and the best line of ascent is to start from the Succoth road-fork at the north-west head of Loch Long and strike steeply uphill by path to a Hydro-electric Board track running south to a dam on the Buttermilk Burn. Follow the burn and cross it to the Cobbler corrie. The summit ridge is reached by grassy slopes between the peaks. The centre peak is free of difficulty as far as the cairn under the summit crag.

The Cobbler boasts nearly 70 rock-climbs, the longest being

370 feet on the North Peak. All tops have good views down the Firth of Clyde to Ailsa Craig. The mountain is linked to its higher neighbours, Beinn Narnain, 3036 feet and Beinn Ime, 3318 feet, by the Bealach a' Mhaim at 2000 feet, from which both are easily climbed. The usual approach to Narnain is from Succoth over its south-east top, or else up the right bank of the Sugach burn to the Sugach corrie. A' Chrois, the north top, has several caves on its lower slopes, about 350 feet above Glen Loin, on the left side of the burn draining the east corrie. A torch is needed to explore the deeper passages. Beinn Ime, the highest of the group, is most quickly climbed from Butterbridge (600 feet) in Glen Kinglas by way of its north saddle and ridge.

Between Ben Vane, 3004 feet, and Ben Vorlich, 3092 feet, lies Loch Sloy, which has been dammed and its water taken by tunnel through Ben Vorlich to power a generating station on Loch Lomond-side. Ben Vane is easily reached by the Hydro-board access road from Inveruglas. Ben Vorlich is best climbed from Loch Lomond into Coire Creagach.

Tyndrum and Crianlarich

From the head of Loch Lomond, the long narrow pass of Glen Falloch (616 feet) leads in 8 miles to Crianlarich at the junction of Strath Fillan and Glen Dochart. Here the Perth and Stirling road comes in from the east. To either side of the Falloch lie two mountain groups: the Tyndrum group to the west, bounded northward by the Fillan, and the Crianlarich group to the east, bounded by Glen Dochart.

Lower Glen Falloch is splendidly wooded; the river loud with waterfalls, which in spate demand inspection. The mountains cannot be properly seen, for the lower flanks hide all tops except Beinn Dubhchraig, 3204 feet, the first of the Tyndrum hills. It is linked by broad ridges to Beinn Oss, 3374 feet, Beinn Laoigh, 3708 feet, and Beinn a' Chleibh, 3008 feet. They may be reached from lower Glen Falloch by walking west up the Dubh Eas burn – a long, rather dull route. A much better approach to Oss and Dubhchraig goes up Fionn Ghlinne, which is entered opposite the Falls of Falloch. Best of all is the north approach from the river Cononish, which joins Strath Fillan 3½ miles north of Crianlarich. The river Fillan is in fact the river Cononish under a new name – it later becomes the Dochart and finally the Tay. The flat ground beyond the

Cononish bridge is named *Dail Righ*, King's Field, after Robert the Bruce, who was attacked here by the MacDougalls of Lorn in 1306, but escaped down Glen Dochart. From the Cononish bridge, the route to Beinn Dubhchraig goes by track across the railway line then through an old wood of Scots pine, and so to the mountain's north-east flank.

Glen Cononish gives the best approach to Beinn Laoigh – the mountain's east face is seen in full stature, soaring to double tops. The ridge between the tops is short and sharp, throwing out two craggy spurs that enclose a bowl-shaped corrie, the floor of which lies 1,000 feet under the summit. The rocky wall at the back of the corrie is split by a central gully, which gives a good snow-climb in winter, often with a cornice. Snow lingers here till late June. Thus although the summit lies 5 miles from the Tyndrum road, it refreshes the eye and draws one on. The most enjoyable line of ascent is straight up to the eastern corrie, which is well known for its arctic-alpine plants, then on to the north-east spur. If the south spur is chosen instead, a track will be found leading from its crest to the main south-east ridge, thus avoiding the spur's upper rocks. The quickest route of ascent ($3\frac{1}{2}$ miles) is from the west by Glen Lochy. Midway between Tyndrum and Dalmally, cross the river Lochy by a footbridge under Beinn Dubh, then go south and into the Eas Daimh glen, which leads on to Beinn Laoigh's broad north ridge. A feature of the wide-ranging summit view is the Cruachan horse-shoe across Strath Orchy.

The Crianlarich mountains are a bigger, more numerous, and complicated group of 7 Munros and 14 tops, all accessible from the roads at Balquhidder, Glen Falloch, and Glen Dochart. The highest peaks – Ben More, 3843 feet, and Stobinian (Am Binnein), 3821 feet – rise at the north end. These are the highest mountains in Britain south of Strath Tay, and seen to great advantage from Strath Fillan, where the broad river and birch trees give a foreground. Although grassy and shaped as a blunt pyramid, the mass of Ben More is impressive, for it sweeps 3,300 feet up from the glen. Stobinian is distinguished by a more tapered cone, cut flat on top. The usual route of ascent starts at Glenmore Farm in Glen Dochart. The ascent by this north-west ridge is safe and easy in summer, but both mountains catch the first of the winter snow, which they carry into summer. Care is needed in winter on the upper ridge above 2,500 feet, for the west flank is surprisingly steep and stony, often carrying ice that may be veiled by soft snow. Numerous accidents have occurred here. Stobinian may be climbed more easily from Balquhidder by way of Glen Carnaig.

West of Stobinian, Cruach Ardrain, 3428 feet, presents a big horse-shoe corrie to Crianlarich. At its back under the summit, a Y-shaped gully gives several hundred feet of snow-climbing. Access has been much hindered by widespread planting of sitka spruce on the north and west slopes. The best starting-point is the footbridge over the railway half a mile south of Crianlarich. Lanes can be followed through the young trees to the upper corrie, from which there is an easy way on to the north-west ridge and summit. A south ridge links it to Beinn Tulaichean, 3099 feet, which is more quickly climbed from Balquhidder. The last three Munros of the group, Beinn Chabhair, An Caisteal, and Beinn a' Chroin, are all climbed from Glen Falloch by long north-westerly ridges.

Loch Earn

Eleven miles east along Glen Dochart, at the Killin road-fork, Glen Ogle rises south to a pass at 945 feet and drops to Lochearnhead at 320 feet. Callander gives access from the south by road through Strathyre, and Crieff from the east through Strath Earn. Loch Earn is a beautifully wooded loch 6½ miles long, whose river flows east to the Firth of Tay south of Perth. The loch's north and south shores have full-length motor-roads. The north road is the main one. Two well-known mountains rise above the loch 3 miles to its south: Ben Vorlich, 3231 feet, and Stuc a' Chroin, 3189 feet. Their bold outlines stand high amid the ruck of lower hills around, and thus are well seen from every point of the compass. They look of simple construction as seen from a distance, Ben Vorlich a cone and the Stuc a buttressed castle. In fact they are complicated mountains, joined together at the Bealach an' Dubh Choirein, radiating eight high ridges and hollowed by at least eight corries. They may be climbed from every direction, but the shortest and most enjoyable routes are from Loch Earn, either up Glen Vorlich on to the north ridge, or up Glen Ample on to the north-west ridge of either hill.

Several hill tracks pass close under both mountains. One from Callander goes north up the Keltie Water, across the lower spurs, and down Glen Vorlich to Loch Earn (10 miles); another by Glen Ample connects Lochearnhead to Loch Lubnaig (6 miles); and a third links Comrie to Callander by way of Glen Artney (16 miles). All southern approaches to the mountains have to go by these tracks.

North of Loch Earn, between Strath Earn and Loch Tay, lie more than 200 square miles of moorland and flat-topped hills, many of which exceed 2,000 feet. They reach their highest point on Ben Chonzie (Ben-y-Hone), 3048 feet. The plateau is cut by seven large glens, all with roads, and several of great beauty. They are worth exploring. The two principal glens are the Sma' Glen running north from Crieff to Amulree, and Strath Bran running south-west from Dunkeld to Amulree. From Amulree, Glen Quaich contains in its lower farmland the lovely Loch Freuchie, before rising over a pass of 1672 feet to the foot of Loch Tay. From the Sma' Glen, Glen Almond runs west into the highest central hills. At the road-end, access can be had to the open slopes of Ben Chonzie. The summit gives a fine view of the Lawers range across Loch Tay. A delightful extension to this north route can be made by starting from Loch Freuchie, and taking the footpath up Glen Lochan (containing several lochans and steep walls) to Auchnafree in Glen Almond. Ben Chonzie can be approached from Strathearn either from Crieff up the deep-cut Glen Turret, or from Comrie up Glen Lednock. Either way, a car can be taken to within 3 miles of the summit.

Glen Dochart to Rannoch

North of the Dochart–Tay glens, in an area comprising only a fifth of the Southern Highlands, are congregated more than half its mountains – 25 Munros including the highest, Ben Lawers. They fall into four groups: the Mamlorn and Lawers groups to the south, Orchy group to the west, and the Glen Lyon group to the north or Rannoch side. Their distinguishing feature, apart from dense concentration and size, is an interior wildness and remoteness, more characteristic of the Central Highlands, with which they here overlap. They are bounded by three great furrows that carry motor-roads: Rannoch–Tummel to the north, Tay–Dochart to the south, and Strath Fillan–Auch–Tulla to the west. Only two roads penetrate far into the interior, by way of Glen Lyon and Glen Lochay at either end of Loch Tay. A third minor road links upper Loch Tay to mid Glen Lyon across the bealach (Lochan na Lairige) between Ben Lawers and the Tarmachans.

The Mamlorn Forest

Mamlorn is by old definition the mountains around the 10-mile length of Glen Lochay. Six Munros are linked by numerous lesser tops of 2500 to 3000 feet; Beinn Heasgarnich, 3530 feet, and Meall Ghaordie, 3410 feet, the two highest points, on the Glen Lyon divide; Creag Mhor, 3387 feet, and Beinn Chaluim, 3354 feet, around the headwaters of the Lochay; and Meall Glas, 3139 feet, and Sgiath Chuil, 3000 feet, on the Glen Dochart divide.

Beinn Chaluim is best climbed from Strath Fillan through Auchtertyre Farm, and Sgiath Chuil from Glen Dochart by crossing a footbridge over the river to Innishewan Farm. All the others are most conveniently reached from Glen Lochay. Heasgarnich and Creag Mhor are the least accessible and in winter carry a heavy snow-cover. Both are noted for their large number of white hares, ptarmigans, and snow-buntings. For the most part they are undistinguished mountains, of sheep-country character, but rich in bird-life on steep moorland of coarse grass and heather.

Lawers Group

East of Glen Lochay, the Tarmachan ridge and Ben Lawers are moated for 15 miles by Loch Tay. The loch, wooded and grassily green along the shores, lies at only 350 feet; the mountains when seen from the Glen Ogle road, or better still from Ben Chonzie, lift to their full height. Meall nan Tarmachan, 3421 feet, has a well-defined ridge of five tops running two miles east to west. It narrows at the east end, where the summit stands over Lochan na Lairige, which lies on the bealach to Ben Lawers. The narrow road across the pass gives convenient access to both mountains. Meall nan Tarmachan is best approached from the south end of the lochan at 1,600 feet by way of the mountain's burn, then by turning the summit's north side. Half a mile south of the lochan, a road (locked) contours the Tarmachan slopes for 2 miles to a quarry at 2,150 feet in Coire Fionn Lairige. To climb the mountain from its west end, leave the Loch Tay road a mile east of Bridge of Lochay. Climb direct either to the west peak, Creag na Caillich, or to the summit by its south ridge. The winter traverse of the Tarmachans is one of the two most airy ridge-walks in the Southern Highlands – the other being the A' Chir ridge in Arran.

Ben Lawers, 3984 feet, is the biggest mountain of the Southern Highlands, and not only in height. It fills 42 square miles in the angle between Loch Tay and Glen Lyon with 8 tops above 3,000 feet, and several lesser ones on the Glen Lyon side. Six are Munros. The schist of Ben Lawers is a soft or friable variety rich in lime, which breaks down to calcareous soil on which arctic-alpine plants flourish as on few other mountains. The summit escaped the last glaciation. The ascent is easy and best taken from Loch Tayside. These southern slopes are held by the National Trust for Scotland, who (with the help of the Nature Conservancy and the Countryside Commission for Scotland) have built a visitor centre and exhibition alongside the car-park off the Lochan na Lairige road on the slopes of Meall Corranaich. The area is a National Nature Reserve. Excellent skiing can be had on the slopes of Coire Odhar, where the Scottish Ski Club has a hut between Meall Corranaich and Beinn Ghlas. The col between the two is reached by a path from the car-park. Alternatively, strike left or right on to the south ridges of either summit.

The crowds at the tourist centre are avoided and a more interesting route found 4 miles east. Take the path up the Lawers burn to Lochan nan Cat (3 miles), and from there on to the mountain's east ridge. The summit view extends across Scotland from the Atlantic to the North Sea, and from Ben Wyvis (north of Inverness) to the Lothian hills – nearly 150 miles. The traverse of all the Munros involves 4,000 feet of ascent along 7 miles of the main ridge.

Orchy Group

Between Loch Lyon and Bridge of Orchy lies a high twisting ridge 7 miles long, four times lifting its crest in Munros. From the south to north they are Beinn Dorain, 3524 feet, Beinn an Dothaidh (pronounced Doe), 3267 feet, Beinn Achaladair, 3404 feet, and Beinn a' Chreachain, 3540 feet. They are called the Orchy group since they form a huge barrier separating the headwaters of the river Orchy from those of the Lyon. Close to their east, directly above Loch Lyon, stands Beinn Mhanach, 3125 feet. All are best approached from the west.

Whether travelling by road or rail over the Tyndrum pass to Bridge of Orchy, you get a splendid first view of Beinn Dorain, which sweeps 3,000 feet up from Glen Orchy as a huge cone, its west slope appearing like the leech of a mainsail. It may be climbed up its south ridge from Auch, or by its north ridge from Bridge of Orchy – the start of the latter route also giving access to Beinn an Dothaidh from the col between the two. The views are indifferent, being screened by neighbouring peaks, whereas Achaladair and

Chreachain, especially the latter at the north end, give wide panoramas across the Moor of Rannoch and south over Breadalbane.

Beinn Achaladair, as seen from the Black Mount across the wide valley of the Water of Tulla, has a long, undifferentiated face, which may be climbed from Achallader Farm, starting up the Achaladair burn. A much better route is to go up the Water of Tulla to Crannach Wood, which is a famous remnant of the old Caledonian forest. The summit is there sculpted by a craggy north corrie, seen through a foreground of Scots pines. The mountain can then be climbed by its north ridge, or the north-west slopes of Beinn a' Chreachain taken instead. The traverse of the Orchy ridge gives 3,000 feet of ascent over its four Munros.

Beinn Mhanach is easily reached by a 2-mile walk from the south top of Achaladair, or from Auch by the path up Auch Gleann (5 miles). The top gives a fine view over Loch Lyon, but approach from there is not recommended since the extension of the loch of a Hydro-electric dam.

Glen Lyon Group

The Lyon group has 7 Munros and 6 tops above 3,000 feet, all to the north of the glen and south of Loch Rannoch. Intermixed are at least two dozen tops above 2,000 feet. The Munros from west to east are Stuchd an Lochain, 3144 feet, Meall Buidhe, 3054 feet, Carn Gorm, 3370 feet, Meall Garbh, 3150 feet, Carn Mairg, 3419 feet, Creag Mhor, 3100 feet, and to the north of the latter, the highest mountain Schichallion, 3547 feet.

The river Lyon drains 25 miles east to the Tay through one of the most beautiful of all Highland glens. It is remarkable for exhibiting in that great length four distinct kinds of glen scenery. From the remote hills of Loch Lyon, it falls between bare mountain flanks for 8 miles to Gallin, where the glen suddenly widens and levels. Over the next 4 miles the pace of the river slows through woodland, where the mountain slopes are clothed half a mile deep in a perfect combination of Scots pines, oaks, birches, sycamores, and beeches. They appear first on one side then the other, while the river flows past Meggernie Castle, built in 1593 by Mad Colin Campbell. Here there is a long avenue of limes beside the river. The foothills of the Carn Mairg range, and of the Tarmachans and Lawers, now wall the glen to either side and appear to close the distant foot of the glen. At Bridge of Balgie, where the Lochan na Lairige road comes in from the south, the scene changes again to a strath of rolling grassland grazed by cattle. The river broadens and winds 5 miles to Invervar, where it narrows and becomes closely screened by avenues of beech, ash, oak, and sycamore, whose leaves cast speckled light across the road. Spurs of Carn Mairg project rocky talons to the river, and each bend of the road discloses some new change in the woodland, mountain, meadow, and water scene. Rock closes in to the bed of the glen at the Pass of Lyon, the river bursts through, and the ground opens out to wide and prosperous farmland above Fortingall. No other glen shows such variety between its upper desolation and lower fertility.

In the churchyard at Fortingall, a yew tree 3,000 years old is said to be the oldest in Europe. Close to the south-west of the village are the earthworks of a Roman camp. In the Pass of Lyon, MacGregor's Leap (signposted) is worth visiting. In the sixteenth century, Gregor MacGregor, pursued by the Campbells, jumped the river across a rock gut. A later attempt to emulate his feat ended fatally. Between the Loch Lyon dam and Cashlie are the remains of four round forts sited at intervals along 2 miles of the river. They were built as massive towers, probably by the Celts, but are now only circles of overgrown stone. The mountain above them, Stuchd an Lochain, has one of the earliest recorded ascents in the Highlands. It was made by Mad Colin Campbell around 1590, and perhaps earned him his soubriquet.

All the mountains of the group, except Schichallion, are easily climbed from Glen Lyon. Meall Buidhe and Stuchd an Lochan, to north and south of Loch Giorra, are two of the most remote mountains of the Southern Highlands and rarely visited. Nine miles east, the four Munros of the Carn Mairg range are swelling, flat-topped hills, high and central enough to retain snow and give excellent ski-touring. The Glen Lyon flanks are steep, but once up the hill-walker can enjoy a long day traversing the four tops, which form a crescent with Invervar conveniently placed at the tips. The round is 9 miles (excluding outliers) with an aggregate ascent of 5,500 feet from Invervar.

Schichallion is a totally isolated mountain of quartzite, which has weathered evenly to a most distinctive cone. It is thus a familiar sight over long distances, for example from Glen Coe, 30 miles away across Rannoch Moor. When seen across Loch Rannoch, the cone has perfect shape, and can look in winter like an ivory tusk.

The approach from Aberfeldy or Fortingall is by the road running north through Coshieville and west to Kinloch Rannoch; if from Pitlochry, west along Loch Tummel. The former road circling the east and north slopes allows several choices of route. The north and south slopes are best avoided, since they are covered by mixed boulders and heather. The footpath marked on maps as starting from White Bridge on to the Aonach Ban (east ridge) is no longer recommended, for it crosses a hillside recently planted by the Forestry Commission. The easiest route now starts nearly 2 miles farther north, a short way east of Braes of Foss Farm, by a path running south and then south-west to the east ridge. The time for this route should be $2\frac{1}{4}$ hours to the summit. Among the several alternatives, you may start from the west up the Templar Burn (2 miles short of Kinloch Rannoch), from which a path goes all the way to the top. Your view south from Schichallion is a dull one across the barren mass of Breadalbane hills, but west and north the far-running lochs and heathery moors and wooded valleys of Rannoch and Atholl spread wide beneath your feet. You look deep into the Central Highlands and the Cairngorms.

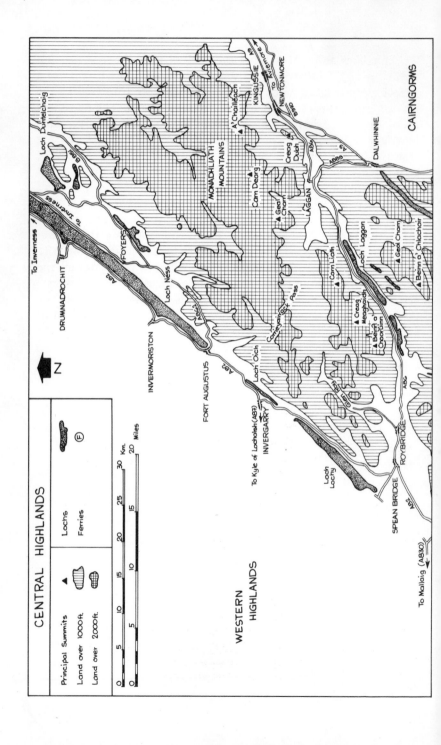

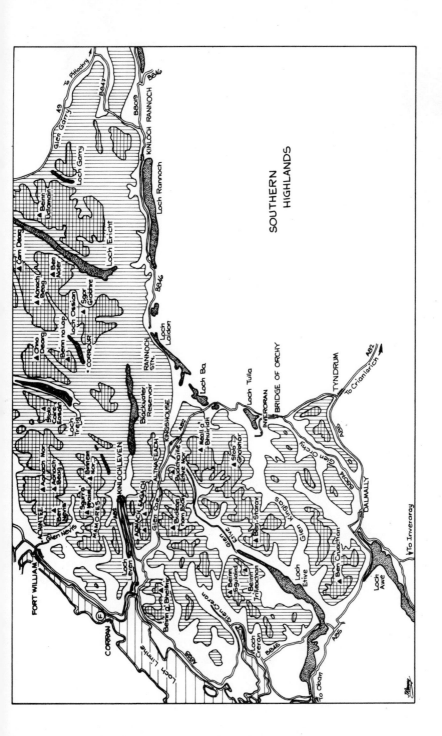

6   Central Highlands

The Central Highlands are bounded on the west by Loch Linnhe and the Great Glen, on the east by Strath Spey and Glen Garry, and to the south by a line from Loch Rannoch through Glen Orchy to the head of Loch Awe. The area is a little less than the Southern Highlands, but contains twice the number of mountain-tops – 143, of which 72 are Munros.

The rocks of the district are Moine schists, with big granite intrusions around Loch Etive, the Black Mount, and Rannoch Moor, and smaller ones on the Monadh Liath. The structure is complex, but the higher hills are generally of granite, quartzite, mica-schist, gneisses, and lavas and volcanic ashes. The mountain shapes are commonly massive humps, like the Black Mount hills, Ben Alder, Ben Nevis, Creag Meaghaidh, and all the Monadh Liath, but great corries have been gouged out of their north and east faces, and huge cliffs often exposed. Where granite crags crop out on the north face of Ben Cruachan, or in corries of the Black Mount or Lochaber, they lie at a lower angle than other rocks and are poor in quality for climbing purposes – a notable exception being the Beinn Trilleachan slabs at the head of Loch Etive, where the angle may be relatively low but the granite is among the best in Scotland. Again, many of the tops have caps of resistant quartzite, which have given them a pointed form, as on the Pap of Glen Coe and on several Mamore tops. Some of the glens, like Glen Nevis, Glen Etive, and Glen Coe, have a splendour of scale and setting unknown to the Southern Highlands, and the hinterlands conceal a greater plenty of remote wilderness country. Thus the Central Highlands offer far greater variety of scene and shape than their overall structure might imply. The cliffs of Glen Coe, Ben Nevis, and Creag Meaghaidh give much of the country's best rock, snow, and ice climbing, while the long crests of Glen Coe, the Mamores, and the Grey Corries of Lochaber, some of the best ridge-walking.

The Central Highlands have four principal districts: Upper Lorn and Lochaber to the west, and Badenoch and the Monadh Liath to the east.

Upper Lorn

Upper Lorn extends from Loch Etive to Loch Leven, and from Loch Linnhe to Bridge of Orchy. The district is circled from Tyndrum by roads that go north by Glen Coe and west by Loch Awe. The diameter of this circle is cut by Glen Etive and Loch Etive, to which a minor road strikes south from Kingshouse on Rannoch Moor. Loch Etive is 18 miles long in a dog-leg form. Footpaths go down either shore, but the best way to see the loch as a whole is to sail up it on the motor-vessel from Achnacloich, 3 miles west of Taynuilt. It cruises every forenoon in summer to Kinlochetive. A dozen big mountains stand round the inner 10 miles. These are the Cruachan and Black Mount ranges on the east shore, the Glen Coe hills to the north, and the Glen Creran hills to the west.

The west coast is pierced by Loch Creran, which punches out two big peninsulas, Benderloch and Appin, between Loch Etive on one side and Loch Leven on the other. From the head of Loch Creran, Glen Creran runs far into the mountainous interior, delimiting Appin to its north-west, and giving access to 3 Munros on its east side: Beinn Sgulaird, 3059 feet, Beinn Fhionnlaidh, 3145 feet, and Sgor na h-Ulaidh, 3250 feet, all of which have 2-mile-long summit ridges. The glen opens as a wide strath, with a road running 3 miles to Elleric. There it forks into narrower glens. Glen Ure, the wooded right-hand branch, gives a trackless pass to Kinlochetive. The bealach at 800 feet is the best point from which to climb Beinn Sgulaird if approaching from Kinlochetive, but the shorter ascent is from the head of Loch Creran up the mountain's west ridge. The left fork of Glen Creran has a good track, which crosses a ridge of 1,300 feet to Ballachulish on Loch Leven (6½ miles). Two miles up this track, access can be had to Sgor na h-Ulaidh – a mountain more quickly climbed from Glen Coe by way of Fionn Ghleann to the north ridge. Directly under the summit, the rock face of Coire Dubh is split by Red Gully, which in winter gives a good snow and ice climb of 650 feet.

Appin, although mountainous throughout, has only one mountain over 3,000 feet, and that one of the shapeliest and best sited. Beinn a' Bheithir (pronounced Vare), the Peak of the Thunderbolt, stands at the corner of Loch Linnhe and Loch Leven. Four of its six tops form a gracefully shaped horse-shoe around a huge north-facing corrie, Glen a' Chaolais, which is heavily wooded in its lower half. The usual ascent is up the corrie by a forest track on to the main ridge. Two peaks on the crest are Munros, about a mile apart: Sgorr Dhearg, 3361 feet, and Sgorr Dhonuill, 3284 feet. If a descent is made down the pleasant north ridge of Sgorr Dhearg, you will have trouble finding a way through the plantations. The complete traverse from east to west is most satisfying. Start up Beinn Bhan and enjoy a high-level walk of 5 miles to Creag Ghorm, from which a steep descent through woods leads to the Ballachulish narrows. The views are across Loch Linnhe to the peaks of Ardgour and Morvern, past Mull to the open sea, across Loch Leven to the whale-back of Ben Nevis and the pointed Mamores, and east through the pass of Glen Coe. There is only one better viewpoing in Appin, and that is the lowly top of Barr More, 417 feet, on the island of Lismore.

You may ferry across to the north tip of Lismore from Port Appin, or better still, since it lands you at the centre of an island 10 miles long, sail from Oban on the daily motor-vessel. Barr More is Lismore's highest point, rising out of farmland between the Lynn of Lorn and Lynn of Morvern. The skyscape is made vast by the throng of distinctive mountain tops. They lift high out of the sea above congregations of other peaks standing close enough to shadow each other in dark blues. No other island grants a view of Highland mountains to equal this one.

Between Loch Etive and Loch Awe, 20 square miles are occupied by Ben Cruachan, 3695 feet. Two of its 8 tops are Munros. Seven big corries hollow the flanks, not counting lesser ones between lesser tops. Loch Awe forms a crescent round the south flank, tapering westward into the Pass of Brander, where it becomes the river Awe, now blocked by a small dam. The pass was the scene of a famous battle, where Robert the Bruce was ambushed by MacDougall, who suffered defeat and the loss of most of his Lorn territory. The pass is so narrow and the walls so steep and wooded, that no glimpse of the Cruachan tops can be had. They are strung on a long ridge with several spurs that enclose the corries. Two of these (the eastern horse-shoe and the great south corrie drained by the Allt Cruachan) are the usual routes of ascent from Loch Aweside. The summit stands above the south corrie and is climbed over its south spur, Meall Cuanail. One of the shapeliest tops is Stob Dearg, 3611 feet, at the west end, often called the Taynuilt Peak. It is climbed by way of the Allt Cruinich, half a mile east of Bridge of Awe. The traverse of all eight peaks is best accomplished from the south corrie, to which a Hydro-electric Board access road runs 2½ miles uphill near the Kirk of St Conon. The corrie is dammed at 1,200 feet. The Board does not normally give permission for cars to visit the dam. Summer tourists may join a bus tour from Oban to visit both the dam and power station (see p. 100).

Cruachan's north side falls steeply into the remote and bare Glen Noe, which gives a pass at 1,800 feet from Loch Etive to Loch Awe. Its north side is flanked by another mountain mass with a summit ridge 3 miles long bearing 2 Munros, Beinn Eunaich, 3242 feet, and Beinn a' Chochuill, 3215 feet. Both mountains are nearly always climbed by their south ridges. Rock-climbs may be had on a buttress of Beinn Eunaich at 1750 feet east-south-east of the summit.

Glen Kinglass divides the Cruachan–Eunaich group from the Blackmount group. The glen rises eastward from Loch Etive to a bealach at 800 feet above Glen Dochard, which falls gently to Loch Tulla. The whole gives a pass of 14 miles with a track running all the way from Forest Lodge, at the head of Loch Tulla, to Kinlochetive (21 miles). The Blackmount has 18 principal summits above 3,000 feet, 10 of which are Munros. There are many lesser tops, and all lie in the great angle between Glen Etive and the Kinglass–Dochard pass. Rannoch Moor gives the base of the triangle.

This Blackmount Forest is a wild tangle of long ridges and deep corries, with bold granite peaks and craggy outcrops on the north and east faces. A splendid roadside view is had from the east side of Loch Tulla, showing them fringed by Scots pines massed around the western head of the loch. Out of Loch Tulla flows the river Orchy. Bridge of Orchy, where the old Glen Coe road leaves the new road, gives the best approach from the south. You may drive a car 3 miles along the old road to Victoria Bridge, and follow the rest on foot for 9 miles to Kingshouse, at the entrance to Glen Coe. This old road is exposed in winter where it reaches 1,454 feet on the shoulder of Meall a' Bhuiridh. The new road keeps to lower ground (1,150 feet).

The name Black Mount is strictly applied only to the high ground below the great Corrie Ba of Clach Leathad (pronounced Clachlet). As soon as you top the Black Mount, the Moor of Rannoch spreads out before you eastward. It occupies 56 square miles to Loch Rannoch, and is for the most part so flat that the river draining east from Loch Ba loses less than 100 feet of height in 10 miles. The hollows left by the ice cap are filled with lochs, which linked by the

Ba river stretch all the way to the base of Schichallion and the Tay. The moor gives good walking along the shores of this waterway, and excellent views of the Blackmount and Glencoe hills.

The most distinguished of the Blackmount Munros are Stob Ghabhar, 3565 feet, Clach Leathad, 3602 feet, Meall a' Bhuiridh, 3636 feet, and Ben Starav, 3541 feet. Starav at the head of Loch Etive is best climbed from there by its north ridge. The top is finely shaped. Stob Ghabhar above Glen Dochard is usually climbed by its east ridge, which is reached by a track 1 mile west of Forest Lodge up the Allt Totaig. A deep eastern corrie has one good ice-climb close under the summit. Clach Leathad has 3 Munros on its long ridges, the highest being Meall a' Bhuiridh. Its principal feature is the vast Corrie Ba, whose river drains to the North Sea. The traverse of the ridge from Stob Ghabhar to Sron na Creise is one of the classic winter hill-walks, especially in April, when the snow has hardened after thaw and frost.

Sron na Creise, a lower north top of Clach Leathad, presents to Kingshouse what appears to be (but is not) a formidable rock wall, much more impressive than Meall a' Bhuiridh to its left. The north slopes of Meall a' Bhuiridh (pronounced Mellavoory) are the principal skiing grounds of the Central Highlands, with chairlift and ski-tows. The lift goes to a small plateau at 2,250 feet, where the tow takes you up the last 1,350 feet. In good snow years, skiing is possible on these upper slopes until late June.

Kingshouse on the banks of the river Etive is one of the oldest Highland inns (modernized), once an important droving stance where cattle herds were rested after crossing the Devil's Staircase from Kinlochleven, and before moving on to Inveroran at Loch Tulla. It is dominated by the powerful presence of one mountain, Stob Dearg of Buachaille Etive Mor, 3345 feet, commonly called the Buachaille (Herdsman). It confronts the moor with a wall of grey and pink rock (black under cloud) shaped like an arrowhead. The rock is rhyolite split by gullies into ridges and buttresses, which make it one of the most popular rock-climbing centres in Scotland. The mountain is in fact a ridge 3 miles long rising in 4 tops, with Stob Dearg as the summit. It stands in the angle between Glen Etive and Glen Coe. Glen Etive is a grassy glen, 10 miles long and once famed for its cattle-grazing, but now planted in its lower part with Forestry Commission sitkas. The river has no good waterfalls, but many deep pools. An easy way from the glen to the top of the Buachaille can be found by climbing to the Coire Cloiche Finne between the two north tops.

The headwaters of the river Coe rise about 4 miles west of Kingshouse, but by long custom the whole trough from Glen Etive to Loch Leven is named Glen Coe. Its 11-mile length is flanked on the south side by only 3 mountains – Buachaille Etive Mor, 3345 feet, Buachaille Etive Beag, 3129 feet, and Bidean nam Bian, 3766 feet – but these have 16 tops and other outliers ranked in depth to the south. Two Munros line the north flank, Meall Dearg, 3118 feet, and Sgor nam Fiannaidh, 3173 feet; these have 10 tops, all save one strung on a long thin ridge 9 miles long. The central part of the ridge from Am Bodach, 3085 feet, to Stob Coire Leith, 3080 feet ($1\frac{1}{2}$ miles) is the Aonach Eagach, one of the narrowest mainland summit ridges. It can be difficult and time-consuming in winter.

Three miles west of Kingshouse, the croft of Altnafeadh is an old droving stance under the Devil's Staircase. The track zig-zags up the hill behind Altnafeadh to an easy pass of 1,800 feet above Kinlochleven.

The true head of the glen is called the Study (not named or marked on 1-inch maps). The name is derived from the Scots Stiddie, meaning Anvil, taken from the far better Gaelic name, Innean a'Cheathaich, the Anvil of the Mist, given to the flat-topped rock on the old road, which is here 100 feet higher than the new. Immediately below is a high waterfall where the Allt Lairig Eilde joins the Coe. The Study is famous for its view of the Three Sisters, which are butt-ends of three long spurs of Bidean nam Bian. In descending order they are Beinn Fhada, Gearr Aonach, and Aonach Dubh. They project into the glen as huge bulges of black rock, contrasting sharply with the green fields around Loch Achtriochtan in the bed of the glen. The upper face of Aonach Dubh carries the long dark slit of Ossian's Cave, which can be reached only by a rock-climb of 200 feet. Far behind and between the first and second Sisters appears the summit of Bidean, the highest peak of Argyll. It has 11 tops, notably Stob Coire nan Lochan, 3657 feet, which appears above the second Sister's back. The mountain has a complex structure, with 5 great corries and 10 miles of summit ridges, all with much crag on the flanks. Numerous accidents occur to walkers on these tops, especially in winter. The safest route of ascent is up Coire nam Beith, opposite the Clachaig road-fork, and then on to the col between Bidean and Stob Coire nan Lochan. The summit view is excellent. The Central

Highlands are spread out like a relief map, from the Atlantic to Rannoch, and Cruachan to Ben Nevis.

There is much good rock-climbing on Bidean, both close to the summits and down on the lower buttresses. Across the glen directly above Clachaig hotel, Sgor nam Fiannaidh is split from top to bottom by Clachaig Gully, which gives 1,735 feet of rock-climbing. Close beside the hotel, a small wood rings the lochan of Torren and a hillock called the Signal Rock. The MacDonalds inhabited the glen between Loch Achtriochtan and Invercoe. In February 1692 they were massacred here during a blizzard, not by the Clan Campbell but by Scottish troops of an Argyll regiment commanded by Campbell of Glen Lyon, who in turn acted under command of Sir Thomas Livingstone, the officer commanding the army in Scotland, whose orders came from the Secretary of State, Sir John Dalrymple. MacDonald by mischance had failed to take the oath of allegiance to William of Orange within the prescribed time. He was six days late. His enemies, the Campbell chiefs, were friends of Dalrymple, and the rest followed. Massacres were not uncommon in the Highlands and many took greater toll of life. This one has been particularly abhorred because the troops had been given hospitality by the people of Glencoe for nearly two weeks before the mass murder, and the treachery had been deliberately encouraged by a minister of the crown.

Lochaber

Lochaber extends from Loch Leven north to Loch Garry, and west to east from the head of Loch Arkaig to Loch Laggan, where it joins Badenoch. The Central Highlands exclude the part west of the Great Glen. Its principal mountain ranges are the Mamores, the Ben Nevis group, Aonach Beag and Mor, and the Grey Corries. They comprise 42 principal tops of which 19 are Munros. Three of these rise above 4,000 feet: Ben Nevis, 4406 feet, Aonach Beag, 4060 feet, and Carn Mor Dearg, 4012 feet; Aonach Mor, 3999 feet, might well be added. Four great glens penetrate the mountains, apart from many lesser ones. Glen Nevis divides the Mamores from the Nevis and Grey Corrie groups, and provides a through route of 22 miles from Fort William to Loch Treig. Glen Spean, where the river Spean drains west from Loch Laggan, provides a pass from the west coast to Strath Spey. Glen Roy runs 10 miles north from Glen Spean to near the headwaters of the Spey. And the water-filled pass of Loch Treig gives Lochaber its eastern boundary; although roadless, it allows the West Highland railway a pass between Rannoch Moor and Glen Spean. Both Loch Treig and Loch Laggan have been dammed, and a 15-mile pipe taken through the lower slopes of Ben Nevis to feed the power-house serving the British Aluminium Company's factory in the Great Glen. The company have likewise dammed the Black Water to feed their factory at Kinlochleven.

From Glen Coe, Lochaber is approached by road either across the new bridge at Ballachulish or round Loch Leven, then up Loch Linnhe to Fort William, which rivals Oban as a chief tourist centre for the Highland coast. The big pulp mill at the head of Loch Linnhe, several housing schemes, factories, new hotels, filling stations, shops, and a tangle of hydro-electric wire and pylons, have made the northern outskirts of Fort William the Highland's monumental example of the ills attending haphazard planning. The Kinlochleven approach is recommended for the excellent view of the Mamore range from the south side of Loch Leven. The range has 16 tops, 10 are Munros, and these are linked by a continuous main ridge that zig-zags 8½ miles from west to east. A dozen spurs projecting north and south bear several of the summits and enclose the corries. They offer superb ridge-walking, especially on the firm snow of spring. The rock is mica-schist and quartzite, the latter forming several sharp tops, including Binnein Mor, the highest at 3700 feet. Some of the quartzite caps are white enough to be mistaken for snow, as on Stob Ban and Sgurr a' Mhaim. All can be climbed from either flank. The Kinlochleven approaches are aided by tracks along the whole base of the range. The western base is traversed by the old military road to Fort William, which you can reach after rounding the head of Loch Leven by a right-of-way path slanting uphill from the school.

Glen Nevis has several unique features. It gives access to 40 mountain tops, is walled on the north by Scotland's highest mountain, which links up with 16 peaks of the Grey Corries stretching east to Loch Treig, and has in the central sector a gorge scene of Himalayan character, above which the Steall waterfall plunges over the lower cliffs of Sgurr a' Mhaim in one surge of 350 feet. The equally high Falls of Glomach and the higher Eas a' Chual Aluinn near Kylesku do not have Steall's volume of water. The lower glen is a pastoral scene of riverside meadows flanked by the immense bare slopes of Ben Nevis on one side and by forested slopes on the other. The uppermost reach is desolate moorland. The central 3-mile sector carries the gorge, where spurs of Ben Nevis and Sgurr a' Mhaim pinch off the upper glen from the lower. The river Nevis has cut a deep twisting channel through the barrier, carving pots and cauldrons out of solid rock in a drop of 400 feet. The walls are wooded in oak, pine, birch, and rowan.

A road from the Great Glen runs 6 miles up Glen Nevis to a car-park at 450 feet at the base of the gorge. The slope from there to the summit of Ben Nevis is 4,000 feet at an angle of 35°. Down it flashes a sometimes spectacular waterslide, the Allt Coire Eoghainn, issuing 1,500 feet above. The gorge is traversed by a rough footpath along the right bank. It winds through the woodland, giving clear views of Steall waterfall through the gorge, and of the wild river below churning past gigantic boulders. At the top comes a sudden transition to flat meadowland, where the river snakes in slow bends past Steall waterfall.

Ben Nevis is usually climbed by the path from Achintee Farm, reached up the right bank from Bridge of Nevis. A normal time to the top is $3\frac{1}{2}$ hours. The summit plateau is flat stony desert. A sharp look-out must be kept in mist, for gullies in the north cliff cut deeply into the plateau, and snow-cornices can mask their mouths far into the spring. The summit Observatory is now a total ruin. Built in 1883 to collect meteorological data, it closed down in 1904. The records over 17 years show a mean annual rainfall of 157 inches and a maximum of 240 inches. The mean monthly temperature is $\frac{1}{2}$°F below freezing. Snow can fall on any day of the year, and the permanent winter falls start in October. Not until July does melting usually leave the plateau clear, but snow-beds underneath the cliffs linger on until renewed by the autumn fall. The summit has an average of 261 gales, many of which reach hurricane force, often with gusts up to 150 mph in winter. It follows that no one should climb Ben Nevis (or any other mountain) without warm and windproof clothing, good boots, food, torch, whistle, and an O.S. map and compass. Turn back when the weather deteriorates.

The summit view in fine weather ranges from Ireland to Torridon, and from the Outer Hebrides to the Cairngorms. South across Glen Nevis, the Mamores bare pointed teeth, otherwise the scene is a revelation of the Highlands as a featureless plateau, fascinating the eye more by its boundless space than by any mountain-shape.

At the south-east shoulder, a thin ridge sweeps east and north to

Carn Mor Dearg, the two forming a huge corrie open to the north-west. This in its uppermost part is Coire Leis, from which the Allt a' Mhuilinn flows 5 miles to the river Lochy. The ridge walk to Carn Mor Dearg shows the magnificent rock architecture on the north-east cliffs of Ben Nevis. They stretch 2 miles to a maximum height of 2,000 feet, riven by gullies and projecting as towers, ridges, pinnacles and buttresses, which offer a great variety of rock, snow, and ice climbs (see Chapter 10). The cliffs can also be seen if you walk up the Allt a' Mhuilinn through the grounds of the distillery at its foot, or by a track starting midway between the distillery and Torlundy, or from Achintee by way of Lochan Meall an t-Suidhe (pronounced Mellantee). The climbers' hut in the glen under the cliffs belongs to the Scottish Mountaineering Club.

Aonach Beag and the west end of the Grey Corries are best climbed from Steall, but Aonach Mor and all the rest from Glen Spean. The crest of the Grey Corries offers an easy but long ridge walk of 5 miles with impressive views of the other Lochaber hills, especially from Stob Choire Claurigh, 3858 feet, at the east end. The eastern approach is made by driving from Spean Bridge along the Coire-choille road on the left bank, then $1\frac{1}{2}$ miles up the Lairig Leacach track (which leads to Loch Treig in 8 miles). The lairig divides the main body of the Grey Corries from a big eastern mountain, which rises steeply from Loch Treig. Its twin tops, Stob Coire Easain, 3658 feet, and Stob a' Choire Mheadhoin, 3610 feet, are both Munros. They are taken from Inverlair, a mile west of Tulloch Station.

North of the Spean, in the angle it makes with the Great Glen, lie a mass of hills containing some two score tops over 2,000 feet. Their north boundary is the Corrieyairack pass between Glen Tarff and the headwaters of the Spey. In the south they lift up over Glen Spean and Loch Laggan in a 10-mile-long wave, on the crest of which 14 tops exceed 3,000 feet. They culminate in Creag Meaghaidh, 3700 feet. This long wide ridge straddles the Lochaber–Badenoch frontier. On its north side, Glen Roy and the river Spey form a 20-mile trough. The lower part of Glen Roy has a lowland character, wide and green with low, sparsely wooded hills. The Parallel Roads (see Chapter 2) are best seen from the highest point of the road, where there is a car-park. There you overlook the grasslands of the upper glen, which rises into scree-covered mountains. On your left hand, the successive mountain flanks are traversed by three parallel terraces that stand out brightly green (grass and bracken) against the heather. On your right-hand side, three identical roads on the farthest hill appear to meet the left-hand roads where the opposing walls converge.

The Creag Meaghaidh range looks a dull group from Glen Spean, rounded and flat-topped with broad ridges, but they are redeemed by deep corries with tall cliffs. One of these, Coire Ardair, is famous for its rock, snow, and ice climbing. All the tops are best approached from the shores of either Loch Laggan or Lower Loch Laggan (the latter being a 4-mile reservoir formed by the damming of the river Spean. The summit of Creag Meaghaidh is a plateau of which a square mile lies above 3,250 feet. The north-eastern edge falls 1,500 feet in great cliffs of mica-schist to a lochan in the floor of Coire Ardair. The burn flowing from it into Loch Laggan gives the best route of ascent by a footpath above its east side.

Western Badenoch

To either side of Loch Laggan, the old region of Badenoch stretches east to Braemar. The Monadh Liath give its north boundary (to Aviemore); its west is a line from the headwaters of the Spey to the hills of Loch Treig East; and its south is Rannoch. It thus includes a great part of the Cairngorms, but its Central Highland area is the western part bounded eastward by the Drumochter pass, between Glen Garry and Glen Truim. The heart of western Badenoch is the Ben Alder range between Loch Ericht and Loch Laggan, including the Corrour Forest around Loch Ossian. The only other high mountain group is the Drumochter range.

Access from the north is by road to the head of Loch Laggan, from the east by road or rail to Dalwhinnie, from the south by road to Loch Rannoch, and from the west by rail to Corrour; thereafter by private roads into the interior from Kinloch Laggan, Dalwhinnie, and Corrour, and by footpath from the west end of Loch Rannoch to the foot of Loch Ericht.

A feature of western Badenoch is the ring of big lochs around the perimeter, and the absence of public roads in the 150 square miles of the interior. In this limited sense, it is a wilderness area almost free of houses and people, a region that represents every wild aspect of the Central Highlands – high, flat-topped mountains with rocky corries, from which strong rivers flow down to wooded lochs, wide sweeps of grassland rather than the heather of the Cairngorms, broad bealachs, and good tracks through the peat-bog. While readily accessible around the fringes, the interior is for those who like solitude. The exploration of its 28 tops, of which 16 are Munros, is generally left to experienced walkers.

The fringe areas are particularly beautiful. The whole length of Loch Laggan is wooded, as also the lower half of Lochan na h-Earba, which runs parallel to Laggan in a fold of the hills. Close behind rise the pointed hills of Binnein Shios and Binnein Shuas, whose craggy flanks and pinewoods look like Canadian Rockies in miniature. Loch Ossian at the edge of Corrour Forest has its eastern half enclosed by woodland and rhododendrons. There is a youth hostel at the west end, good skiing on the mountains around, and access by tracks to Loch Ericht and Ben Alder. The finest of all the fringing lochs are Rannoch and Tummel, where the busily prosperous scene makes an extreme contrast with the loneliness of Loch Ericht. From Pitlochry westward, the Tummel valley is heavily inhabited. Farms, hotels, cottages, and villages are widely spread along its length. Pitlochry is a tourist centre, pumping out a daily tide of car-borne traffic. The shores of the lochs and the Tummel river are wooded richly – pine, birch, oak, ash, larch, holly, cypress, chestnut and more – outstandingly on the south shore where the Black Wood of Rannoch is another relic of the Caledonian forest. Its dark pines are lightened by clumps of birch, which set off tall single redwoods that tower above them. The best view-point over the full length of the Tummel valley is the hill of Craigower, 1300 feet, close to Loch Faskally's east shore.

Ben Alder, 3765 feet, stands over the southern part of Loch Ericht. Its huge flat top is lined to the north-east by cliffs that plunge into long and deep corries. The rock is schist on the lower slopes, capped by granite. The easiest approach is by road from Dalwhinnie down the north shore of Loch Ericht to Ben Alder Lodge. A private road then runs west to Loch Pattack, a mile short of which a footpath encircles Ben Alder. The easiest climb is by the broad west ridge. At the south base of the mountain, Benalder Cottage is often used as an overnight bothy, best approached from the west end of Loch Rannoch.

Between Loch Ericht and Drumochter Pass (1500 feet) lie the 6 main tops of the Drumochter Hills. They include a horse-shoe of 4 Munros around Coire Dhomhain, with Geal Charn as an outlier to the north. The highest top, Beinn Udlamain, 3306 feet, lies at the inner end. All may be traversed in one 11-mile walk from Dalnaspidal to Drumochter Lodge. Several other tops to north and south are linked by high passes to the Dhomhain horse-shoe. They give good ski-running, as do the hills east of Drumochter in the Cairngorm district. The two groups combine to make Dalwhinnie an excellent centre for ski-touring.

The last of the Central Highland groups, the Monadh Liath, or Grey Moors, lie between the Spey and Loch Ness. Their south boundary is the Corrieyairack and the head-waters of the Spey, from which the main range comprising 18 tops and 6 Munros runs north-east between Strath Spey and the upper Findhorn to the Slochd Mor (1189 feet) – the pass crossed by the road from Carrbridge to Inverness. West of the Findhorn, a score of tops around 2,500 feet extend to Strath Errick and Strath Nairn, but are not reckoned as Monadh Liath. The main range is built of schists (mica, gneiss, and quartz) of the Moine series, with one pink granite spur between Aviemore and the river Dulnain. Rock outcrops appear in the Speyside glens and corries, but the Findhorn slopes are peaty wastes; in poor weather they can fascinate the mind by their interminable, dreary monotony. The summits are rolling stony plateaux – dull mountains with extensive but not excellent views. They offer moorland walking and ski-touring in winter. All are best approached from their Speyside glens. The highest top is Carn Dearg, 3093 feet, on the north side of Glen Banchor, which meets the Spey at Newtonmore. Short rock climbs can be had on the south face of Creag Dubh, 2350 feet, 3½ miles south-west of Newtonmore. The cliffs lie above Lochain Ovie on the Laggan road.

In 1731 General Wade made his military road from Drumochter and Laggan Bridge over the Corrieyairack Pass (2507 feet) to Fort Augustus in the Great Glen. This was one of the old drove roads. Access by car is gained half a mile west of Drumgask, then up the right and left banks of the Spey to Melgarve (9 miles). Thereafter the road becomes a rough footpath. The view from the pass (spoiled by a big pylon) extends from the Moray Firth to the Cuillin. The descent goes down Glen Tarff to the Great Glen near Cullachy House (20 miles from the Laggan road). At Melgarve, a track branches west past Loch Spey over the Spey–Roy bealach to Turret Bridge (9 miles) at the road-head in Glen Roy.

General Wade's road from Fort Augustus to Inverness went up Strath Errick on the east side of Loch Ness, and the modern secondary road holds to its line. This slow road is more pleasant by far than the busy main road on the west side: it is worth following to enjoy the Falls of Foyers, which are among the finest of the Highlands. The river Foyers drains Loch Killin and Loch Mhor, then drops to Loch Ness in an upper fall of 30 feet and a lower of 90 feet. The volume of water was reduced in 1896 by the damming of Loch Mhor for Britain's first hydro-electric scheme, but is still considerable. Excellence is given by the woodland setting.

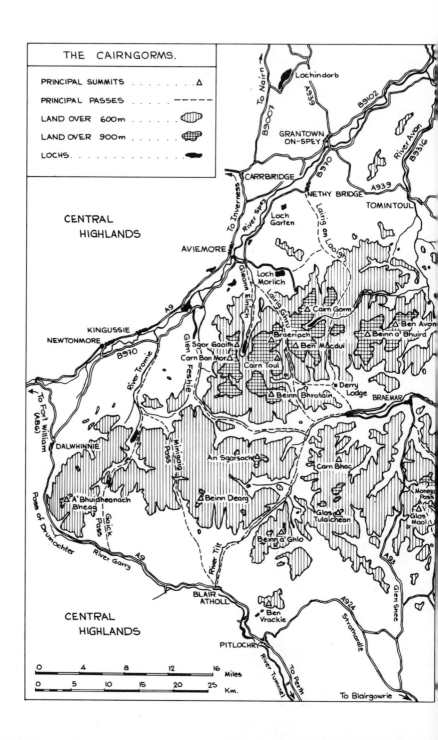

THE CAIRNGORMS.

PRINCIPAL SUMMITS . . . . . . △
PRINCIPAL PASSES . . . . . – – –
LAND OVER 600m . . . . . .
LAND OVER 900m . . . . . .
LOCHS. . . . .

Lochindorb

To Nairn

B9007

A939

B9102

River Avon

B9316

GRANTOWN-ON-SPEY

B970

River Spey

CARRBRIDGE

NETHY BRIDGE

A939

TOMINTOUL

To Inverness

CENTRAL HIGHLANDS

Loch Garten

Lairig an Laoigh

AVIEMORE

Loch Morlich

Gleann Einich

Lairig Ghru

△ Cairn Gorm

△ Ben Avon

A9

Braeriach

△ Beinn a' Bhuird

Sgor Gaoith △

△ Ben Macdui

KINGUSSIE

Glen Feshie

Carn Ban Mor △

Cairn Toul

NEWTONMORE

B970

River Tromie

△ Beinn Bhrotain

Derry Lodge

BRAEMAR

To Fort William (A86)

DALWHINNIE

Minigaig Pass

An Sgarsoch △

Carn Bhac

Monega Pass

△ A' Bhuidheanach Bheag

Gaick Pass

Beinn Dearg △

Glas Tulaichean △

Glas Maol △

Pass of Drumochter

River Garry

A9

River Tilt

Beinn a' Ghlo

A93

Glen Shee

BLAIR ATHOLL

A924

Strathardle

CENTRAL HIGHLANDS

Ben Vrackie

PITLOCHRY

River Tummel

To Perth

To Blairgowrie

0   4   8   12   16   Miles

0   5   10   15   20   25   Km.

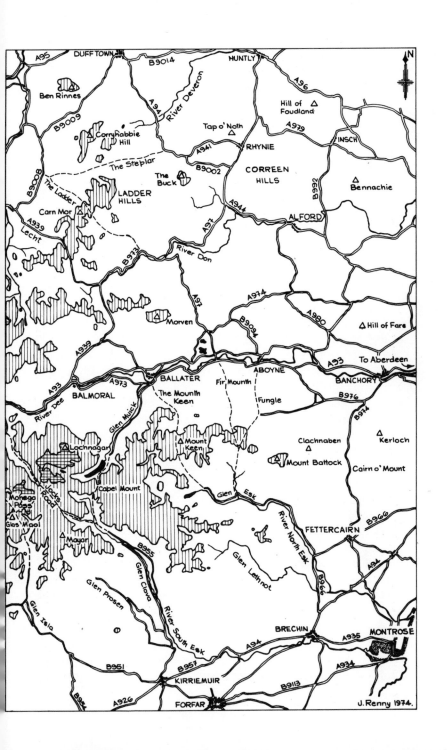

7 Cairngorms

The Cairngorm district is the whole North-east Highlands between the rivers Tay and Spey. At its heart lie the Cairngorms proper, the granite plateaux between the Spey and the Dee. It contains the biggest group of high mountains in Scotland, spreading nearly 24 miles east to west and 16 north to south. Ben Macdhui, Braeriach, Cairn Toul, and Cairn Gorm all exceed 4,000 feet, and many outliers like Beinn a' Bhuird and Ben Avon come close to that height. The main plateau is semi-circled by other high ranges south of the Dee – Lochnagar, the Braes of Angus, and Glen Ey Forest; to the west of these, Atholl, Gaick, and Feshie. The river and forest scenery fringing the district is unsurpassed in the Highlands, especially at Balmoral and Mar Forests on the east, the rivers Tummel, Garry, and Tilt on the south, upper Glen Feshie on the west, and Rothiemurchus and Abernethy on the north or Spey side. The Cairngorm plateau by contrast is a featureless waste of stone. It has no immediately obvious appeal, yet is the most splendid thing of its kind in Scotland. When you walk the tops you appreciate the vast scale, the immense corries ranging along the faces, the massive slopes, the long passes, the wide skies, and the very bareness of the ground: they all cast a spell on the mind. Until recent years they have given a wilderness experience that could be found nowhere else in such fulness. But every man-made road driven to the interior, and every building put there, diminishes that experience. The process has gone far and should be halted; the loss is becoming irreparable.

From Drumochter pass, the main Grampian range zig-zags 100 miles eastward, coming to its highest point on Lochnagar, 3789 feet, and ending on the coastal lowlands near Aberdeen. Some 19 miles east of Drumochter it throws off a northern spur, which is the high Cairngorms. The spur runs 50 miles from the headwaters of the Feshie to fan out on the Banff and Aberdeen moorlands, where the terminal points of Ben Rinnes, Tap o' Noth, and Bennachie, are far-known landmarks. The chapter-heading *Cairngorms* might, it would seem, more properly be *Grampians*. But the people of our country do not in speech accept that latter term. They prefer to think of the range south of the Dee as the southern Cairngorms. In former days it was called The Mounth (pronounced Munth) from the Gaelic *Monadh*, meaning heathy hills, and the name is still applied to the old tracks crossing it.

The entire Cairngorms, north and south, comprise 2,200 square miles, of which nearly 400 are the northern Cairngorms between the Feshie bealach and the Lecht road, and 160 square miles the high Cairngorms, the heartland between the Feshie and the big bend of the river Avon at Inchrory.

The Lecht is a road crossing a pass at 2,114 feet between Cock Bridge and Tomintoul. It is the second highest road in Scotland, exceeded only by the Cairnwell, 2,199 feet, between Braemar and the Spittal of Glen Shee.

Rock topography

The Cairngorms are underlain and ringed by crystalline schists of the Moine and Dalradian series, through which a mass of granite has been intruded to form, by erosion of surrounding rocks, the principal summits. In former days the Cairngorms were named Monadh Ruadh, the Red Hills, in contrast to the Monadh Liath, the Grey Hills west of the Spey.

Moine schists occupy the whole western periphery from the north to the south-west, where they compose the Monadh Liath and much of the Gaick and Atholl Forests. The Dalradian series take the whole eastern arc from Banffshire in the north through Aberdeenshire, Angus, and Perthshire, and then sweep on through Argyll. Dalradian quartzite is the most conspicuous mountain builder on the southern sector, where the highest point is Beinn a' Ghlo, 3677 feet, in Atholl. The high Cairngorms and the Lochnagar–Broad Cairn massif east of the Dee are the largest of the granite intrusions. The trend of the main valleys is south-west to north-east. Little bare rock is exposed on the mountain sides facing south and west; these have long since disintegrated into rounded mounds with flat tops and no sharp ridges. That general rule is modified by the many granite hills taking pyramid shape, as on Devil's Point and Carn Eilrig at either end of the Braeriach massif, or the Meikle Pap of Lochnagar; great tors often project along the ridges, best seen on the Mither Tap of Bennachie, Ben Avon, or Ben Mheadhoin.

The evidence of the Ice Age is seen not in striated rock like the Cuillin but in the moraines and hillocks of the glens, dammed lochs like Loch Callater, huge erratic boulders strewn on ridges, and above

147

all in the splendid corries and their cliffs plucked out of the north and east sides of the plateaux.

The plateaux are bare, except for moss and lichen, and the occasional pink cushion of moss campion blossoming on the edge of the summer snowfields, but heather is luxuriant on the flanks, bell heather and cross-leaved heath from June onwards, and ling in August and September. The southern Cairngorms, where the rocks are mainly schists and quartzites, are much grassier and graze large herds of sheep (as well as deer), especially in Atholl and the Braes of Angus.

Access

The Cairngorm district is completely ringed by roads. Only one, from Aberdeen to Braemar, penetrates by way of the Dee to the interior. This Deeside road is joined by four others that cross the spines of the ranges to north and south. Only one crosses the northern range: the Lecht road that links Speyside to Ballater. Three cross the Mounth from the coastal lowlands: the Cairnwell road from Blairgowrie to Braemar, the Cairn o' Mount from Fettercairn to Banchory, and the Slug road from Stonehaven to Banchory. No other access roads cross the watershed. Several go up the glens in the Braes of Angus, two in Atholl up Glen Tilt and Glen Bruar (private roads although rights-of-way for walkers), and three on the north side up Glen Tromie, Glen Feshie, and Glen More. The latter now goes right up to Coire Cas of Cairn Gorm, in aid of skiing and tourism. Apart from these, very numerous rights-of-way tracks, old drove roads and stalking tracks, criss-cross the mountains. The most famous are the Mounth tracks, which go right over the tops between Strathmore and the Dee, and the three great passes from Dee to Spey by the Lairig Ghru, the Lairig an Laoigh, and Glen Feshie.

The Cairngorms have 124 tops over 3,000 feet, of which 54 are Munros. These are divided among three mountain groups: Gaick and Atholl with 14 Munros, the Mounth and Braes of Angus with 18, and the high Cairngorms, which have 22 Munros and more than half the tops.

Gaick and Atholl

At the Drumochter dip in the Grampians, Gaick is the deer forest north of the spine, bounded by Glen Feshie and the Spey. Atholl is the far greater district on the south side, extending east to the Cairnwell and Glen Shee. At the headwaters of the Feshie, the Gaick and Atholl spine rises to 3,276 feet on Cairn an Fhidleir (Carn Ealar), but thereafter keeps below 3,000 feet westwards until it ends above Drumochter on two featureless Munros.

The Gaick hills are remarkable for the flatness of their tops and ridges, and the multitude of white hares thereon. The principal feature of Gaick is the loch-filled pass between the Spey and Glen Garry. From near Kingussie, Glen Tromie strikes deep into a jungle of mountains astride the broad spine, where a long flat trough, shaped by glacial action, holds a chain of three lochs linked by river. From the farthest of these, Loch an Duin, the Gaick pass at 1,600 feet allows a way down the Edendon Water to Dalnacardoch in Glen Garry (24 miles from Kingussie).

A still more famous pass is the Minigaig, an historic drove road from Kingussie to Blair Atholl by way of Glen Tromie and Glen Bruar (26 miles). This is one of the true Mounth tracks, named in Gaelic *Monadh Miongaig*: like most others it has no bealach but goes over the broad ridges on firm open ground. On the Glen Garry side, it may be started from the Errochty road-fork, a mile west of Bruar Water, or from Old Blair a mile north of Blair Atholl. The descent to the Spey goes down the Allt Bhran to the Tromie. The imposing ruins seen on the Spey opposite Kingussie are those of Ruthven Barracks, built by Wade in 1716 and sacked by the Highlanders in 1746.

Between Glen Bruar and the Cairnwell road, the range spreads out in 24 tops over 3,000 feet. The highest and best known is Beinn a' Ghlo, 3677 feet, which lies 6 miles south of the watershed and is separated from its neighbours by deep glens. One of these, Glen Tilt, is a famous right-of-way pass from Blair Atholl to Braemar (27 miles). Blair Castle at the foot of the glen is the seat of the duke of Atholl and open to the public. It is worth visiting. Cars cannot be driven up Glen Tilt without permission from the estate office. The walker in this glen will not find his interest flagging. The river is one of the liveliest, the woods are well grown and varied in species, and there is a continuous change from the lower fertility to an upper desolation. The glen is narrowly enclosed and the flanking mountains are not well seen.

The lower glen has roads up each side. The right of way goes up the left bank from Bridge of Tilt to Marble Lodge (there is marble in the glen), then by the right bank to Forest Lodge (8 miles). The road ends shortly after and a path continues past the Falls of Tarf.

The river Tarf, flowing in from the west, once turned north to the Dee, but now south as the Tilt captured its waters by eating back the land. The rise from here to the watershed at 1,580 feet is only 280 feet in 2 miles. The pass is the lowest between Drumochter and Cairn o' Mount, with a good view to the high Cairngorms and deep into the Lairig Ghru. The descent goes by the Bynack and Geldie burns.

Beinn a' Ghlo has 4 tops, of which Carn nan Gabhar is the highest. The ascent from Blair Atholl starts up Glen Fender to the highest point of the road, 1,443 feet, under Carn Liath. Permission is needed for a car.

Atholl is famous for its deer forests, grouse moors, and sheep runs. The estates are active, and inquiries about access should be made at the estate office in April–May and September–October.

The peaks of the main spine are best climbed from the north side, by the Geldie and Ey burns, or from the Cairnwell road.

The longest and most important of the southern glens is Glen Shee. Five miles above Blairgowrie, where Strath Ardle branches west at Bridge of Cally, Glen Shee strikes north to the Cairnwell at 2199 feet, from which Glen Clunie falls to Braemar. This was the old Mounth track and drove road from the upper Dee to Strath More. A military road was built in 1750 and now it is the highest motor-road in Scotland. It used to be notorious in winter for its double bend called the Devil's Elbow, which has been recently straightened.

Glen Shee is a green glen, with wide meadows by the river and grass-slopes above. In the lower half, two branch roads break east to Glen Isla, the first of which passes under Mount Blair, 2441 feet. It is believed that in this neighbourhood the battle of Mons Graupius was fought between the Picts and Romans. The head of the glen at 1100 feet is named the Spittal of Glen Shee (from *hospital* meaning refuge for travellers). It was an early droving stance and later a stage for coach-and-horse. The hotel on the site has been rebuilt in Scandinavian style. The glen forks at the Spittal. The left fork, Glen Lochsie, gives a pass by way of Loch nan Eun, 2500 feet, to Glen Ey, and also access from the loch to a circle of four Munros. The right branch, Gleann Beag, carries the Cairnwell road. The pass between Cairnwell, 3059 feet, on the west side, and Meall Odhar, 3019 feet, on the east, is undistinguished except by height, history, and good ski-slopes. Chair-lifts and tows have been set up to either side. The mountains are dull walking but swiftly climbed.

Those around Loch nan Eun can be climbed from the Cairnwell, or Glen Ey. The Ey Burn takes its source from this group and meets the Dee at Inverey, where the Cairngorm Club has a hut. Glen Ey is a deer sanctuary, once famed for its cattle until the people were cleared. It has limestone with hill-slopes richly grassy. The five 3,000 foot tops round its head offer good walking on short grass and fine views. The long hill ridge dividing Glen Ey from Glen Clunie terminates on Morrone, 2819 feet, above Braemar. The top offers a splendid panorama of the high Cairngorms from Cairn Toul to Ben Avon.

The Braes of Angus to Braemar

The Aberdeen–Angus hills form a broad, rolling tableland, which except for Lochnagar, which lies out on the Balmoral limb to the north, hardly appears to the eye as split into separate mountains. As seen from the tops, even Lochnagar merges with the rest, for a line 10 miles long can be drawn from the Meikle Pap to Craig Leacach west of Glen Isla at a height everywhere above 3,000 feet, except for a slight dip around the Tolmount. The mountains are fatly massive, and their backs grassily smooth. They take up much room. Only 14 Munros with 17 tops occupy the land from the Cairnwell to the Kincardine frontier. The Angus frontier runs along the main spine. This whole southern tableland is Dalradian schist and gneiss, hence its grassy character, distinct from the heather-covered granite of the Lochnagar–White Mounth massif – from which it is separated only by the Dubh Loch–Callater col at 3050 feet.

The Braes of Angus, which fall to Strath More, are deeply cut by five parallel rivers. Three of these, the North and South Esk and the Isla, fall from cliff-walled corries under the lip of the plateau. The finest of these is Glen Clova (the valley of the South Esk) placed at centre. All have motor roads, up to but not into the corries, from which Mounth tracks cross the plateau to the Dee. The northern Deeside slopes are likewise penetrated by Glen Muick and Glen Callater, to either side of Lochnagar. Between all these corries the plateau is more irregularly shaped and gives many miles of delightful walking around 3,000 feet or more, with much choice of route for ascent and descent.

The roads into Glen Isla start from Kirriemuir or Alyth. The double corrie at its head has the Caenlochan glen to the west and Cannes glen to the east, both within the Caenlochan National Nature

Reserve. A larch forest once covered their lower slopes, and crags ring the walls at the back. Below Monega Hill to the west, a Mounth track climbs the ridge to 3318 feet on Glas Maol, 3504 feet, and descends north-west to Sheann Spittal Bridge in Glen Clunie (6 miles). The Spittal was an old hospice, not marked now on maps, where the road crossed the Clunie Water.

Glen Clova is the biggest and most interesting of the southern glens. The motor road ends at Braedownie, 816 feet, 17 miles from Kirriemuir. On the last 7 miles the glen is cut straight by glacial action, which has left a remarkable series of hanging corries on either flank. At Braedownie the glen divides under the forested slopes of Craig Mellon: the left-hand branch is Glen Doll, and the right-hand branch ends in a corrie under Broad Cairn, 3268 feet. Eastward, a moorland plateau undulates 20 miles to Glen Esk. From Brae-downie, the Capel Mounth path crosses the plateau at 2275 feet to the Spittal of Glen Muick (6 miles). Glen Doll is flanked to the south by Driesh and Mayar, in whose sides are Corrie Kilbo and Corrie Fee. The entrance is commanded by a rock buttress called The Scorrie, 2512 feet, bearing the Winter Corrie high on its east side. The back and sides of Corrie Fee and Glen Doll are lined by the cliffs of Craig Rennet, Craig Maud, and others, which give excellent rock-climbing. This whole area is noted for its arctic plants. Down Glen Doll flows the White Water, and up the left bank goes the Tolmount track to Loch Callater and Braemar. Its lower part from Braedownie to the plateau is known as Jock's Road. It crosses the plateau at 3,000 feet east of Tolmount, 3143 feet, then turns down Glen Callater to the foot of the loch (9½ miles), from which there is a road to Braemar (5 miles).

Glen Esk is the valley of the river North Esk, which has its source in the hills above Glen Muick and Glen Clova. The road in goes 17 miles north from Edzell to Invermark, near Loch Lee, where the glen branches right and left into Glen Mark and Glen Lee. The lower part of Glen Esk is pleasantly varied farmland, and the hills around the upper parts rugged but low, rarely exceeding 2,500 feet except on Mount Keen, 3077 feet, close above Glen Mark. Three Mounth tracks cross to the Dee. The Mount Keen track leaves the Water of Mark up the Ladder Burn, and crosses the west shoulder of Mount Keen at 2504 feet, then down to the Water of Tanner and across the hills on its west side to Glenmuick House and Ballater (12 miles). The Fir Mounth tracks starts less than 4 miles lower at

Tarfside. It starts up the Water of Tarf, then up the long south ridge of Tampie, over its top at 2363 feet, and finally down the north side through old firs to the Burn of Skinna, Glen Tanar, and Dinnet (13 miles, or 14 to Aboyne). The Fungle track has the same start as the Fir Mounth, but leaves the Tampie ridge to cross the col between Tampie and Mulnabracks at 1961 feet, then down the Water of Feugh to the Castle of Birse, where it goes north to the Allt Fungle and Aboyne (14 miles).

The valley of the Dee, winding between the Grampian range and the high Cairngorms, is richly wooded along its green floor and over the flanking hillocks, more especially between the town of Ballater at 658 feet and the village of Braemar at 1,112 feet, which are sited to either side of Balmoral Forest. Balmoral includes Lochnagar and all its northern slopes. The most famous wood along the foot is the forest of Ballochbuie, said to be the most ancient of Highland pine forests, for it has bever been felled. When due to be cut it was saved by Queen Victoria's purchase of Balmoral in 1878, when she referred to Ballochbuie as 'The bonniest plaid in Scotland' – an allusion to a previous sale in exchange for a tartan plaid. Balmoral Castle stands on the right bank of the Dee near Crathie.

Lochnagar is the central feature of Balmoral, separated from the Grampian range behind Loch Muick, the Dubh Loch, Loch Callater, and their deep glens. On Lochnagar as nowhere else in the Highlands, are such vast sweeps of hillside purpled by the heather of late August. The spectacle is more brilliant than is likely to be imagined before it is seen. In June, acres of the summit may be coloured red with creeping azalea; moss campion fringes the melting snow, and rare arctic-alpine plants grow around the head of Loch Callater. Above 2,000 feet, the mountain is sculpted by two great corries and several lesser ones. The most splendid by far is the north-east corrie, topped by Cac Carn Beag, 3789 feet, and 3 other tops. Granite cliffs fall 600 feet beneath the steep screes, which plunge an equal height to the lochan from which Lochnagar takes its name. A few centuries ago the mountain's name was White Mounth, a name now reserved for its south plateau above the Dubh Loch. 'Lochnagar' is most probably derived from *Loch nan Gabhar*, the Loch of the Goats.

The cliffs of Lochnagar tend to be vegetatious, but provide much good climbing not only in summer but more especially in winter. Excellent rock and ice climbing may also be had on the south side of the mountain on Creag an Dubh Loch, where the cliff face, 700 feet high, runs straight for nearly three-quarters of a mile.

The eastern approach to Lochnagar goes 9 miles by road from Ballater to the Spittal of Glen Muick, then 5 miles by a path across the river up to the Meikle Pap and the summit. The western approach goes 5 miles miles by road from Braemar to Loch Callater, then by path on to Carn an t' Sagairt Mor and so to the summit (6 miles). In ideal weather, the view covers the length and breadth of the Scottish mainland – from Caithness to the Cheviot and from Aberdeen lighthouse to Ben Nevis.

The High Cairngorms

The high Cairngorms are split north to south into three plateaux by the two long passes of the Lairig Ghru and Lairig an Laoigh. Each group is dominated by a pair of mountains around 4,000 feet high: Braeriach and Cairn Toul between the Feshie and Lairig Ghru; Cairn Gorm and Ben Macdhui east of the Lairig Ghru; and Beinn a' Bhuird and Ben Avon east of the Lairig an Laoigh. These three pairs are the crests of their plateaux, the shallow troughs of which never fall as low as 3,000 feet. Together they form the largest mass of high land in Scotland. The traverse of all six has occasionally been made in one day. Each group has important outliers.

The high landscape quality of the Cairngorms is given by their forests, glens, and corries. Rothiemurchus forest in Speyside, although worked for centuries, retains its beauty in the combination of old gnarled pines with drooping birches. By the Spey there is great variety of tree and grassland; nearer the hills, the Scots pine predominates, with space for full branching and a carpet of blaeberry and heather. Small lochans like Loch an Ard with reeds and water-lilies, or Loch an Eilein with its castle, or Loch Morlich with sandy beaches, and innumerable little hills like the Tor of Alvie, and burns like the Druie, add to the woodlands' endless diversity. Much new planting has been done by the Forestry Commission in Glen More Forest Park around Loch Morlich, but until thinned and matured these plantations lack interest. The same can be said of the new plantations by Nethy Bridge, but the old woodlands where the Lairig an Laoigh track passes through to the hills still delight the eye.

At Deeside, the woodland approaches are quite different. The Speyside forests are on flat land, but the Deeside approaches are the glens. The route in from Braemar traverses high above the Dee, giving fine views of the Cairn Toul-Braeriach plateau from a fore-ground of birchwood, then of Douglas fir and pine. The river narrows to the Linn of Dee, where it bursts through a rock-gut – a famous salmon leap. The tracks in then go west by the treeless Dee to the Geldie, or north either through the magnificent pinewoods of Glen Quoich to Beinn a' Bhuird, or by the Lairig an Laoigh track up Glen Lui and Glen Derry. The Derry Wood is one of the finest in the country. All these glens have been scarred through the bull-dozing of tracks by the owner of Mar Forest.

The main glens carry right-of-way passes to Speyside. The Glen Feshie pass goes 26 miles from Braemar to Kincraig. From the Linn of Dee, the track continues west up Glen Geldie, a broad moorland strath where the only refuge is the ruin of Geldie Lodge. The bealach at 1800 feet is wild and exposed. A mile beyond, the Eidart must be crossed at its junction with the Feshie. This burn is notoriously dangerous in spate, when a footbridge should be used 400 yards upstream. Glen Feshie then narrows. The burn is always lively, but with deep salmon pools. Screes and splintered crags rise close above. Landslides falling from high ravines have swept the woods and track, tumbling big pines. The track traverses steep, precarious screes before emerging from the gorge on to flat ground, where it winds among juniper on to wide grassland covered sparsely in old pines. The stone bothy of Ruigh Aiteachain (Landseer's old cottage) still offers shelter. A short way beyond, the river spreads wide and stony, but is crossed by bridge below Feshie Lodge, where you join the road to Kincraig. The flat bed of the glen here used to be a drovers' cattle market. All this land is now deer forest, although sheep and cows are kept lower down.

The Lairig Ghru track penetrates the heart of the Cairngorms between Braeriach and Ben Macdhui. At the Linn of Dee, the best route diverges from the Dee to go up Glen Lui to Derry Lodge, then through the Luibeg glen to rejoin the Dee near Corrour bothy under Devil's Point. The slopes of Macdhui look dull, but Cairn Toul across the glen is the most graceful peak of the Cairngorms, with aid of a hanging corrie under its summit (one of three). Beyond Angel's Peak, on the far side of Cairn Toul, the Dee is left behind where it swings west into An Garbh Choire, the enormous corrie between Cairn Toul and Braeriach. The scene has no equal in the Cairngorms for wildness on the grand scale. The glen narrows to a trough full of boulders, and the burn runs partially underground to form the Pools of Dee. The crest of the pass is now close, at 2733 feet. A mile and a half down the north side, at the foot of Braeriach's Sron na Lairig, the Sinclair refuge hut sits above the left bank. The track goes down the Allt Druidh into the pinewoods and heather of Rothiemurchus, where the burn joins the bigger Am Beanaidh flowing out of Glen Einich. A short way before, the track splits into three, one branch east to Loch Morlich, one to Coylumbridge, and the left branch more directly down the Beanaidh to Coylumbridge: 19 miles from Linn of Dee, or 27 from Braemar to Aviemore.

The Lairig an Laoigh is 30 miles long from Braemar to Nethy Bridge. In upper Glen Derry it passes under Coire Etchachan, where the track to Ben Macdhui diverges westward. The Lairig track climbs to the bealach between Beinn Mheadhoin and Beinn a' Chaorruinn at 2446 feet, and descends past the Dubh Lochan to cross the river Avon at Ford of Avon. The name in Gaelic is said to be *Ath nam Fiann*, the Ford of the Fiann (Fingal's men), or *Ath-fhinn*, Fingal's ford, and to have given name to river, loch, and ben. The O.S. map marks the ford as bridged, but the bridge was swept away a few years ago and has not yet been replaced. There is an emergency refuge on the north side. Cross and climb at first up the Allt Dearg, then close under the flank of Bynack More. Take care in winter not to wander north-east down the Caiplich headwaters. Hold to the Bynack slopes, finally crossing Bynack's north ridge at 2526 feet, the highest point of the pass. Vast and desolate moorlands stretch away to the east. The track is now good and forks short of the river Nethy – the Lairig an Laoigh north to Nethy Bridge, and the west fork across the Nethy (bridge and bothy) by way of the Ryvoan pass to Glen More.

A good-weather alternative from the river Avon goes west to Loch Avon and up to the Saddle, 2707 feet, between Cairn Gorm and A' Choinneach. The Saddle commands a view of the cliffs around the head of the loch. The descent down Strath Nethy, which is rough with stone fallen from the crags, leads in 4½ miles to the Nethy Bothy, now called Bynack Stables. The end part is kept open.

Another important track from Ford of Avon goes down the Avon's left bank 12 miles to Inchrory. There is a bothy 3½ miles down at Faindouran. The route gives clear views into the Slochd, the magnificent north corrie between Beinn a' Bhuird and Ben Avon (pronounced A'an). The river is famous for its clear water and deep rocky pools, best seen at the Linn of Avon near Inchrory. Several other tracks from Deeside to Inchrory converge on Loch Builg, at the east end of Ben Avon.

The granite corries, which give such strong character to the Cairngorms, have among their multitude several of the most remarkable of the Highlands. Three at least are unique of their kind: Loch Avon for its deep-sunk site between Cairn Gorm and Ben Macdhui, invisible from either and therefore still a mountain fastness despite the chairlift on Cairn Gorm; Lochnagar's north-east corrie, outstanding for the grace of its sculpting under huge cliffs; and the Garbh Choire of Braeriach for remoteness and the immense scale of its craggy amphitheatre, which curves 4 miles around four corries to Cairn Toul (pronounced Towl). Down the cliffs of one upper corrie, the river Dee cascades from its source in the Wells of Dee at 4,000 feet on the plateau. The main spring is marked by a cairn of quartz stones. The gush is powerful, and reinforced by others close below. Where it goes over the edge of Garbh Choire Dhé it is spanned by a big snow-bridge, usually until the end of July. The snowfield under the cliffs normally persists through the whole year. The Garbh Choire's only possible rival is the Slochd Mor of Beinn a' Bhuird.

The six high tops of the Cairngorms, not to mention their 58 satellites, can all be climbed by a variety of routes, of which only the most commonly used are given here. The best of all the high level walks is that over Cairn Toul and Braeriach around the Garbh Choire. If starting from Braemar, climb from the Corrour bothy west up Coire Odhar by a zig-zag path to the neck between Devil's Point and Cairn Toul. If from Speyside, approach by Glen Einich – one of the best glens of the district, wooded below and wild above – until the Allt Beanaidh Bheag comes down from Braeriach, then move up to Loch Coire an Lochain and climb one of the ridges to either side of the bowl. An easier but duller route up Braeriach goes from the Lairig Ghru up Sron na Lairig. The walk along the tops keeps for $2\frac{1}{2}$ miles to 4,000 feet or above. The route is hard to follow in mist and there is no easy descent to the Dee until either end is reached.

Ben Macdhui, 4296 feet, and Cairn Gorm, 4084 feet, are climbed from the Dee by way of Glen Derry and Corrie Etchachan. A shorter route is by Luibeg up Macdhui's south ridge, but this route reveals too little of the mountain. Macdhui is Scotland's second highest summit, and the view spans nearly 200 miles from Ben Hope to the Lammermuirs. From Speyside, the easiest route to Cairn Gorm is by road through Glen More up to Coire Cas, where there is car park and chairlift, and a track to the summit. Those for whom the route is spoiled by car and bus traffic, crowds of tourists or skiers, kiosks, hut, and mechanical uplift with pylons and wires, will find a much more interesting route, and a more varied scene, if they climb from the Lairig Ghru over Creag an Leth-choin to Cairn Lochan, 3983 feet, and so along the tops of the north corries. The view south is indifferent, but northward over the Spey excellent across dark forests and bright waters. A good route of descent from Cairn Gorm is down the long north ridge to Ryvoan. The best way from Cairn Gorm to the Shelter Stone of Loch Avon is down Coire Raibert, where some hillcraft is required in mist to turn the lower crags. From Macdhui, the easiest way is down to Loch Etchachan, then through the gap on its north side. The Shelter Stone at the head of the loch is a few minutes up from the shore and as big as a square-topped cottage.

Beinn a' Bhuird, 3924 feet, and Ben Avon, 3843 feet, form a broad sprawling ridge running 7 miles east to west between the Dee and Glen Avon. They throw off spurs in all directions, enclosing corries big and small. They are connected and divided by the bealach of the Sneck, 3190 feet, which gives a right-of-way pass between Deeside and Inchrory.

Ben Avon with its spurs has 10 tops over 3000 feet, of which only the summit is a Munro. The mountain's outstanding feature is the large number of granite tors on its back and sides. Some are big enough to be seen even from the Dee. The shortest route from Braemar goes from Invercauld up Gleann an t-Slugain to the Sneck (9 miles), from which the sudden view into the Slochd Mor wilderness has startling effect. The traverse is best appreciated by starting from Inchrory up the north-west ridge, thus passing (at 2700 feet) the Clach Bhan, the most weathered of all the tors, deeply sculpted into pot-holes by wind-rotated water, which has then removed some of the sides to give chair or pulpit shapes. The most spectacular tors are seen later, about 500 feet down the north ridge of Stob Bac an Fuarain – horns 80 feet high, mapped as *Clach Bun Rudhtair*. On the summit ridge, the biggest tor forms the highest top, *Leabaidh an Daimh Bhuidhe*, the couch of the yellow stag (6 miles, 3½ hours).

The main body of Beinn a' Bhuird lies north and south at right-angles to the Sneck ridge. To west and south its convex slopes make it one of the dullest-seeming hills, but the eastern face is carved out in a series of rock-bound corries, which, to either side of the main ridge leading off to Ben Avon, rival those of Braeriach's Garbh Choire. The most direct and revealing route from Deeside goes up Gleann an t-Slugain to its head, then on to the south ridge by Carn Fiaclach, and so along the cliff-tops of the corries (9 miles to summit, 4½ hours).

All three plateaux have important outliers. From west to east these are; the Carn Ban Mor plateau between Braeriach and Glen Feshie; the Beinn Bhrotain–Monadh Mor ridge south of Cairn Toul; the Bynack Mor ridge east of Cairn Gorm; and Beinn a' Chaorruinn west of Beinn a' Bhuird.

The Carn Ban plateau has three Munros, which are widely separated rollers on a high featureless expanse called the Moine Mhor. Between Glen Einich and Feshie it extends a long ridge northward to Rothiemurchus, bearing a distinguished mountain, Sgoran Dubh. It has 4 tops and 2 Munros. The summit is Sgor Gaoith, the peak of the wind, 3658 feet. Its lesser top, Sgoran Dubh Mor, lies a mile north, and the two present to Loch Einich a line of cliffs split into 5 buttresses. Sgoran Dubh is a well-formed, impressive mountain as seen from Glen Einich. All the tops can be reached from above or below Loch Einich, or from Glen Feshie, where a track from Achlean climbs past the Badan Mosach wood (in which there is a nature trail) to Carn Ban Mor, 3443 feet.

Beinn Bhrotain, 3795 feet, and Monadh Mor, 3651 feet, lie at opposite ends of a 3-mile ridge, which Glen Geusachan separates from Cairn Toul except where the col at its head gives a link, and an easy route of ascent from the Dee. The glen has good grass that used to graze cattle before it became a deer sanctuary. The south-east slopes of Bhrotain may be climbed from White Bridge.

Bynack Mor, 3574 feet, with its lower Munro, A' Choinneach, 3345 feet, lie east of Strath Nethy, and are climbed across the Saddle or else from the Lairig an Laoigh. About 400 feet below and south-east of the summit stand the Barns of Bynack, which are three groups of granite tors from 50 to 100 feet high. The rocks have weathered into pillow shape.

Beinn a' Chaorruinn, 3553 feet, and Beinn Bhreac, 3051 feet, are two Munros facing Ben Macdhui across Glen Derry. Their tops are connected by a 3-mile-long stretch of flat bog and turf, favoured only by herds of deer. It extends even to Beinn a' Bhuird. The most direct approach is from the Lairig an Laoigh. The walk along the top gives the best possible sight of Ben Macdhui's construction, showing how the massive dome is supported by corries, cliffs, and buttresses. The most interesting route of descent goes south through the pinewoods of Dubh Ghleann and Glen Quoich.

The eight principal rock-climbing centres of the high Cairngorms are on Sgoran Dubh above Loch Einich, in the Garbh Choire of Braeriach, Coire Sputan Dearg and Coire Etchachan of Macdhui, the Shelter Stone Crag of Loch Avon, Coire an Lochan and Coire an t-Sneachda on the north face of Cairn Gorm, the Coire an Dubh Lochan between the north and south tops of Beinn a' Bhuird, and the Garbh Choire north of the Sneck. In general, the rock tends to be rounded and rather holdless, and to weather along the fracture lines into blocks, but these are not invariable rules.

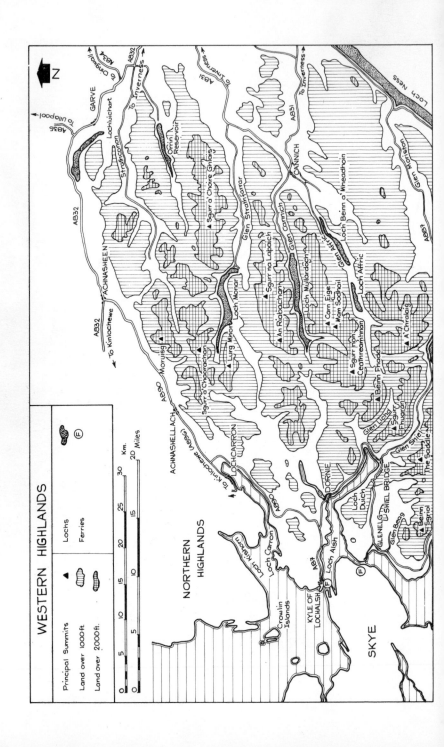

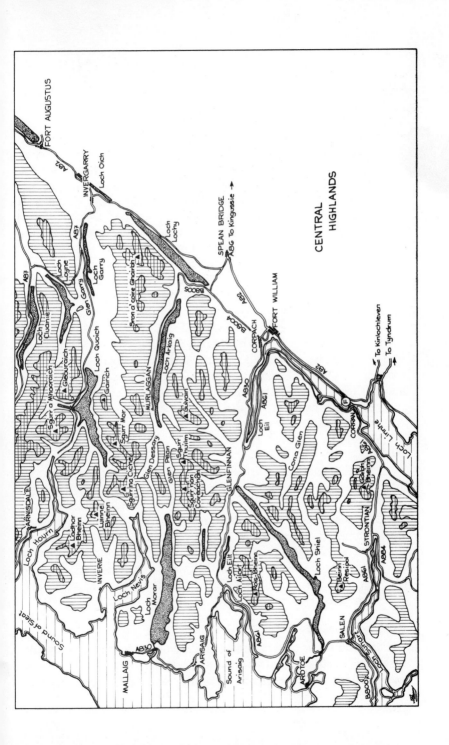

8 West Highlands

The West Highlands include all land west of the Great Glen and south of Strath Bran and Glen Carron. The seaboard from Morvern to the Kyle of Loch Alsh is fretted by lochs of which the greater are Sunart, Nevis, Hourn, Alsh, Duich, and Carron, and by over eighty islands, of which the principal are Mull, Rum, and Skye. The mountain spine lies not far inland from the heads of the sea-lochs; down its length the rainfall is extremely high: 170 inches is locally common, rising to over 200 inches at the head of Glen Garry. But variation within a short distance is also extreme, and peninsulas have a low fall: 40 inches at Ardnamurchan Point or the west shore of Knoydart.

The spine is repeatedly split east to west by long parallel glens, allowing passes from the Great Glen and Cromarty Firth to the west coast. The most important of these are Loch Eil to Loch Aline, which carries the Mallaig road and rail; Loch Arkaig to Morar; Glen Garry to Lochs Hourn and Nevis; Glen Moriston and Glen Shiel (the road to Skye); and Strath Bran and Glen Carron, which take road and rail to Kyle of Lochalsh. Valuable footpaths and passes across the watershed are given by the three upper glens of Strath Glass: Affric, Cannich, and Farrar.

Access

All the big glens give access to the mountains between by road and path. The west coast has no south to north road, being so involuted by lochs that it measures 330 miles between Morvern and Loch Carron compared with the Great Glen frontier of 85 miles up Loch Linnhe to Inverness. Mallaig is served by the West Highland railway from Glasgow through Fort William; and Kyle of Lochalsh by railway from Inverness and Dingwall. Ferry services connect Morvern, Ardnamurchan, and Oban with Mull; Mallaig with Skye and Rum; and Glenelg with Skye.

Rock topography

The mainland rocks are almost entirely of the Moine series, while basalt with gabbro intrusions form the better part of Skye, Mull, and the Ardnamurchan peninsula. The mountains above 3,000 feet are all of these three rocks. On the mainland they number 119 tops, of which 62 are Munros; on the Hebrides 22, of which 13 are Munros. The number of other hills that fall just short of 3,000 feet is even larger, some of them of other rocks, like the Red Cuillin of Skye (granite).

The mountains, closely packed and trenched, are generally steeper and more pointed than the Central Highland ranges. From the low hills of Morvern they gradually increase in height northward to over 3,800 feet around Glen Affric. An outstanding feature is their deep penetration by the sea and their views across the Hebrides from the western tops in Knoydart, Morar, and Moidart. In short, mountains pack the district so heavily that on first inspection they appear maze-like, yet are given order by the parallel glens. Most of the land is deer forest and sheep-run, with crofting and forestry in the glens, and big-scale fishing concentrated at Mallaig.

Morvern, Ardgour, Ardnamurchan

These three districts formed one of the larger Scottish islands before the isostatic rise of land at the close of the Ice Age. They are still nearly separated from the mainland by Loch Linnhe, Loch Eil, and Loch Shiel, for the watershed between the two latter is only 50 feet above sea-level. The rectangle thus enclosed is split again by Loch Sunart, which separates the Morvern and Ardnamurchan peninsulas. From the loch's head, Glen Tarbert runs 8 miles east, carrying the main access road to all three. They have 15 notable tops, of which the highest are Sgurr Domhnuill, 2915 feet, and Garbh Bheinn, 2903 feet, both in Ardgour. The Ardgour hills seen from Glencoe or Ballachulish are one of the most attractive groups of the West Highlands, and no disappointment follows a closer approach. The most direct route in from the south is across the Corran Narrows of Loch Linnhe by car ferry (4 miles north of Ballachulish bridge) to mid-Ardgour. If the ferry is not running, you go from Fort William around the head of Loch Eil, which is a western dog-leg of Loch Linnhe. If you start from Oban, you may cross to Mull and taken the car ferry from Fishnish to Loch Aline in Morvern.

Morvern's interior is all moorland and low hills of no distinctive shape. The road in from the head of Loch Sunart, after crossing the moors at 800 feet, runs south down Gleann Geal to Loch Aline on the Sound of Mull. Loch Sunart has given Morvern its name, *A' Mhorbhairn*, the sea-gap. Loch Aline takes a bottle-neck shape, and the little village at the outer narrows has an excellent setting, with the hills of Mull on one side, the wooded loch on the other, and a view down the Sound of Mull to the Lorn coast. Kinlochaline Castle, once the seat of the Clan MacInnes, stands at the head of the loch, and the ruin of Ardtornish Castle, held by the Lords of the Isles, at the outward point. The MacInnes motto, *Work gives pleasure*, must seem to some ironic since Loch Aline is much spoiled by sand-mining (see p. 101). From Lochaline, a low valley holding three lochs curves west to Loch Sunart, thus dividing the south-west hills, which are Tertiary basalt and grassy, from the metamorphic rocks that reach their highest point on Creach Bheinn, 2800 feet, above Glen Tarbert.

Across Glen Tarbert, Ardgour is the most highly mountainous of the three areas. At the Loch Linnhe end of the glen, near Inversanda, Coire an Iubhair runs 3 miles north into the hills below 1,000-foot cliffs that wall Garbh Bheinn's north-east face. They give excellent rock-climbing on a mixture of quartzite and gneiss. At the foot of the corrie, which in fact is a glen, there is good camping beside the river (ask permission at Inversanda House). The best route up Garbh Bheinn goes 2 miles into the glen then leftward into the high eastern corrie. The principal feature of the cliffs is the eastern buttress, which rises 1,200 feet to the summit, and gives Garbh Bheinn a splendid appearance when seen across Loch Linnhe. The summit reveals a vast spread of sea and mountains.

An even better viewpoint will be found on a much inferior mountain, Ben Resipol, 2774 feet, in west Ardgour. Two miles down Loch Sunart, at the first of 30 bays in its north shore, the village of Strontian lies at the foot of Strontian glen. At the head of the glen, a ridge links Ben Resipol on the west with Sgurr Domhnuill, 7 miles to its east. The glen forks a mile up, and both branches have roads leading to old lead mines. The main or right-hand glen gives the best approach to Sgurr Domhnuill. For Ben Resipol, leave the road at the fork, strike uphill north-west, when a third lead-mine road will be found leading to the crest of the hill-ridge, from which Resipol's summit is easily gained. The ridge gives a perfect view across Loch Shiel and Loch Moidart to Eigg, Rum, Muck, and the Cuillin. The Scuir of Eigg seen from here thrusts out of the sea like a tusk.

Loch Sunart is beautifully wooded for 10 miles along its shores to Salen Bay, where the road turns north across a 2-mile neck of land to Loch Shiel, and to the village of Acharacle. All land to the north of Shiel River and loch is Moidart, and to the west, Ardnamurchan. Loch Shiel runs 17 miles east and north to Glenfinnan on the Mallaig road and railway. On the green fields at the head of the loch, the clansmen rallied to Prince Charlie in August 1745, when the Stewart banner was unfurled for the rising. The scene is commemorated by a tall round pillar bearing a stone Highlander who represents not Prince Charlie but his clansmen. The view down the loch is given unusual beauty by a wooded island in the foreground and the frame of mountains receding into the distance down either side. The Forestry Commission have made a road 11 miles down the Ardgour shore to Polloch (not open to car traffic), giving easy access to the hills on foot. From Acharacle, a road strikes 3 miles north-west across Kentra Moss to the clachan of Ardtoe on a craggy and hillocky shore with sandy coves, one of which has a fish-farm.

From the Salen neck, Ardnamurchan peninsula (average width 5 miles) thrusts 17 miles into the Atlantic. Its farthest point is the most westerly of the British mainland (on the same longitude as Dublin). The hills are peculiarly bare, scoured to the bone by a big glacier. The highest hill is Ben Hiant on the Sunart shore, 10 miles west of Salen. Thus far the rock is all of the Moine series, but the last 7 miles west of Hiant is gabbro and lava – the site of a Tertiary volcano. The best gabbro hill of the peninsula is Beinn na Seilg, 1123 feet, 2 miles west of Kilchoan. Many short climbs may be enjoyed.

The only motor road into Ardnamurchan goes by the south shore. It is narrow, bumpy, twists between trees and crags, and is one of the district's important scenic assets. A footpath goes all the way in by the north coast, and is no less excellent for its view up the Moidart coast and to seaward. The local authority unhappily plan to make it another motor road. Footpaths of this quality are rare in the West Highlands. The peninsula has numerous points of interest: the thirteenth-century Mingary Castle by the shore near Kilchoan; the series of sandy beaches along the north-west shore; the lighthouse tower, 118 feet high, on the west point (visitors welcome); prehistoric remains on the lower slopes of Beinn na Seilg; and a surprising variety of plant and wild life.

Loch Eil to Glen Shiel

North of the Mallaig road, the West Highlands grow highly mountainous. The seaboard is indented by Loch Moidart, Loch

Ailort, Loch Nevis, Loch Hourn, and Loch Alsh, between which lie Moidart, Morar, Knoydart, and Glenelg. The inland side is likewise indented by Loch Eil, Loch Arkaig, Loch Garry, and by Loch Cluanie which drains through Glen Moriston to the Great Glen. All these parallel inland lochs are linked by glens to all the parallel sea-lochs, except Loch Moidart. Neither Moidart nor Morar rise to hills of 2,000 feet, but the other groups have 39 tops of 3,000 feet, of which 25 are Munros.

Moidart

Entry can be made on foot anywhere along the road between Glenfinnan and Loch Ailort, or by the coast road that runs south from the head of Loch Ailort to Glenuig, where it crosses the hill pass to Loch Moidart, Loch Shiel, and Ardnamurchan. The higher hills are all at the north end.

From Glenfinnan, an ascent should be made of Beinn Odhar Mhor, 2853 feet, on the west side of Loch Shiel, preferably up the north-east slope. The view down Loch Shiel from the summit is a prize worth winning, as also that from Sgurr Giubhsachan, 2784 feet, on the opposite shore of the loch. Moidart's highest hill is Rois-bheinn, 2887 feet, near the outer end of Loch Ailort. The summit is gained in 2 miles by way of its west ridge, and is worth climbing for its wide view of the coast, the sea-lochs, and the Inner Hebrides.

The low ground of the south half is the more beautiful part of Moidart. Loch Shiel hotel at Acharacle or the camp-site at South Langal on the north shore make good centres. The road north across Shiel Bridge immediately forks. The main road goes over the hill to Kinlochmoidart, and a side road down the wooded river to outer Loch Moidart at Dorlin, where the fourteenth-century Castle Tiorram of Clanranald stands on a tidal island. A motor-boat calls at the Dorlin jetty twice a week to take visitors cruising. The outer loch is largely filled by the island of Shona, dividing it into north and south channels – the latter with several smaller islets and wooded shores.

Glen Moidart, running 6 miles east from Loch Moidart to the base of the Rois-bheinn ridge, is surprisingly fertile and wooded in lime, beech, and chestnut. You can drive 2 miles up and walk by a good path to the still more lovely upper glen.

25.
Loch Nevis
to Isle of Eigg,
from Sgor na Ciche.

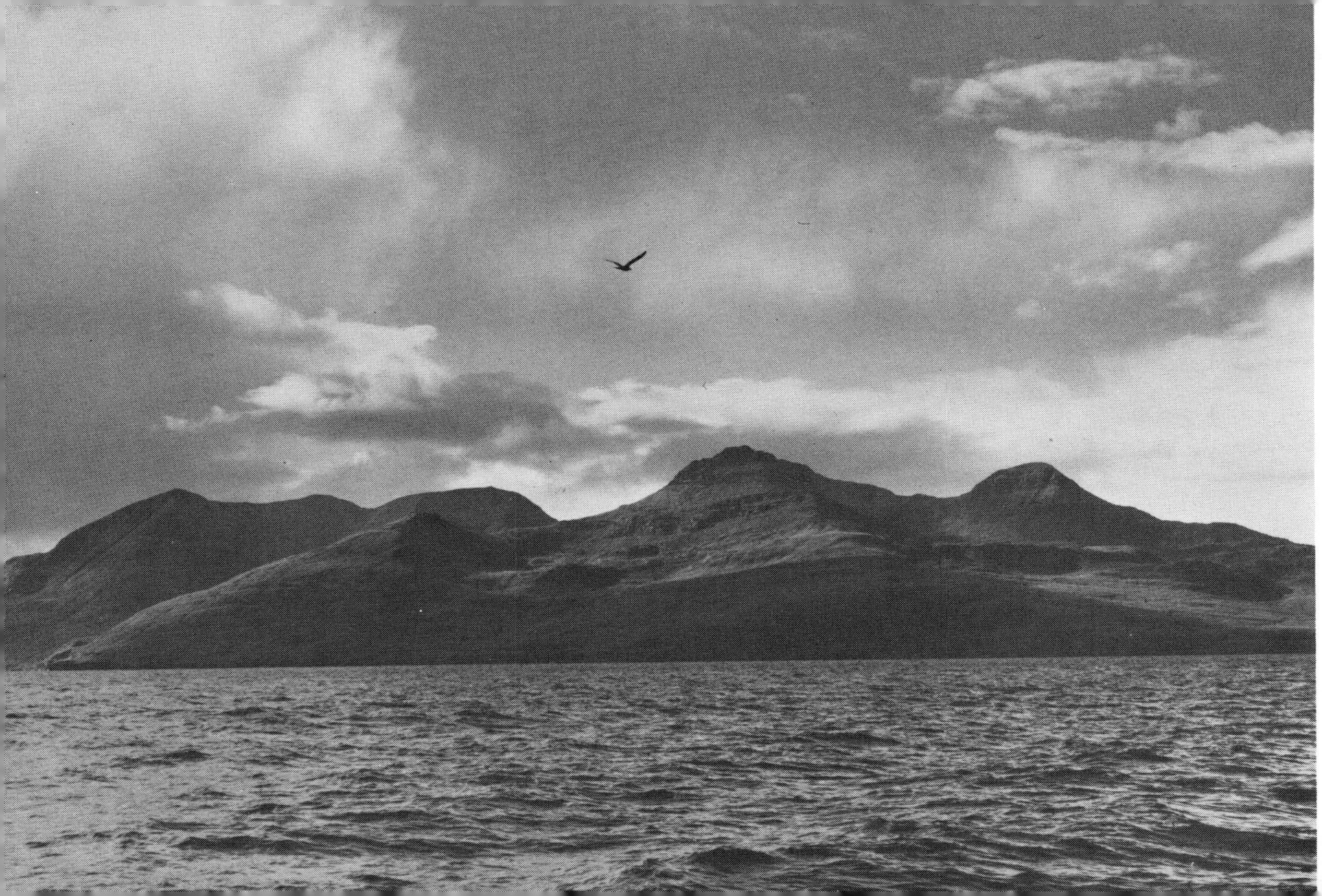

27. The Cuillin of Rum.

28. Applecross. Coire na Poite, Beinn Bhan.

29. (*below*) Sgurr nan Gillean, Rum.

30. (*opposite*) Loch Coruisk, Skye.

31. Fuar Tholl and Loch a' Bhealaich Mhor, Glen Carron.

Morar and Locheil

These districts are bounded on the north by Loch Arkaig and Glen Dessary. They have only two roads: the Mallaig road and one up Loch Arkaig. Large as this mountain territory is, it has only 3 Munros, 2 at the head of Glen Finnan, and 1, Gulvain, 3244 feet, above Glen Fionnlighe. All are best climbed from the south, and have long ridges. Among them stands a much finer hill, the Streap, 2988 feet. It has 5 tops, steep sides, a narrow south-west ridge, and a good view down Loch Shiel. A right of way to Kinlocharkaig goes by a good track up Glen Finnan, then across the bealach at 1,586 feet. Another footpath from Lochailort to Loch Morar leaves the foot of Loch Eilt northward across the 1,000-foot watershed to Loch Beoraid, where there is a Prince Charlie's Cave among several big boulders that have fallen off a cliff, and so down the Meoble to the trackless shore of Loch Morar.

Morar is low country, famous for its beaches of silver sand, which stretch in successive bays along 5 miles of machair. The Prince's beach, where Charles landed in July 1745 and embarked for France fourteen months later, lies farther south in the Sound of Arisaig, where the Borrodale Burn flows into Loch nan Uamh – a shingle and rock shore marked by a cairn. Loch Morar, 12 miles long, divides Morar from west to east. Only a narrow land-barrier separates it from the Sound of Sleat (pronounced Slate), to which the river once burst through in a heavy fall now vanished – harnessed by dam to a hydro-electric scheme. Loch Morar is the deepest inland water of Britain, 1,017 feet. It is inhabited by Morag, a monster who appears only before the death of a MacDonald of Clanranald. A motor road goes 3 miles up the north side to Bracora, whence a footpath continues to the head of the loch and on to Arkaig by two passes, Glen Pean and Glen Dessary. Half-way along Loch Morarside a side track strikes half a mile north to Tarbert Bay on Loch Nevis, and then east to Kylesmorar. The high ground above Tarbert gives a splendid view of Sgurr na Ciche, 3140 feet, the highest and sharpest peak of the West Highlands south of Glen Shiel.

Mallaig at the north end of Morar is a highly specialized fishing port. The scene of intense activity on the pier when the boats unload herring and prawns, or lobsters are auctioned, is one not to be missed – the liveliest of its kind on the seaboard. Motor-boats cruise up and down the coast and may be privately hired. Car ferries ply to Skye, and a mailboat to Inverie in Knoydart.

Knoydart

Knoydart is the big, hilly peninsula between Loch Nevis and Loch Hourn, which are each 13 miles long, and of typical sea-loch form – a broad outer loch separated by narrows from a long and narrow inner loch penetrating deeply into the mountains. Loch Nevis is flanked by low hills to its south, therefore is sunny and open. Its shores are roadless, and so too is its head, which is graced by Sgor na Ciche. Loch Hourn by contrast is more closely crowded by mountains, which rise on both sides of the outer loch to above 3,000 feet, while the inner loch is unusually narrow, twisting and steeply flanked by wooded crags. Loch Hourn is the only Scottish loch to bear close resemblance to a Norwegian fiord. It tends to be sunless. The two sea-lochs give Knoydart much of its quite distinguished character, which is that of remoteness and isolation. No public road penetrates the fastness, although there are short estate roads around Inverie Bay on outer Loch Nevis. No touring motorists pollute the air of its five main glens and their passes, or its 36 miles of coast. Scenically, its mountains do not match the best to north and south, but the latter cannot rival Knoydart's unsullied peace, nor its freedom from man-made blemish. The principal land-use is sheep-farming, crofting, deer-stalking, and some forestry work.

Normal access is by daily motor-boat from Mallaig to Inverie. Camping is necessary for exploration. There is no accommodation.

The numerous glens and tracks of the interior give excellent walking, and ready access to 3 Munros. The tracks should be used as far as practicable, for the going is unusually rough away from them. To reach the head of Loch Nevis from Inverie, for example, it is better to go by Gleann Meadail although this involves an ascent to 1,709 feet, than to walk along the shore, which is trackless beyond Kylesknoydart. The old name, the Rough Bounds of Knoydart, was given to the peninsula for good reason. The head of Loch Nevis can also be reached by track from Loch Arkaig through Glen Dessary, or by hiring the Mallaig mail-boat.

Ladhar Bheinn (pronounced Larven), 3343 feet, is the most westerly Munro of the mainland. The north-east face presents to Barrisdale Bay on Loch Hourn a splendid corrie ringed by great cliffs. The quickest approach to these is by mail-boat (thrice weekly) from Arnisdale in Glenelg to Barrisdale Bay, which may be reached alternatively from Kinlochhourn at the Glen Garry road-end by a 6-mile track. From Inverie, a track to the south base of the mountain goes

3½ miles over Mam Uidhe, 445 feet. A pass between Inverie and Barrisdale is given by Gleann an Dubh Lochain, which is the central axis of Knoydart, dividing Ladhar Bheinn from the two easterly Munros, Luinne Bheinn, 3083 feet, and Meall Buidhe, 3107 feet. The latter rise from a 4-mile ridge enclosing a north-west corrie, which contains a spectacular example of glaciated rock. All the tracks mentioned here are rights-of-way.

Loch Arkaig

The approach from the Great Glen starts from the wooded bay of Bunarkaig, 3 miles from the foot of Loch Lochy, then through the once-famous Dark Mile to Loch Arkaig. The Dark Mile was named from its close-set beech trees, where Prince Charlie hid in August 1746, but many have since been felled by storm and the narrow road has been widened. The road goes 12 miles farther along the north shore of the loch among deciduous trees to the bare upper stretch at Muirlaggan, where Jacobite treasure is alleged to have been buried. From Strathan, the stalker's cottage at the head of Loch Arkaig, five rights-of-way radiate through the surrounding mountains.

After Culloden, Prince Charlie escaped by Glen Pean to Morar and the Hebrides. The Pean track is on bog. Glen Dessary to its north has a good track for 4 miles, degenerating to a rough path over the wild pass of Mam na Cloiche Airde at 1000 feet, close below Sgurr na Ciche. This remote mountain is most easily climbed not from Dessary but from the head of Loch Nevis by its south-west ridge.

Glen Garry

Loch Hourn is linked to the Great Glen by Glen Garry, which splits the West Highlands for 26 miles to Invergarry, where its river joins Loch Oich at the summit of the Great Glen, 105 feet. The damming of Glen Garry has filled it almost from end to end with Loch Quoich (pronounced Kooich), Loch Poulary, and Loch Garry. Glen Garry used to rival Glen Affric as the finest of Scottish glens, but the widening of the road, erection of dams, wires, and pylons, and the flooding of old woodland, has robbed both of their greatest beauty. Loch Garry still offers a woodland and water scene of top quality, and the huge irregular sheet of Loch Quoich, ringed by the mountains of the Knoydart border, is one of the most splendid water-scapes of the Highlands, especially when viewed from the new high road to Kintail and Skye, which rises north over the hills about 5 miles west of Invergarry. The road down by the shore of Loch Quoich gives access to 3 Munros on the north side, and on its south (cross underneath the Quoich dam) to the shapely peak of Gairich by way of Glen Kingie.

Glen Shiel

A principal geographical feature of the West Highlands is the deep trough 50 miles long across the Highland watershed from Loch Ness to the mouth of Loch Alsh. Its eastern half is Glen Moriston, which drains Loch Cluanie. Its western half is Glen Shiel, which drains into Loch Duich. Glen Moriston is flanked by relatively low hills, but from Cluanie westward the south side of Glen Shiel is lined by 9 Munros on one continuous ridge, with many other tops of 3,000 feet and less. The north side has 11 Munros. None offer rock-climbing, but their distance from the sea allows them to carry a good snow cover until late spring, when the traverse of the south ridge becomes one of the country's better hill-walks. The two most westerly tops, Sgurr na Sgine, 3098 feet, and the Saddle, 3314 feet, are usually left to another day. The Saddle is the finest mountain of the range, and one to be lingered over. Its east (or Sgurr na Forcan) ridge is the most interesting route. Its neighbour, Sgurr na Sgine, has a 3000-foot north top named Faochaig (whelk), whose lance-like shape draws the eye when seen from upper Glen Shiel. It appears to block the exit from the glen. These three mountains lie on the border of Glenelg, the great peninsula between Loch Hourn and Loch Duich.

Glenelg

Glenelg has only one road in. It breaks west near the head of Loch Duich and climbs steeply up to the Mam Ratagan, 1116 feet. The pass has a clear view over tree-tops and across the head of Loch Duich to the Five Sisters of Kintail. The long descent on the west side allows a glimpse of Glenelg's interior – rough and mountainous ground like Knoydart, where old tracks give the best hope of exploration. The road meets the coast at Glenelg Bay, where a fork leads to the summer ferry across Kyle Rhea to Skye. (The principal ferries to Skye sail from Kyle of Lochalsh farther north, where the boats are numerous and bigger.) In earlier centuries the Skye cattle bound for the Falkirk and Crieff trysts were swum across Kyle Rhea (named from *Riadh*, a Fingalian hero), which is 500 yards wide.

They were tied nose to tail in strings of five. The main Glenelg road skirts the Sound of Sleat to Loch Hourn, where it passes under the vast and abrupt scree-slopes of Ben Sgriol, 3196 feet, to end at the clachan of Corran, just beyond the village of Arnisdale. A rough path goes 4 miles farther along the shores to the narrows. From the crofts of Corran, you get a clear view of the Black Cuillin – nearly every peak can be seen. If you want to climb Ladhar Bheinn, inquire at Arnisdale post-office about the mail-boat to Barrisdale.

Ben Sgriol is best climbed from Gleann Beag to its north. Enter the glen at Eileanreach on the coast-road, where a narrow side-road runs 3 miles east to Balvraid Farm, from which the river may be followed to the shoulder dividing the two north corries. The summit view to the turreted Cuillin, Loch Hourn, and Knoydart is unusually wild. Below Balvraid, the Pictish broch of Dun Telve stands on grassland by the river. It is the best Highland specimen and dates from the first century BC (see pp. 73-74).

Kintail and Glen Affric

Kintail is named from the Gaelic *Cean da shaill*, the head of two seas. These are Loch Duich and Loch Long, each a branch of Loch Alsh. The Kintail hinterland extends from Glen Shiel north to the river Ling, and includes the headwaters of the rivers Affric, Cannich, and Elchaig. Parallel to the Shiel–Moriston trough, a series of five lesser ones give east to west passes across the Highland watershed: Affric–Lichd, Cannich–Elchaig, Strathfarrar–Monar, Strathconon–Fhiodaig, and Strath Bran–Carron. Between them are four clearly marked ranges, comprising 37 Munros.

The first group of 11 mountains spreads 20 miles along the north side of Glen Shiel. The three highest tops (A' Chralaig and its neighbours, all above 3,600 feet) lie north of Cluanie; the more famous if lower group are the Five Sisters of Kintail at the seaward end. They extend 6 miles, reaching their highest point at centre on Sgurr Fhuarain, 3505 feet. Their traverse from east to west facing the Hebrides is the most popular hill-walk of Kintail. Most of south-west Kintail from the Five Sisters to the Falls of Glomach belongs to the National Trust for Scotland, so that public access can be had at all seasons. North and east Kintail belong to shooting proprietors, who ask the public to respect their privacy in the shooting season.

Besides Glen Shiel, two other shorter glens run east from the head of Loch Duich. The first is Glen Lichd, between the Five

Sisters and Beinn Fhada. Its flat bare floor carries the river Croe. Near its foot at Morvich, the Trust has a camping and caravan site. Its steep upper reach by the Allt Granda gives a pass of 1065 feet to Glen Affric. The second is Gleann Choinneachain, Kintail's finest glen with a tumbling burn and clear pools under the north corries of Beinn Fhada. It forks half-way giving a pass to Glen Affric over the Bealach an Sgairne, 1600 feet, or to the top of the Falls of Glomach by the Bealach na Sroine, 1700 feet.

The source of the Allt a' Ghlomaich (the burn of the chasm) is the Loch a' Bhealaich at 1,200 feet above the head of Glen Affric, from which it flows 3 miles north to 1,100 feet, then drops 500 feet down a chasm. The top fall is 350 feet – the same height as Steall waterfall. (Scotland's highest waterfall is Eas a' Chual Aluinn, 658 feet, in Sutherland.) But no other has so dramatic a site as the Hidden Falls of Glomach. As the name implies, a full-length view is hard to get. If you approach from the top, you climb down a steep zig-zag track on the west side of the chasm to a platform from which only the upper half of the fall can be seen. A much better approach starts from the head of Loch Long at Killilan. The road up Glen Elchaig is private, but the owner permits cars to drive 5 miles on to the Allt a' Ghlomaich. Boots are then essential. Climb up the left bank till the track divides at a point where the top of the falls can be glimpsed. One branch goes high on the outer slopes (giving a pass to Glen Affric); instead, take the lower branch, which traverses along the precipitous west flank into the upper chasm. The route could be dangerous in wet weather. The narrow path ends on a rock-rib from which you can look down into a cauldron below the waterfall. The scene is unique in the Highlands for its mighty plunge of water within a cauldron of such extreme narrowness and depth.

Near Dornie at the mouth of Loch Long, the castle of Eilean Donan projects out of Loch Alsh. It was built around 1230 by Alexander II for defence and attack against the Norsemen, who held Skye. His son gave it to the MacKenzies of Kintail. In 1912 it was rebuilt by the family of MacRae, who since 1520 had been hereditary constables. The castle is open to the public. A bridge and causeway lead out.

The road to Skye continues along the shore of Loch Alsh to Kyle of Lochalsh. Side roads branch off north across the peninsula to Loch Carron.

Glen Affric, Glen Cannich, and Strath Farrar are the three great inland valleys of the river Glass, named Beauly in its lowest part.

Entry to them by road must be made either from Inverness or from Drumnadrochit near the Urquhart bay of Loch Ness, for all are roadless at their western ends. Yet all carry right-of-way tracks to the west coast, and many others to their north and south. These three glens were long regarded as the most beautiful in the Highlands. Hydro-electric dams, and the flooding and felling of woodland, have removed Cannich and Strath Farrar from that category. Affric too has been shorn of its intimate quality, but remains excellent landscape. The river Affric rises on the hills of Kintail and Glen Shiel, and flows 20 miles east through a wide glen to join Strath Glass at Fasnakyle. Its north side is flanked by the highest range west of the Great Glen – Carn Eige, Mam Sodhail, and Sgurr nan Ceathreamhnan (pronounced Kerrenan), all around 3800 feet. Three great changes of scene mark the glen's course. Stark mountains stand around the heather-moors of the head. The central sector of 10 miles is occupied by Loch Affric and Loch Beinn a' Mheadhoin, which are ringed by a forest of Scots pine. The lower part is a narrow glen of river, gorge, and mixed birch and pine. The public road now ends 2 miles short of Loch Affric, whence a track continues 17 miles to Loch Duich. There is a youth hostel half way at Alltbeath.

Glen Cannich and Strath Farrar are entered by road lower down Strath Glass, and Strath Conon by the road north-west of Muir of Ord. The mountains of their upper reaches are massive, numerous but widely spread, and often hard of access. Old paths, drove roads, and rights-of-way thread the main and the side glens; they link Beauly with Kintail, and allow entry to the interior from several points along the West Highland's northern frontier – Strath Carron-Bran. The longer expeditions require a tent.

Islands

The four mountainous islands that lie off the coast - Mull, Eigg, Rum and Skye – are relics of the old igneous plateau. Their hill-rocks are mostly basalt, gabbro, or granite. Skye and Mull were part of the mainland until ploughed off by glaciers. Both were well wooded in historic times. Now all are bare except where planted, and these plantations have become extensive in east Mull and in pockets of Skye. The island hills attract a heavy rainfall of 80 to 120 inches, but the ground is well drained.

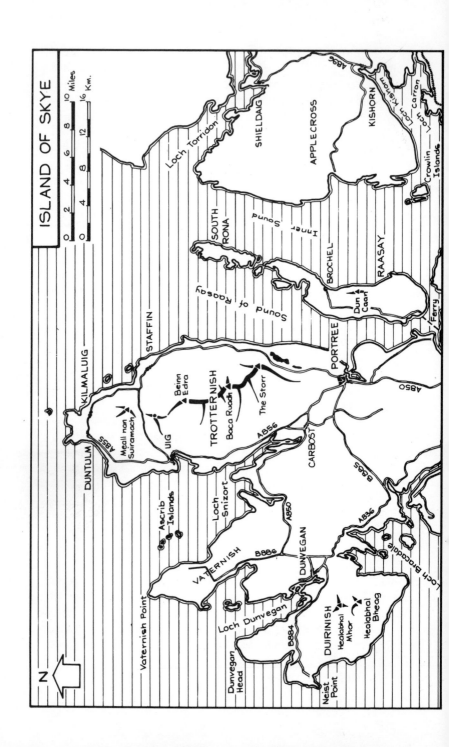

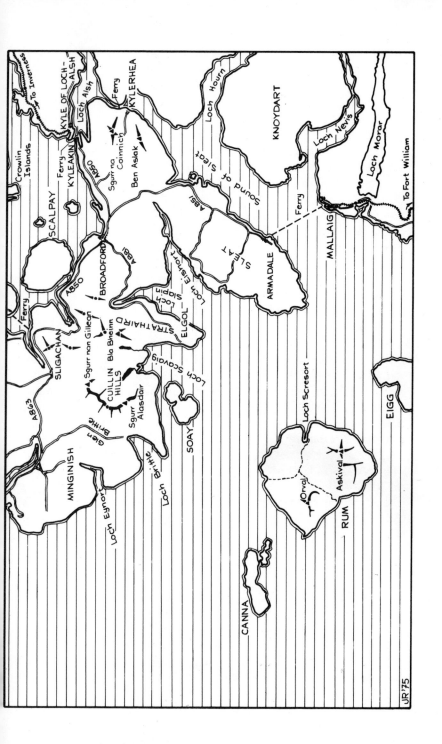

Mull

Mull is a big island of 224,000 acres with many lesser islands off its hugely bayed west coast. Access from Oban and Morvern is to the sheltered east ports. The great western sea-lochs have given Mull a big head and tail, which rarely lift above 1,000 feet. But the central area (where the old volcano was sited with a crater 6 miles wide) has 4 mountain groups above 2,000 feet, rising in the west to 3169 feet on Ben More, which is the only Munro.

The eastern group lies behind Craignure. Dun Da Ghaoithe, the Fort of Two Winds, 2512 feet, is the highest hill after the tops of Ben More. The south and central groups rise to either side of Glen More, above the heads of Loch Buie and Loch Ba respectively. All three are readily accessible from roadways and give good walking along the summit ridges.

The Ben More group stands separate to the west, between Loch na Keal and Loch Scridain. The quickest route of ascent is up its north-west shoulder from Dishig on Loch na Keal ($2\frac{1}{2}$ miles). The more interesting route ($3\frac{1}{2}$ miles) is over its north-east top, A' Chioch, which is best reached up the burn between Ben More and Beinn Fhada. The ridge over A' Chioch to the summit gives an easy scramble, sometimes narrow and rocky. Care must be taken if leaving the summit in mist, for the rock is magnetic and the compass unreliable close to the cairn. The summit view across nearer islands to the outer, especially to Rum and the Cuillin, is among the best of the west seaboard.

The sea-cliffs do not offer good rock-climbs, but they have interesting walking underneath, for example, from Carsaig Bay on the Ross of Mull to the natural arches at Malcolm's Point, or from Burg on the Ardmeanach peninsula to the fossil tree in the Wilderness. Staffa and the Treshnish Isles may be visited by motor-boat from Ulva Ferry.

Eigg

Eigg, Rum, Muck, and Canna are known collectively as the Small Isles. They lie 12 to 25 miles west of Mallaig, from which Caledonian MacBrayne's steamer gives a passenger service four days a week (Monday, Wednesday, Thursday, and Saturday). Eigg is the chief island with 40 people (1975) on its 5,000 acres. Eigg's chief feature seen from the north is a V-shaped cleft or glen cutting its back. But

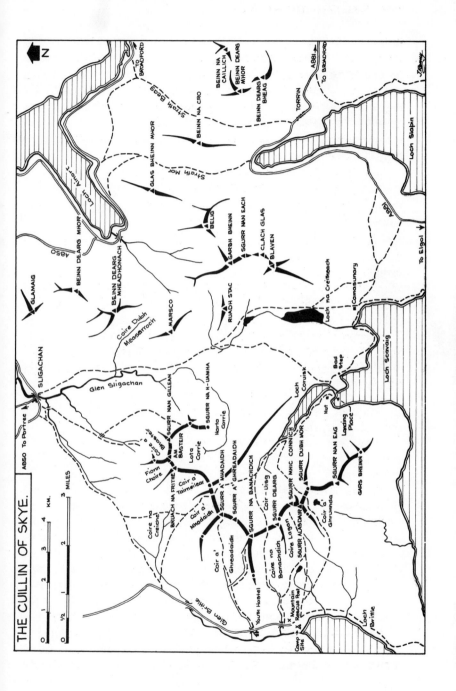

THE CUILLIN OF SKYE.

more eye-catching from the south is the Scuir, a great tusk of 1289 feet. Its summit is a 300-foot block of pitchstone lava, which offers several severe rock-climbs on its south face. Ascent from the west is easy. The hills to either side of the main glen approach 1,000 feet and give enjoyable walking. Accommodation can be had at Laig Farm on the north-west shore.

Rum

Rum takes a diamond shape, 8 miles by 8, ringed by sea-cliffs that rise on the west to 1,000 feet. Its northern part is a hilly moorland of Torridonian sandstone, but the rock of the south half is mainly gabbro, which lifts to 2,500 feet along the coast in a zig-zag ridge bearing 7 peaks. They have good rock-climbing on the flanking buttresses, especially Askival, 2659 feet, which is the highest and shapeliest peak. The best expedition in Rum is the traverse of the main ridge from Allival to Sgurr nan Gillean, returning by Glen Dibidil and the coastal track (8 or 9 hours). Rum has no accommodation other than a bothy at Dibidil. The island is owned by the Nature Conservancy, to whom application for permission to land and camp must be made well in advance at 12 Hope Terrace, Edinburgh 9, preferably through a club secretary. 'Rum' is the island's oldest known Gaelic name, spelled thus since the earliest written records (Annals of Ulster and Tigernach, with reference to events of the seventh century). The recent O.S. spelling of 'Rhum' is incorrect, in so far as there is no *rh* prefix in Gaelic.

Skye

Skye is the largest of the Inner Hebrides, 429,000 acres in a length of 60 miles. A dozen sea-lochs bite deep into the land, so that no part of the interior is more than 5 miles from a shore. The coasts are heavily crofted, the hinterland stands high in moorland, and 40 rock peaks of the Cuillin rise in the south-west to a maximum height of 3257 feet. The principal village is Portree, on the east coast facing Raasay. South Skye is divided from the mainland by the Sound of Sleat. Car ferries cross from Kyle of Lochalsh to Kyleakin, from Glenelg to Kylerhea, and from Mallaig to Armadale.

The Norsemen held Skye for nearly 470 years and named it *Skuy-ö* (pronounced Skya), meaning Island of Cloud. It is most probable that the name Cuillin also derives from the old Norse

Kjölen (pronounced Coolin), meaning keel-shaped ridges – the name given to a Scandinavian range.

Twenty Cuillin tops exceed 3,000 feet, of which 12 are Munros, but one of these, Blaven, lies east of the main ridge, from which it is separated by Glen Sligachan. The main ridge swings $7\frac{1}{2}$ miles around Coruisk, reaching its highest point on Sgurr Alasdair, 3257 feet. The ridge is narrow for the most part, and the peaks sharp, for the corries have been deeply gouged by glaciers. The rock, left bare of soil and grass, is a mixture of coarse crystalline gabbro and smooth basalt, both present in equal surface quantity. Few summits can be reached without aid of the hands. The traverse of the pinnacled ridge gives 10,000 feet of ascent and the best day's mountaineering in Scotland, for the diversity of scene is equalled by no other range. Rock-climbs abound on the walls, spurs, buttresses, and ridges, but the four summits that give the most enchanting panoramas can easily be reached by walkers. These are Sgurr Alasdair, by way of the Great Stone Shoot of Coire Lagan from Glen Brittle; Bruach na Frithe, 3142 feet, by its north-west ridge from Sligachan; Blaven, 3044 feet, by its south ridge from Camasunary; and Sgurr na Stri, 1623 feet, from Loch Coruisk or Glen Sligachan. Since much of the rock is magnetic, compass bearing cannot be relied on for route-finding.

The centres from which the Cuillin are best climbed are Sligachan (hotel) for access to the north end, and Glen Brittle (youth hostel and climber's hut) for access to the south, and Loch Scavaig (club hut) which can be reached either by motor-boat from Elgol or by the path along the east shore past Camasunary. The old track across the Strathaird peninsula, from Kilmarie to Camasunary and Coruisk, was destroyed by Army bulldozers in 1969. Between Camasunary and Coruisk the 'Bad Step' – a rock slab – has to be crossed 15 or 20 feet above the sea. People tend to get into trouble by crossing too high up.

The Red Cuillin form two groups, one east of Glen Sligachan but north of Blaven, and the other between Loch Slapin and Broadford. Their half-dozen peaks above 2,000 feet and many lesser tops are all granite, scree-covered and rounded, and without rock-climbing. Their highest point is Glamaig, 2537 feet, above Sligachan. They offer pleasant, high-level walks.

The northern peninsula of Trotterish has a basalt spine with fantastic rock spires on the east flank at its either end. In a corrie at the south end stands the Old Man of Storr, which can be seen against the sky from Portree. It stands 160 feet on a rock plinth. A dozen other shorter pinnacles of weird shape are grouped around the rim of this corrie, which is unique in Scotland. The Old Man was climbed in 1955 by Don Whillans. The north end has a natural fortress called the Quiraing (pronounced Kooraing), caused by a down-slipping of the uppermost rocks. An obelisk of 100 feet called the Needle guards the entrance.

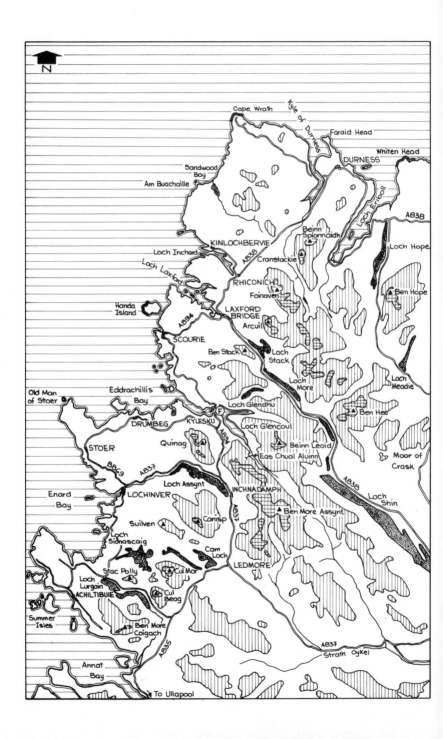

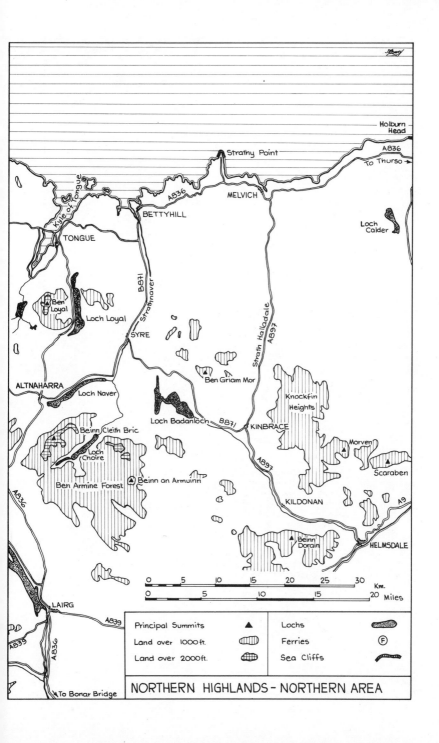

NORTHERN HIGHLANDS - NORTHERN AREA

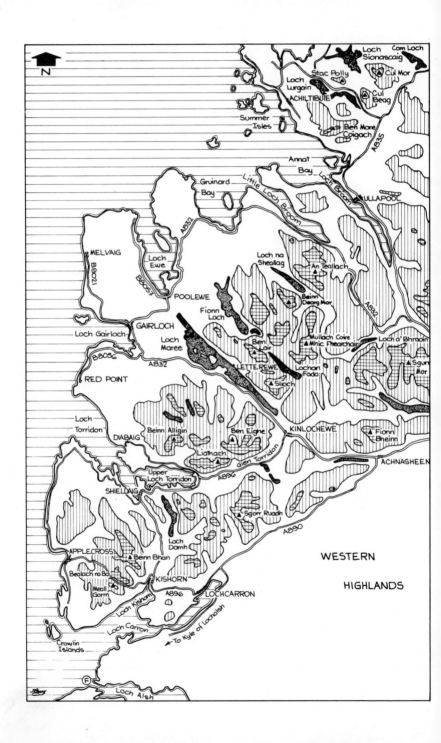

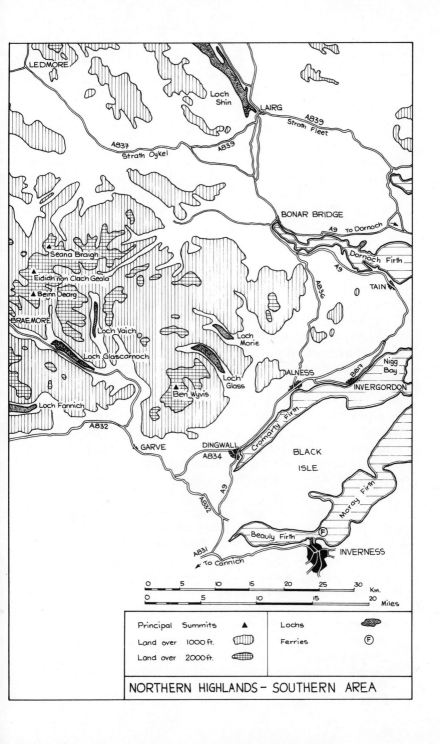

NORTHERN HIGHLANDS – SOUTHERN AREA

9 Northern Highlands

The Northern Highlands include all Sutherland, and Ross and Cromarty north of the Strath Conon–Bran–Carron pass that links the Cromarty Firth with Loch Carron. Caithness is lowland, but has two hills of 2,000 feet at its south end. The coastal islands have no mountains, and the seaboard is much less indented than that of other Highland districts. Only three of the 10 sea-lochs (Torridon, Broom, and Cairnbawn) penetrate deeply.

Rock topography

The Strath Bran–Carron pass is the most decisive of Highland frontiers. To its north, in the lands west of the Moine Thrust (Glen Carron to Loch Eriboll), there is an abrupt change of rock and topography. A broad coastal strip, 10–20 miles wide, is occupied by Torridonian sandstone, which predominates from Applecross to the south edge of Assynt, and by Lewisian gneiss from Assynt to Cape Wrath. The gneiss forms a rolling floor from which mountains of sandstone or Cambrian quartzite project as monoliths. None of these rocks yields a fertile soil. Even at low levels the rock crops out increasingly to form a peculiarly wild landscape, largely empty of human life, for this is the most thinly populated part of Britain. (Sutherland has a population of 11,900 in 2,028 square miles.)

East of the Moine Thrust, the rocks are the metamorphic schists and gneisses that form on the Fannaichs and Inverlael groups the district's highest mountains, closely above and below 3,600 feet. But these do not begin to equal the lower sandstone mountains of the west, which take every shape from arrowy towers and corkscrew crests to long swinging ridges and flat-topped plum-puddings. They spring from gneiss moorlands congested by lochans, or in Wester Ross from wooded glens, sea-lochs, or high peninsulas. The variety is endless and embodies some of the best landscape in Scotland. To the south of Loch Carron the hills are relatively grassy; northwards from Applecross, heather clings to the flanks but the tops remain stony deserts. The change is less sudden in the glens, where in Torridon a West Highland softness overlaps the northern harshness. But north of Loch Maree the scene is simpler; rock and water set on bog. Here are two of the most splendid wilderness areas of the High-lands: Achaniasgair, hidden between Loch Maree and An Teallach, where the gneiss rises to a mountainous maze; and the Inverpolly and Glen Canisp forests of Coigach and Assynt.

The undifferentiated structure of the schist mountains spreads through Easter Ross to Ben Wyvis. In Sutherland the mountains lie to the west and sink eastward to desolate moors that rarely rise above 1,000 feet. In that monotonous landscape 3 mountains project all the more effectively: Ben Hope, Ben Loyal, and Ben Klibreck. They get dignity from isolation, and redeem the moor-scene.

The district has 65 tops above 3,000 feet, of which 35 are Munros. Many of the more spectacular sandstone or quartzite mountains in Applecross, Assynt, Coigach, and the Reay Forest are well below that height.

The climate is drier than that of the West Highlands. No ground has more than 120 inches of rainfall, which mostly varies from 30 to 80 inches according to land-height; thus the wettest area is around the head of Loch Broom. Sutherland has the windiest coast of the mainland. The hinterland is bare of trees except in protected glens – a bareness that uncontrolled heather-burning exacerbates.

Access

Strath Bran forks at either end, at Garve and Achnasheen, to give roads over three trans-Highland passes. The Garve fork goes over the Dirrie Mor pass to Loch Broom, Ullapool, and Assynt. The Achnasheen fork, besides giving the pass to Glen Carron and Applecross, also gives one through Glen Docherty to Loch Maree, Gairloch, and Torridon. From Bonar Bridge on the Dornoch Firth, three other passes lead to the north-west. One goes by Strath Oykell to Assynt, the second by Loch Shin to Laxford Bridge and Durness, and the third by Strath Tirry over the Crask moor to Altnaharra and the Kyle of Tongue.

Applecross

Applecross is a broad peninsula between Loch Kishorn and Loch Torridon. Loch Kishorn, the largest and most beautiful bay of Loch Carron, has since 1975 been defaced by a construction yard for oil production platforms. The Applecross coast facing Raasay is 16 miles long, indented at centre by Applecross Bay, to which a road crosses the Bealach nam Ba from Kishorn. The ground is all deer forest, rising from the sea in three steps, the first to 1,000 feet and the second to 2,000; finally to a plateau of Torridonian sandstone, which has been broken by deep corries into three flat-topped mountains, Beinn Bhan, 2936 feet, Sgurr a' Chaorachain, 2600 feet, and Meall Gorm, 2325 feet.

From the head of Loch Kishorn a pass goes north through a fold in the hills to Shieldaig on Loch Torridon. The west side of the pass is flanked by bold cliffs of Beinn Bhan, from which several corries have been sculpted. (Rock-climbing.) Their cliffs have weathered like Cyclopean masonry. The middle one, Coire na Poite, has a lochan in its lower bowl enclosed by spurs, between which a burn cascades over a rock step from a higher corrie, whose floor of glacier-worn rock cups two green but crystal-clear lochans. The purple cliffs behind them rise to 1,200 feet.

Sgurr a' Chaorachain to its south has two tops each at the crest of terraced spurs running east. The north spur, A' Chioch, has several rock-climbs – the best on its north wall. The huge screes on the face of the mountain's south corrie are threaded by a zig-zag road, which climbs on to the Bealach nam Ba, the Pass of the Cattle, at 2,053 feet – the highest road on the west side of Scotland. To its south stands Meall Gorm, like its fellows dipping steeply south and east into Loch Kishorn. The view from the pass is across Raasay to Skye, and south to Glenelg. The hill-tops to either side are readily accessible; but flat as they are give exceedingly rough walking on a desert of stone. The landscape is lunar.

The people of Applecross live in crofting communities along the shore of Loch Torridon, and along the west coast between Applecross village and Toscaig, where there are clachans at the small bays. Applecross has a small unlicensed hotel. Accommodation may also be had at Lochcarron and Shieldaig, or at a youth hostel at Loch Kishorn. Shieldaig is linked to Applecross Bay by a coastal road and by a hill-track over a pass at 1,213 feet.

Torridon

Torridon is the district name for the mountain ranges to either side of Glen Torridon and Upper Loch Torridon. They include 18 tops of 3,000 feet, of which 6 are Munros, and an abundance of lesser mountains. Nearly all are sandstone, many with Cambrian quartzite strata sometimes forming the summit caps. Only two are entirely quartzite.

Between Glen Carron and Glen Torridon, the Bendamh and Coulin Forests comprise a dozen mountains, amongst which lie scattered a score of lochs, many of them in beautifully sculpted corries placed high on the hills. The lower slopes are nearly as rough as Knoydart, but access is greatly aided by 50 miles of old stalking tracks and rights-of-way, which enter from all sides. The three most valuable routes are: (1) From Achnashellach railway station in Glen Carron, a path goes up a wild torrent of the river Lair into Coire Lair, giving access to rock-climbs on the cliffs of Fuar Tholl and Sgorr Ruadh, 3142 feet. (2) Also from Achnashellach, a right-of-way path crosses the Coulin Pass to Loch Clair in Glen Torridon ($7\frac{1}{2}$ miles). The views through the woods and across the Coulin lochs to Beinn Eighe and Liathach, whose white summits are reflected in water fringed by birch, pine, heather, and bracken, have few rivals in Wester Ross. (3) From Annat, at the head of Loch Torridon, a right-of-way path runs south-east under Maol Chean-Dearg, 3060 feet, to Coulags in Strath Carron ($7\frac{1}{2}$ miles). This track connects at the watershed, Bealach na Lice, 1300 feet, with the Coire Lair path.

The Torridon mountains proper are the higher sandstone ranges to Glen Torridon's north side. Liathach (pronounced Leeagach), 3456 feet, and Beinn Eighe (pronounced Ay as in bay), 3309 feet, are narrow ridges bearing 7 and 8 tops respectively in 5 and 7 miles' lengths. These are two of the finest ranges in Scotland, with good rock-climbing in their northern corries. Both are sombre sandstone with several quartzite caps – Beinn Eighe's eastern tops are entirely quartzite. The two mountains are divided by the narrow glen of Coire Dubh (it is a local tradition to name hill-glens as corries). Liathach in turn is divided on the north by Coire Mhic Nobuil from Beinn Alligin, 3232 feet, and Beinn Dearg, 2995 feet. These ranges are held for the nation by the National Trust for Scotland, except for 7 tops of Beinn Eighe, which form a Reserve under the Nature Conservancy.

Beinn Eighe as seen from its Coulin side has a sharp white crest swinging airily from peak to peak. The mountain's most splendid feature is the north-west Coire Mhic Fhearchair (pronounced Veek Errechar), approached by way of either Coire Dubh or from Loch Maree up the Grudie river ($2\frac{1}{2}$ hours). The stony floor of the corrie at 1,900 feet cups a loch, from the back of which 3 buttresses spring 1,250 feet. Their lower halves are red sandstone and their upper quartzite. The left-hand encircling spur carries the summit, Ruadh Stac Mor. This can be climbed direct from the corrie, and the long ridge then traversed to its Kinlochewe end – or vice versa.

Liathach, seen from Loch Clair, is topped by a white arrowhead that soars 3,000 feet above the road. The traverse of the long crest is rivalled only by that of An Teallach and Aonach Eagach. The ridge is most easily gained by taking the path up Coire Mhic Nobuil through a gorge wooded with Scots pines, until a way can be seen to the west top. Broad at first, the ridge narrows for half a mile over the Fasarinen pinnacles, which end close to the summit pyramid. The short pinnacles can be avoided in summer (but not in winter without much trouble) by a ledge on the south side. Their north side falls in great cliffs to the depths of Coire na Caime (rock-climbing). A way off the summit can be found down its north-west ridge, or else to Glen Torridon from the west side of the eastmost top, Stuc a' Choire Duibh Bhig.

Beinn Alligin is a relatively easy mountain, whose four tops tower above lower Coire Mhic Nobuil, from which they are usually climbed by way of the south-east corrie under the nearest top. Its smaller neighbours, Beinn Dearg and four other mountains in the Flowerdale and Kinlochewe Forests to the north, are like Alligin steep-sided and rocky. Beinn Alligin surpasses all other Torridon mountains in a summit view extending from Cape Wrath to Ardnamurchan.

Gairloch

Gairloch is the name of the parish that includes all ground between Loch Torridon and Outer Loch Broom. The coast-line is broken into short, low peninsulas by Gair Loch, Loch Ewe, Gruinard Bay, and Little Loch Broom. Close behind Loch Ewe, Loch Maree runs 12 miles inland. It is one of the three most excellent of big freshwater lochs. Slioch, 3217 feet, has a powerful presence at the head, while the western waters off Slattadale Forest are spattered with wooded islands. The main road from Strath Bran to Gairloch runs along the south shore; the north shore has only a right-of-way track from Kinlochewe to Poolewe at the head of Loch Ewe. On Loch Ewe's eastern shore are the famous Inverewe gardens, owned by the National Trust for Scotland.

The Gairloch mountains number some 35 tops in the 12-mile band between Loch Maree and Little Loch Broom (where Lochbroom parish overlaps). They are grouped in the three deer forests of

Letterewe, Fisherfield, and Strathnasheallag, and include 18 tops of 3,000 feet, of which 8 are Munros. The rock is Torridonian sandstone, Cambrian quartzite, hornblende schist, and Lewisian gneiss, the latter rising here to several summits. Slioch is a sandstone pile on a gneiss plinth.

Access is difficult. The east has no peripheral road, the south is moated by Loch Maree, and the west is guarded by 50 square miles of low moor congested with lochs and burns and the complicated waterways of Fionn Loch, which has innumerable bays and feeder-lochans. Only the north road by Dundonnell gives convenient access, and only to An Teallach. But for those who are prepared to walk long distances, many paths penetrate the glens and cross the bealachs, giving access to all the peaks and lochs. In exchange for these tracks, walkers should respect the proprietors' rights in the stalking season.

Achaniasgair

The Maree–Broom mountains and lochs are the most remote wilderness area in Scotland, 15 miles long by 12 deep. As seen from their own tops, they are naked and bony mountains exposing much rock, but are surprisingly adorned by lochans high up in folds under the summits. They look of maze-like complexity, sandwiched between the high walls of the Letterewe ridge and An Teallach. A map reveals some order. They are furrowed by two parallel lochs, Fionn Loch and Loch na Sheallag; each prolongs the furrow northward by river to Gruinard Bay, and eastward by feeder lochs or rivers. The Fionn furrow is again prolonged east behind Slioch by another and deeper trough, half-filled by Lochan Fada but with a dry west end lined for $2\frac{1}{2}$ miles by tall cliffs of hornblende schist on the north face of Beinn Lair (rock-climbing). Between these main furrows rise, first, the Letterewe ridge, holding five mountains, all of which except Meall Mheinnidh provide rock-climbing on their north or west faces. Then come the central ranges of Achaniasgair – the ancient name of this deer forest (which the O.S. sheets call 'Fisherfield'). Here are 13 mountains with lesser tops. Many provide rock-climbing.

The most remote but eye-catching peak is A' Mhaighdean (pronounced Vyéjen), the Maiden, Scotland's finest mountain of gneiss. From the Dubh Loch at its western base, its rocky pillar lifts to 3173 feet. The highest mountain is Mullach Coire Mhic Fhearchair, 3326 feet, above Lochan Fada. It displays all the chief rocks of the district. The most northerly mountain is Beinn Dearg Mor, 2974 feet, above Loch na Sheallag. Its eastern corrie is so like that of An Teallach in miniature that often it is mistaken for such in photographs.

Finally, the range of An Teallach (the Forge), 3483 feet, fills the Strathnasheallag Forest with 11 tops above 3,000 feet. It and Liathach are the two most splendid of sandstone mountains. The crest is riven and rocky where it curves 2½ miles around the eastern corrie, Toll an Lochain. From the back of a black lochan, dark cliffs rise 1,700 feet to the sinuous summit-ridge, which in its middle section is a sharper knife-edge than any other on the mainland. An easy scramble in summer, it requires a rope in winter. The mountain is most easily climbed by its north-east or south-east ridges.

Tracks leading to the region's interior are: (1) From the Strath Beag road by the Garbh Allt to Strath na Sheallag (Shenavall bothy, 7 miles). (2) From Gruinard Bay up the Gruinard river to Loch na Sheallag (5 miles), or to Strath na Sheallag (9 miles). (3) From Poolewe up the river Ewe to Loch Kernsary and the head of Fionn Loch (9½ miles). (4) From Kinlochewe by the north shore of Loch Maree to Letterewe, then north to the head of Fionn Loch (11½ miles), and to Strath na Sheallag (18½ miles). (5) From Kinlochewe to Loch Fada either north by the Heights of Kinlochewe (7 miles), or farther west by Gleann Bianasdail (6¼ miles).

The bothy at Shenavall may be used by climbers in spring, but not in the stalking season. There is a climbers' hut at Dundonnell, half a miles east of the hotel.

Loch Broom

Loch Broom runs 20 miles into the mainland – the longest sea-loch of the Northern Highlands. The land around forms the district of Lochbroom, 400 square miles including Coigach. Its capital is the fishing port of Ullapool on the inner loch, from which a car ferry sails to Stornoway in Lewis. Ullapool is the best tourist centre for exploring the district.

The quickest approach from south and east Scotland is from Inverness and Garve, then over the bleak moorlands of the Dirrie Mor (Great Divide) at 915 feet, and down through the woodlands of Strath More to Loch Broom. The west coast road from Little Loch Broom is known as the Destitution Road, for it was made in the famine of 1851 to give work to starving men. It climbs to 1,110 feet then falls past Loch a' Bhraon (from which the name Broom is derived) to join the Loch Broom road at the Corrieshalloch gorge. This gorge is a mile long and 200 feet deep, with a most spectacular waterfall named the Falls of Measach. To its north and south are two big mountain groups with 19 tops above 3,000 feet, whose summits reach 3547 feet on Beinn Dearg to the north, and 3637 feet on Sgurr Mor in the Fannaich Forest to the south. These massifs were covered by a big ice cap, whose glaciers sculpted Strath More and Strath Beag and deepened Loch Broom. As the ice melted, the water rushing west cut the Corrieshalloch gorge through solid rock.

Lochbroom displays three very different kinds of landscape. Inland, the Moine schists build the rounded hills and peat-moors that spread from the Fannaichs north through the forests of Braemore, Strathvaich, Inverlael, Freevater, and Rhidorroch to Glen Oykell. West of the Moine Thrust, which runs through Coigach to near the head of Loch Broom, hills of Torridonian sandstone rise to cones and pyramids; even when low as in Coigach they take striking shapes, which make the inland Munros look tame. West again, the low ground towards the coast is ash-grey hillocky gneiss, especially noticeable in Coigach and Gruinard.

The Fannaich Forest

The Fannaichs are 12 tops of 3000 feet, of which 8 are Munros, all to the north side of Loch Fannaich and south of the Dirrie Mor. Sgurr Mor, 3637 feet, is the highest mountain of the Northern Highlands. The most central peak, Sgurr nan Clach Geala, 3581 feet, offers some rock-climbing on its east face, and several other cliffs may be found, but the group as a whole is grassy on top, with easy walking on ridges narrow enough to simplify route-finding in mist. The best lines of approach are from the west by Loch a' Bhraon and from the south by Loch Fannaich. Access to the latter is by a side-road from Grudie in Strath Bran.

Dirrie Mor to Strath Oykell

North of the Dirrie Mor, Beinn Dearg and its five neighbours are lonely, desolate Munros, and as seen from the west shapeless masses. But Beinn Dearg has an impressive south-east corrie, Coire Ghrannda, with big cliffs of schist around a lochan. The four Inverlael Munros of the group may be conveniently approached from the head of Loch Broom by the river Lael, first by car ($1\frac{1}{2}$ miles), then on foot by a good path ($4\frac{1}{2}$ miles to the Bealach Coire Ghrannda). A more direct approach to Coire Ghrannda is from the Dirrie Mor, leaving Loch Droma by a path near its east end and climbing up on the west side of Leac an Tuath. The two outliers of the group, Am Faochagach in Strathvaich, and Seana Bhraigh in Freevater Forest to the north, are usually approached, respectively, up Strath Vaich, 2 miles east of Loch Glascarnoch, and from Ullapool by Glen Achall. Seana Braigh is notoriously remote, unless permission is obtained to take a car 10 miles up the glen on a private road, leaving a 6-mile walk to the summit by way of Allt nan Caorach. Another route to the north side is from Oykell Bridge to Corriemulzie Lodge (6 miles on a private road), then $5\frac{1}{2}$ miles by path to the summit. Seana Braigh has a spacious north-east corrie with cliffs and some rock-climbing.

Easter Ross

Ben Wyvis, 6 miles east of Strath Vaich and 6 west from Dingwall, is an isolated plateau of Moine schists and gneisses, sprawling 6 miles by 3. Seven tops exceed 3,000 feet but the only Munro is Glas Leathad Mor, 3433 feet. This is one of the dullest of all Scottish mountains if climbed from the south. The quickest route is from Garbat on the west, 4 miles north of Garve. But the best (most interesting) route is the eastern. Start from Evanton, and take the public road for 5 miles up Glen Glass to Eileanach, thence go west by Allt nan Caorach into the huge eastern corrie. The northerly branch, Coire Mor, is wildly craggy around a lochan, but allows an easy ascent to the main ridge (6 miles from Eileanach). The plateau is vast and grassy. The moorlands around stretch far and wide without foreground interest, but the view is the most extensive of the Northern Highlands. Coire Mor has some rock-climbing, not of good quality. The mountain has excellent ski-slopes in winter.

The river Glass in its lower reach runs through a unique cleft (the Black Rock of Novar) cut vertically through Old Red sandstone to a depth of 100 feet for $1\frac{1}{4}$ miles. It is only 12 to 20 feet wide at the top.

Coigach

Coigach is the whole district between Outer Loch Broom and the Sutherland frontier, where an east–west furrow filled by Loch Veyatie, Fionn Loch, and the River Kirkaig, divides it from Assynt. The main north road from Loch Broom to Durness follows the

Moine Thrust line, west of which no hill attains 3,000 feet. Coigach is almost entirely Torridonian sandstone, although Lewisian gneiss is widely exposed on the low coastal fringe towards Enard Bay, and Cambrian quartzite often caps the hills thickly. Coigach has south and west coast-lines to either side of the Rhu More peninsula. The south or Outer Loch Broom coast has a score of off-shore islands – the Summer Isles, which partially protect a shore exposed to the North Minch. Midway between Loch Broom and Loch Veyatie, the north road sends a branch 14 miles west to Achiltibuie, facing the Summer Isles. The road follows a chain of freshwater lochs in a great fold of the hills between Ben More Coigach on the south side and the mountains of Inverpolly Forest on the north. Ben More Coigach, 2438 feet, has a long sharp crest. The best line of ascent is by the east ridge, reached from Drumrunie New Lodge across the river Runie. Close to its north, Sgurr an Fhidhleir (pronounced Scooranee-ler) has a big rock buttress of 650 feet above Loch an Tuath (rock-climbing).

The Inverpolly Forest is a Reserve of the Nature Conservancy. It has 3 mountains all most worthy of the name: Cul Beag, 2525 feet and Stac Polly, 2009 feet, above the Loch Lurgain road, and Cul Mor, 2786 feet, 3 miles behind them. They encircle an open grassy strath filled by a dozen lochs, of which the biggest is Loch Sionascaig. The interior is a sanctuary for red deer and greenshanks. The track in from the roadside to Cul Mor starts 400 yards east of the cottage of Linneraineach, crosses a low bealach, and goes round the head of Loch an Doire Dhuibh on to Cul Mor's craggy flank. From the summit, you look west to the Hebrides and north to Suilven and Canisp in Glencanisp Forest, while close under your feet lies the serpentine length of the Cam Loch, the Highland's most sinuous waterway. From here north to Loch Inchard (25 miles) the land is gneiss, except for its sandstone monoliths, and pitted by the many hundreds of lochs and lochans that are its main topographical feature.

Stac Polly, the Stack of the Bog (but no boggier than others) towards the west end of Loch Lurgain, is an old sandstone hill without a quartzite cap and now in the final throes of disintegration. Its half-mile ridge has been shattered by weather into small pinnacles from which steep scree-slopes fall on all sides. The summit ridge gives an airy walk, for the pinnacles can be dodged; an easy scramble is needed to reach the summit at the west end. The summit can be reached direct from the road by way of a tiny corrie, or more leisurely by the long east ridge. Some short rock-climbs may be had on the westmost cliff.

Assynt

Assynt is walled eastward by the range of Ben More Assynt, which spreads north-west almost to the head of Loch Glencoul, one of the twin heads of Loch Cairnbawn. Between that wall and the sea, and between the Cam Loch and Loch Cairnbawn, Assynt measures 14 miles by 12. Under the west flank of Ben More it is twice split: north to south by a swerving trough holding the road and the river Loanan, and east to west by Loch Assynt and the river Inver. Lochinver, at the back of Enard Bay, is the chief village and fishing port. A good road links it to Inchnadamph at the head of Loch Assynt.

The main road access is either from Ullapool to Ledmore at the south end of the Loanan trough, or from Bonarbridge to Ledmore by way of Strath Oykel. A minor west road runs all the way fom Achiltibuie up the Coigach and Assynt coasts to Kylesku, at the narrows of Loch Cairnbawn. It is narrow, tortuous, and slow – and reveals the character of the hinterland much better than the main road, which is too enclosed by the near hills. The land between the roads is an uninhabited desert of rocky hillocks and hollows, between which little glens run here and there, all filled with lochans and burns. The lochans are often edged with water-lilies and lobelia, always out of reach, for they are cropped by deer. On ʳhis choppy moorland three sandstone mountains are spaciously set: Suilven, 2399 feet, to the south; Canisp, 2779 feet to the east; and Quinag, 2653 feet, far north.

As seen end-on from the west, Suilven (and Stac Polly too) lifts its head like a monster from the deep. It was named by the Norse Pillar Mountain, but from north and south where its length is moated by lochs, it resembles a tall ship. The scene has a fantastic quality absent from the Loanan trough. Away from the roads, beware of trying to follow a straight course to gain any objective. Plan your route from the map, by stalking tracks as far as possible, on pain of entanglement in a maze of rock and water.

The route in to Suilven and Canisp from westward starts at the south side of Lochinver by a private road to Glencanisp Lodge, then by footpath to Suileag. An equally good route is to the south-west up the Kirkaig river by path to Fionn Loch. The view from Suilven's three tops has an all-absorbing feature – the numberless tarns that light the moor, a light that changes colour hourly with the skies, from black or white to royal blue.

Canisp is more conical and easily climbed from the east by fording the river Loanan. Quinag, north of Loch Assynt, has 7 sandstone tops, whose bed of gneiss rises to 2,000 feet on the north top, Sail Ghorm. The north-east top, Sail Garbh, confronts the Reay Forest across Kylesku with a splendid buttress (Barrel Buttress – rock-climbing). The traverse of the tops is best started from the road between Loch Assynt and Kylesku. The views include the wooded Assynt valley, varied seascapes, and the wild hills of Glencanisp.

Ben More Assynt, 3273 feet, is not only the highest mountain of Sutherland but built of gneiss rising to the highest level it attains in Scotland. The summit is capped by quartzite, and the lower west slopes are Cambrian limestone. Evidence of the latter is seen on the green pastures of Inchnadamph (Stag's meadow), where some of the croft houses are built of marble. The hotel here is a centre for geologists, botanists, potholers, and archaeologists (apart from anglers and climbers), for the limestone of Ben More has been burrowed by burns and carved into caves. Those most worthy of attention are the Traligill burn at Inchnadamph, which drops underground at the 600-foot contour, and has caves with straw stalactites at 750 feet; and the Allt nan Uamh $2\frac{1}{2}$ miles south, where 3 caves at 900 feet have yielded Mesolithic remains of man and animal (see p. 69).

Ben More has 3 tops of 3,000 feet, of which 2 are Munros. The first of these, Conival, 3234 feet, is climbed direct from Inchnadamph by the Traligill burn to Conival's north col. From Ben More's summit the view north extends past Ben Hope to Orkney.

Assynt has many other landscape features, notably on the great headland spreading north-west to Point of Stoer. That wilderness is congested with more lochs than Glencanisp; the rock-lined coast is interspersed with sandy coves; and the cliffs of the north point are marked by the Old Man of Stoer, a sea-stack 200 feet high – the name is from the Norse for stake. Finally, the narrow deep glen at the head of Loch Glencoul bears on its south flank the highest waterfall in Scotland, the Eas Chual Aluinn, with a vertical drop of 658 feet (O.S. figure). It can be reached from the Loch Assynt–Kylesku road-pass by a 3-mile track starting close to its highest point (849 feet). The fall takes three leaps in 500 feet, then spreads a mare's tail over the last 150 feet.

Reay

Reay (pronounced Ray) is the ancient name for the territory of Clan Mackay, extending from Kylesku to Cape Wrath and from Beinn Cleith Bric (Klibreck) to Dounreay Castle in Caithness. The Reay Forest is the mountain country flanking a chain of lochs and rivers between Loch Shin and the sea-loch of Laxford.

Reay, seen from its tops, might best be described as a vast bog, pimpled by hills, largely uninhabited except sparsely on the coastal margins and one or two principal glens, like Strath Naver. The west coast is little indented, except by Loch Laxford and Loch Inchard, just 4 miles long, but the north coast is more heavily breached by the Kyle of Durness, Loch Eriboll, and Kyle of Tongue. From Eriboll, a broad belt of Cambrian limestone runs south with gneiss land to its west and Moine rocks eastward. The mountains of Reay Forest form the only compact range, running 15 miles south-east from Foinaven to Ben Hee, but nowhere reaching 3,000 feet.

The western peaks, Foinne Bheinn (Foinaven) and Arcuil, stand 9 miles in from the open sea, and between sea and hill the gneiss moors are the roughest, least tractable of low land in the Highlands, far more heavily pocked with lochans than Assynt. Among the works that mitigate the crimes of the infamous duke of Sutherland last century are the only two roads, one from Kylesku to Durness and the other from Lairg to Laxford Bridge.

The west coast is a rocky waste thickly bayed from Loch Cairnbawn to Loch Inchard. Apart from small crofts, there are notable settlements only at Badcall and Scourie, and along the north shore of Loch Inchard, where Kinlochbervie is the most important fishing port of the North Highlands. Two miles north-west of Scourie, the uninhabited island of Handa has a 350-foot sandstone cliff on the north side – a breeding station for guillemots, razorbills, fulmars, and puffins. Access is by lobster-boat from Tarbet, north of Scourie. The RSPB has a bothy on the island, and bird-watchers may use it for a small charge. Within a wedge cut from the cliff stands the Great Stack. The gap is 80 feet wide, and was first crossed in 1876 by Donald MacDonald of Lewis. He stretched a rope over the outer points of the wedge, and thus over the stack, and crossed hand-over-fist with no safety rope – an extraordinary feat. The first ascent from the sea was made in 1969 by Hamish MacInnes. Between Loch Inchard and Cape Wrath, Sandwood Bay has the longest sandy beach of the coast. To its south stands Am Buachaille, a tall sandstone stack where semi-precious stones are embedded in the shore rocks.

The north coast is broken into many big headlands, where cliffs of varied rocks rise high: the Parph moor, ending at Cape Wrath in a 370-foot cliff of red gneiss veined with pink pegmatite, and at Cleit Dubh 4½ miles east on cliffs of red sandstone rising above 800 feet; around Durness, limestone 112 feet high, where the Cave of Smoo has a famous pothole and arch; and at Whiten Head (between Loch Eriboll and Tongue Bay), quartzite cliffs of 600 feet on the Eriboll side, and Moine crystalline rocks eastward. The latter rise to 843 feet, and with Cleit Dubh are Britain's highest mainland sea-cliffs. These northern cliffs have sandy coves, good walking on top, many stacks (some with difficult climbing), natural arches, and numerous great caves, more especially on the west side of Whiten Head – the only place on the mainland where Atlantic seals breed.

The Reay Forest has 5 hills of which Foinne Bheinn and Arcuil are by far the finest if bleakest. They together form a twisting 9-mile ridge with eastern offshoots and many tops. Ganu Mor, 2980 feet, is the north summit (Foinne Bheinn), and Arcuil, 2580 feet, crowns the south end. Both are quartzite. The long west flank of Foinne Bheinn is a blank wall of scree, but the east side has three corries backed by long cliffs and spurred by big buttresses (rock-climbing). The quickest way to the summit is by its north ridge, reached from the summit of the Durness road near Gualin House. The western view across 120 square miles of lochan-riddled moor is unmatched in scale for its kind – glittering desolation. Northward, the surf breaks white on Durness beaches, and close below Loch Eriboll lies still; southward, An Teallach rears up behind Coigach. Arcuil, as massive and hollow as the hull of the Ark, from which Norsemen named it, has high narrow ridges almost completely enclosing a deep-sunk central corrie, at the base of which lies Loch an Easain Uaine, the Loch of the Green Falls. The best way up is from Loch Stack to its south, by a track leading up the Allt Horn and so on to the mountain's east ridge.

The Reay interior has only 2 Munros, Ben Hope and Beinn Cleith Bric, which with their 2 lower neighbours, Beinn Laoghal (Loyal) and Beinn an Armuinn (Armine), are isolated mountains on the great bog between Lairg and the north coast. Ben Hope, 3042 feet, and Beinn Laoghal, 2504 feet, stand up boldly close to Kyle of Tongue. Both are steep to the west, with deep corries and outcropping rock. Ben Hope is climbed from the road to its south-west, and Ben

Laoghal (the only igneous mountain in the north) from the head of Loch Loyal to its east. Its rock is a kind of granite with little or no quartz, called syenite. Beinn Cleith Bric, 3154 feet, and Armuinn, 2338 feet, rise from the Crask moor south of Loch Naver. Their rock is mica-schist. Dull mountains on a dreary bog, they can be approached from the Lairg–Altnaharra road to their west.

Caithness

Caithness is mountainous only on its southernmost border, where 2 hills, Morven and Scaraben, exceed 2,000 feet. Most of the county is Old Red sandstone with low featureless moors inland, but fine sea-cliffs on both coasts, notably at Dunnet Head (346 feet), the most northerly point of the mainland, and Holburn Head, to either side of Thurso Bay, and at Duncansby Head (210 feet), which has pinnacled stacks.

Morven, 2313 feet, is a cone of Old Red conglomerate, and Scaraben, 2034 feet, a rounded ridge of Moine quartzite. They are best climbed either up the Berriedale Water to the north, or by Langwell Water to the south.

10 The Development of Mountaineering

In the narrow, modern sense, mountaineering is the ascent of mountains for sport, and the mountaineer a man of sufficient craft to be free on the hills – free to move efficiently on their many features at all seasons in normal weather. 'Normal' includes much high wind and low cloud, with snow and ice underfoot. In fact, mountaineering has always meant a great deal more than this to many men. Like all open air sports it can give an exhilaration of spirit, but has wider physical range than others. It can release the urge to adventure, but this adventure has so many different facets, meaning such very different things to men of different temperament and levels of awareness, that no man can answer for others the question, 'Why climb?' There is one common factor that all mountaineers share without question – enjoyment.

In Scotland, mountaineering began in the late nineteenth century when men found that the hills and contest with the natural elements refreshed them in body and mind for return to social duties and urban restrictions. The pioneers were men in sedentary jobs. But long before then, the Highlanders living in the roadless hills were mountaineers in a basic sense not now known in Scotland. From the early days of clan life, they crossed the ranges, climbed the mountains by easy routes, traversed the hill passes at all seasons, and scaled cliffs, for a score of well-attested reasons: hunting in high corries, mining, herding, culling sea-birds and their eggs, reiving, driving cattle and sheep to market often over the high tops to save detours, raiding their enemies, escaping pursuit, and collecting crystals. To all this and more clan history gives much evidence. The famous forced march by Montrose in January 1645, when he led his royalist army from the head of Loch Ness over the snows of the western Monadh Liath, then zig-zagged down to the Corrieyairack, Glen Roy and Glen Spean to rout the Covenanters at Inverlochy, could not have been done in two days without an army of mountaineers. Numerous other examples show that the summits themselves were familiar ground to such men. They were inured to travel in blizzard conditions that immobilized Lowlanders. The final break-up of the clan system after 1763, the emptying of the glens, the death of droving, and new roads, so changed Highland life that by the mid-nineteenth century when tourists were coming in some number from the Lowlands and England, the Highland people could no longer be thought of as mountaineers, except for the small number employed as shepherds or gillies.

The discovery of mountains for recreation was made by men from the south. This developed during the eighteenth century out of travel for more utilitarian ends. First came the military map-makers like General Roy, who worked around 1750, then the road map-makers from 1770, and the ordnance surveyors after their establishment in 1791. They were followed by scientific and social explorers like Thomas Pennant, the zoologist (1772), Dr Johnson (1773), Dr John MacCulloch (1811–21), and Professor J. D. Forbes (1836). The two latter geologists climbed mountains far and wide. Forbes's delight in them grew out of his work. He was an Edinburgh Scot, appointed to the chair of Natural Philosophy at Edinburgh when aged twenty-four, but his main work was the study of Alpine glaciers. The Alpine Club, formed in London in 1857, made him their first honorary president. In Skye he made the first recorded ascents of Sgurr nan Gillean and Bruach na Frithe.

The travellers' writings drew attention to the Highlands; still more so Sir Walter Scott's Highland romances published between 1810 and 1820. These led adventurous men and women, including many artists and poets, to embark on the Grand Tour of The Highlands with ascents of distinguished mountains like Ben Lomond and Ben Nevis. They mostly travelled mounted, for Highland roads were steep and stony. Coaches and mail-gigs could be used only for a short season on important routes, when 50 miles could take most of a day. Off the main routes, travel went on foot or by horse, or by hired horse-cart. Some prodigious walking feats were accomplished by the military and ordnance surveyors. Winter ascents were rare. The first record of step-cutting on ice was on Ben Lomond in 1812 by Colonel Hawker, who used knives.

Scotland's first mountaineer in the modern sense was Sheriff Alexander Nicolson, a Skyeman born at Huabost in 1827, but exiled to Edinburgh as a student, editor, and lawyer. He saw the Cuillin with new eyes while on holiday in 1865. Others before him had climbed peaks at the fringes, but he became their first explorer. Among his many ascents were Sgurr Alasdair (named after him), which he reached by the Stone Shoot after traversing Sgurrs Banachdich and Dearg; and Sgurr Dubh Mor from Sligachan by way of Coruisk in rain and mist. He used his plaid as a rope on the descent from the summit by moonlight. His writings in *The Scotsman* and *Good Words* (a widely read magazine) made it plain that he climbed without scientific motive purely for enjoyment, and from deep, aesthetic appreciation of the mountain scene. He climbed rock for the fun of it. This was the first clear sign of a new climate of thought about mountains. Between 1849 and 1875 at least a dozen clubs were formed in the east and central Lowlands, most notably the Cobbler Club of Glasgow (1866), which specifically encouraged climbing rather than rambling.

1880–1914

The needed fillip to mountaineering proper was given from 1880 to 1890 by members of the Alpine Club. They launched a campaign on the Cuillin. The most influential men were the Pilkington brothers, Charles and Lawrence, two of the leading alpinists of the day. They climbed Sgurr nan Gillean by its west ridge, the Inaccessible Pinnacle by its east ridge, and drew to Skye several of the club's best climbers: Slingsby, Hastings, Horace Walker, Clinton Dent, and Norman Collie among others. They found routes up all the peaks in summer, while in five winters they made snow climbs on all but three peaks of the main ridge. Professor Norman Collie, a Scot born in Manchester, was not at first a member of the Alpine Club although later its President. In two years 1887–8, he traversed all the main peaks with John Mackenzie of Sconser, who became Scotland's first real mountain guide. Their partnership lasted nearly fifty years, except when Collie was away in the Alps, Himalaya, Canada, or Norway. Among the many rock-climbs they made together were the face climb on Sgurr Alasdair, the Window Buttress of Sgurr Dearg, and the Cioch Pinnacle of Sron na Ciche.

Thus far all climbing effort had been expended on the Cuillin. Despite Byron's frowning glories, the Cairngorms were not thought to include much rock, while the cliffs of Ben Nevis and Glen Coe had been left untouched. Little was known of the two latter. They were not more accessible by reason of more southerly position.

Skye could be approached by railway from Inverness to Strome, which had opened in 1870, but Glen Coe and Fort William had to be reached by horse-drawn carriage across the Moor of Rannoch. In 1880 a railway was laid as far as Tyndrum (the Oban line) but the road north was an exposed track much blocked by snowfall. From 1890 bicycles were much used to eke out the railway lines – arduous work on rough surfaces. The best Highland maps omitted whole ranges of Munros, and showed rivers flowing the wrong way. The publication of the first O.S. maps in 1880 was a most significant event.

The Alpine climbers were naturally drawn to the Cuillin by their long rock ridges, about which their club was the central source of information. Scotland greatly needed such a forum for exchange of knowledge and discussion. The lack was remedied in 1889, when W. W. Naismith and others in Glasgow founded the Scottish Mountaineering Club under the presidency of Professor George Ramsay. Naismith, aged thirty-three and father of the club, had since 1880 done much climbing in Skye and the Alps (including a solo ascent of the Eiger). The alpine influence was strong in the new club. Fourteen of its hundred members were already in the Alpine Club, among them Norman Collie, G. A. Solly, Clinton Dent, the Pilkingtons, and J. H. Gibson. They had powerful effect in directing their fellow members towards winter climbing and to early familiarity with snow and ice, which gave important practice for the Alps. The pages of the *SMC Journal* and articles written in other magazines widely spread their ideas, which included encouragement to seek out hard ways to the tops. The budding mountaineer naturally took the easy ways first. On emerging from the town-jungle on to the open moor, he delighted first in the sun on his face, the burn-song in his ears, and the rising hills ahead. Rock and ice were secondary thoughts. He carried walking to lengths rarely attempted now (for example, even in his teens Naismith walked 56 miles to climb Tinto). The club was only two years old when it published the Tables of 3,000-foot mountains compiled by Sir Hugh T. Munro, who climbed all but two of the 538 tops on his list. Rock-climbing soon developed, not just because a mastery of rock was needed for the Alps, but for sport, and not only in summer but on the snow-bound crags of winter.

In 1887 the Cairngorm Club was formed at a meeting at the Shelter Stone of Loch Avon – two years before the SMC. While rapidly growing, its early character was that of a field club, exploring, recording, and organizing large excursions to the hills.

The early development of Scottish rock-climbing differed in four ways from that of English. (1) Skills developed more slowly because the Highlands were cast on a much bigger scale, the cliffs more remote, road and rail communications poorer, the approaches longer, the population and therefore climbers smaller in number. England's larger numerical involvement and her climbers' quicker access to rock meant that development of skills came sooner and faster; this initiative in setting standards on summer rock has continued. (2) Yet, contrary to what has been said in modern climbing histories, Scotland had no counterpart of the early English development in three phases – a first period of gully climbing, exploiting the most obvious line of weakness, followed by a move to buttresses and ridges as climbers won free of the gullies' muscle-demanding strictures, and finally to balance-climbing on open slabs and walls. Everywhere in Scotland except on Lochnagar, the gully period was eliminated. All features of the cliffs were attacked from the start. The long, deep gullies often with huge pitches of near-vertical rock were not inviting routes in Scotland, whereas the ridges and buttresses between looked much fairer to the eyes of alpinists or men under their guidance. (3) In Scotland, the rope was used from the start but abhorred in England, where Haskett-Smith, the initiator of the gully-epoch, 'used no ropes or other illegitimate means'. Rope-use in Scotland was taken for granted as correct alpine practice. Whether it added to safety was another matter. (4) A remarkable feature of Scottish climbing was its ardent pursuit in winter despite arctic conditions and lack of adequate clothing and equipment.

Practice: Summer and winter climbing were so inextricably mixed in the early records, which gave little detail of snow and ice conditions or techniques or even of lines chosen, that separate developments of the two cannot be singled out. Nor were the tools and equipment for summer and winter differentiated. The ice-axe, about 44 inches long, was carried at all seasons, again as for the Alps, and used in summer to clear vegetation or rubble off holds, or to jam in a crack for foothold. Rope-lengths were as short as 30 to 50 feet between each man. Prior to 1914, no belays were given or anchors taken, the purpose of the rope being not to stop a fall but to check a slip while the climbers were moving continuously on moderate rock or snow, as in the Alps. On difficult rock, when the leader left a stance his second paid out the rope through his hands, not around the shoulder or waist. After the start of the new century, advanced climbers like the Abraham brothers of Keswick favoured direct belays over rock. No boots were designed for mountaineers. They had to use the labourer's model with wide welts and hobnailed soles. The alpinists of the SMC introduced overlapping nails (clinkers) round the edge of the welt. In the absence of windproof clothing, closewoven tweed jackets, breeches, and waistcoats, and wide-brimmed felt hats or cloth caps, were universally worn.

The Routes: In 1892, Ben Nevis was discovered by the Hopkinson family – three brothers and a son – from the north of England. They walked up the Allt a' Mhuilinn to view the cliff, of which some hint had been given by the opening of the summit observatory in 1883. Their reward was a first sight of that tremendous array of ridges, towers, and buttresses, with snowfields at their base in mid-summer, and rock-corries at their heart. No climb had ever been attempted. Two features stood out: a ridge at centre rising thrice in towers on its 2,000-foot flight to the plateau; and beyond, an apparently steeper ridge of 1,800 feet with a huge west face. These were later named Tower Ridge and North-East Buttress. The Hopkinsons climbed the first to the base of the Great Tower at nearly 4000 feet, where they had to withdraw; but next day walked up to the plateau and climbed down the whole ridge. Two days later, two of them climbed North-East Buttress. The routes were the longest in Britain and must have given intense enjoyment – to this day they are the most popular on the Ben – yet the Hopkinsons chose to make no written report.

Meantime, the Scots were busy in Arran and elsewhere. In March 1893, Douglas and Gibson attempted the 600-foot Douglas Gully of Lochnagar. They were stopped by the 200-foot terminal wall, which lay at an angle of 70 degrees under its plaster of snow and ice. It was destined to remain unclimbed for 57 years, but the fact that the attempt was made shows the mettle of early climbers. Next day they climbed Black Spout Gully by its left fork. In Glen Coe, Collie, Solly, and Collier made the first rock-climb on the north face of Buachaille Etive Mor in March 1894 (no record of snow, if any) and also the first on Bidean nam Bian by the north face of Aonach Dubh. This was during an Easter meet at Bridge of Orchy, when news of the Hopkinsons' climbs on Ben Nevis filtered through to the club. No undue emphasis should be put on its spurring effect, for

33. Gorm Loch Mor from A' Mhaighdean, Letterewe Forest.   *Gneis*

34. Gorm Loch Beag and crags of Carnmore, Achaniasgair.

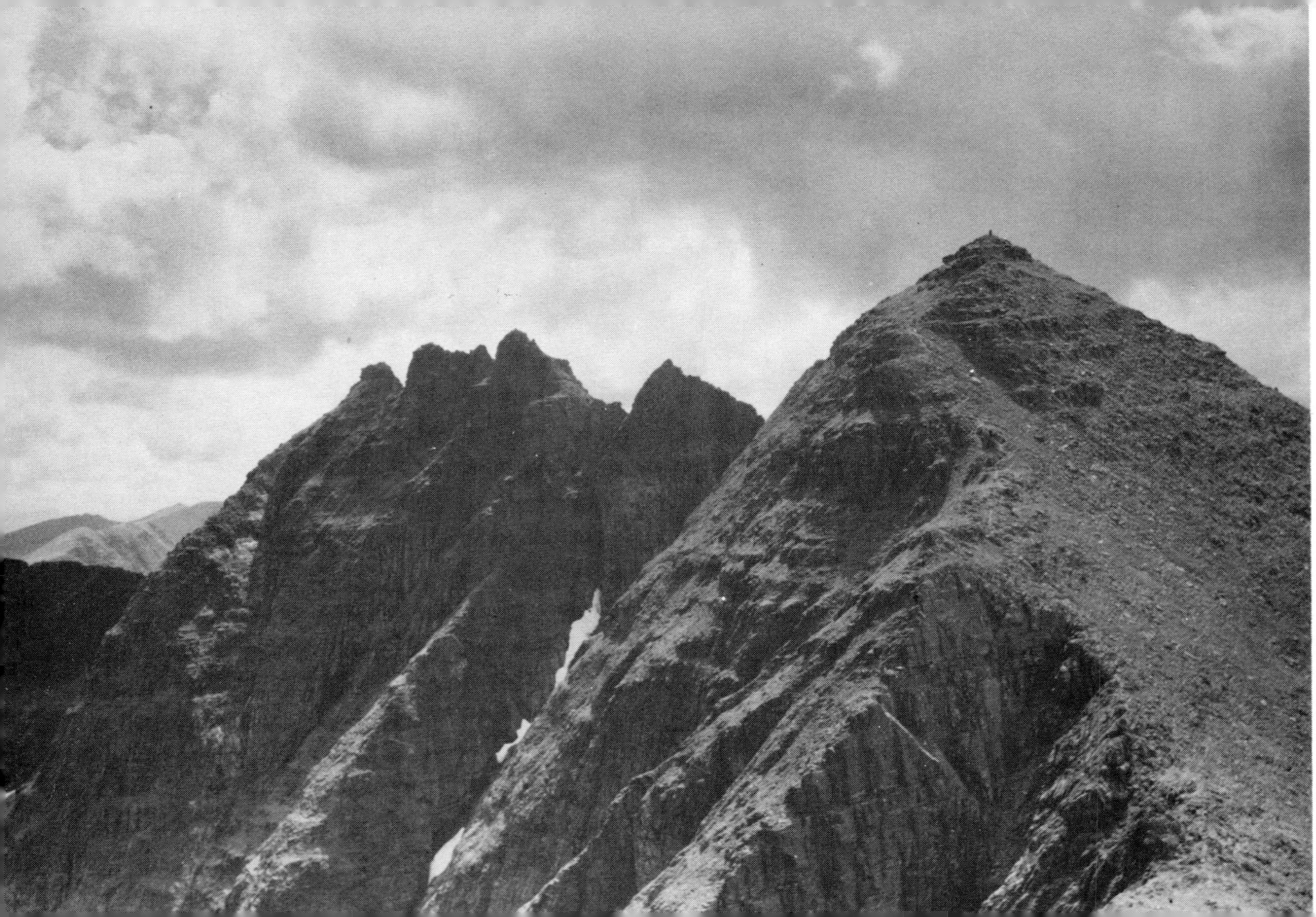

35. An Teallach.

1894 was in any event the year in which members began to record good new climbs far and wide. Collie's party moved to Ben Nevis before the end of March to take up the Hopkinsons' challenge. They made the first winter ascent of Tower Ridge – snow was lying more heavily than it had for ten years (Observatory records) – and Collie likened the climb to the Italian Ridge of the Matterhorn.

The pioneers over the next several years were Collie, Naismith, Tough (pronounced Tooch), and Brown, Douglas and Gibson, and J. H. Bell. Many others were involved, and they were to be joined from 1896 by Harold Raeburn, who ranked with Collie as the two best of Scotland's mountaineers at home and abroad. Such men, it must be remembered, were the hard core of the club. Like all who make history by taking bold initiatives they were few in number. The majority, then as now in most clubs, chose the easiest routes in fair weather. But for the rock-climber this was the golden age. His every ascent was a new route.

In the summer of 1894 Bell and Naismith were in Arran making routes on Cir Mhor, but the event of the year was the autumn opening of the West Highland railway (Glasgow to Fort William). The next Easter meet was held on Ben Nevis. Among the many routes climbed in April 1895 were Castle Ridge by Collie and Naismith, and Aonach Beag up its North-East Ridge by Naismith, Thomson, and others. In May, Tough and Brown climbed the North-East Buttress of Nevis (unaware of the Hopkinsons' climb), and went on to Glen Coe to make the first route up the North Buttress of Buachaille. When winter came, J. H. Bell climbed the North Wall of the Chasm, and next summer Naismith made the first ascent of Crowberry Ridge – a big event.

Most of these routes were repeated by other parties and new ones added. The standard of rock-climbing was rising. It is surprising how few gullies were chosen either in summer or winter. Little ice-climbing was recorded, for the winter routes on ridges and buttresses were not of the kind on which ice tended to accumulate. Climbing on hard snow was much practised, and first ascents of classic routes like the centre gully of Beinn Laoigh began around 1888. The first notable snow-climbs were not done until 1896 on Ben Nevis, when Naismith, Bell, Collier, and Slingsby made April ascents of North Castle Gully, South Castle Gully, and No. 2 Gully (which had a now notorious cornice). Castle Buttress fell at the same time to Brown and Naismith, and the Douglas Boulder Direct to Douglas, Brown, Raeburn, and Hinxman. This was Raeburn's first SMC meet. He had made his mark at once. Tough and Brown took him to Creag Meaghaidh, where they tried the Centre Post of Coire Ardair, but were chased out by avalanches. In August that year, Tough and Brown made the first rock-climb on Lochnagar. They climbed the central buttress, later called the Tough–Brown Ridge. Collie climbed Sgurr Alasdair by an 800-foot route up its Coire Lagan face, and Naismith climbed the Right-Angled Gully of the Cobbler.

The first good short ice-climbs were made in April 1897 by Maylard in the Upper Couloir of Stob Ghabhar, and by Hastings and Haskett-Smith in Gardyloo Gully of Ben Nevis. These were steep snow-gullies, each interrupted by an ice-pitch that could vary in height from 10 to 30 feet, and in angle from 65 to 90 degrees. They were valuable practice-routes for longer, more testing climbs elsewhere, like Crowberry Gully. This, the classic ice-climb of Glen Coe, was climbed in April by Raeburn and Green. There was much snow in the bed but the rocks were clear, and the climb was not a true winter ascent, which Raeburn made twelve years later. He and Bell that summer climbed the Church Door Buttress of Bidean nam Bian. In November, Raeburn led the central gully of Lochnagar, named Raeburn's Gully, and Bell climbed the Waterpipe Gully in Skye in 1898. The standard of climbing had again markedly risen.

The higher standards evolving in England were brought to Scottish rock at the opening of the new century. In 1900 George Abraham led the Crowberry Direct. This required a severe move on a most exposed face – the first of its kind recorded in Scotland, and hitherto regarded as 'impossible' or else 'unjustifiable'. The climb implied an evolution in confidence, or familiarity with the medium won by practice, so that a smooth wall above a long drop could be climbed on tiny or outward-sloping holds, reliance for safety being placed not on the muscle-power of fingers, arms, and shoulders, but on foot-friction, good balance, and the co-ordination of hand and eye, which together allow free, swift movement. To the uninitiated it can look dangerous when it is not. Abraham's 'rashness' was censured by the *SMC Journal*'s omission of any mention, but Raeburn, undeterred, soon made the second ascent. During the next two years he made summer ascents of Observatory Ridge and Buttress, and the severe Raeburn's Arête on the North-East Buttress of Nevis. The first of these he climbed solo, a feat at the time. In

1908 he added Raeburn's Buttress, a tapering pinnacle 600 feet high, to his Nevis list.

Other first-class climbers like Ling and Glover and Inglis Clark were putting up good climbs all over Scotland, aided now by the use of motor-cars. Their winter climbs, sometimes done with Raeburn, included the North-West Gully of Stob Coire nam Beith in Glen Coe (1906) and the more difficult Central Buttress of Stob Coire nan Lochan (1907); their summer routes were in the Cairngorms and Northern Highlands, like the Barrel Buttress of Quinag (1907). Collie in 1906 climbed the Cioch in Skye with John Mackenzie after finding the pinnacle from its shadow on Sron na Ciche.

It was Raeburn, however, who now dominated Scottish climbing until the outbreak of the first world war. Two of his ice-climbs stand out above all others: Green Gully on Nevis done in 1906 with Phildius, and Crowberry Gully done at Easter 1909 with Brigg and Tucker. These were much in advance of his time, and so went unrepeated by contemporary climbers. (Raeburn was also in advance of Alpine tradition when he made the first solo traverse of the Meije, and the first British guideless climbs with Ling up the east face of Monte Rosa, the Viereselsgrat of the Dent Blanche, and the traverse of the Matterhorn by the Zmutt and Italian Ridges. He climbed too with Ling in Norway and the Caucasus, where they made several first ascents.)

The development of rock-climbing had thus far been entirely in the hands of the SMC, aided in summer by standard-setting English incursions, as when Harland and Abraham made the severe direct route on the Cioch in 1907, only a year after the moderate route by Collie and Mackenzie. In 1908 the Ladies' Scottish Climbing Club was founded by Mrs Inglis Clark. Here again the early alpine influence was strong and the club devoted to rock-climbing. The club flourished. Tribute must be paid to the members' moral courage, for women seen wearing breeches were liable to be stoned; they were obliged to wear skirts while in the public eye and to 'stash' them behind boulders at the foot of the climbs.

The publication by the SMC of their Skye Guide, written by Douglas in 1907, followed by the publication of Ashley Abraham's *Rock-Climbing in Skye*, gave a great impetus to exploration there. Scores of new routes were made by SMC members from south of the Border – Shadbolt and McLaren, Steeple and Barlow, and J. Archer Thomson. This culminated in Shadbolt and McLaren's traverse of the Cuillin ridge in twelve hours; a feat long thought impossible not from inherent difficulty but from sheer length. It became practicable because climbers had acquired the needed speed and confidence from familiarity with far harder rock-climbs.

The principal feature of mainland climbing up to 1914 was the high achievement on snow and ice-bound rock. In all Britain there were only a few hundred mountaineers, and only a minority of the SMC capable of rock and ice work to Raeburn's standard. His sketchy accounts of winter routes were inadequate for comparison with other climbs, hence two of his hardest were omitted from early guide-books, and receiving no second ascents went unnoticed for 65 years.

The flowering of climbing skills in the new century was hindered by the lack of advance in equipment and clothing. Tweeds still gave the only protection against storm. Boots remained of bad design, hobs and clinkers the only nailing, ice-axes too long and heavy, rope-lengths absurdly short, rope-belays always given direct across rock if given at all, for the golden rule was that the leader did not fall. Nor did he. The climbers were virtually free of accident while achieving amazingly high standards in relation to gear used. This first high tide in Scottish climbing was showing signs of an ebb when war broke out in 1914. The Scottish mountaineers were engulfed. Climbing died.

1920–1930

The peace of 1919 brought no revival as in England. There was no young leadership left. Mallory, Pye, Carr, Holland, Dorothy Pilley and others of the younger English climbers returned to the Cuillin and made fine summer climbs on Sron na Ciche, like the Crack of Doom and Cioch West. But in Scotland, where even the tradition of winter climbing was dead, there was no one to emulate them. Raeburn, now 55, alone had the energy to try to give a lead. In 1920 he made the first winter ascent of Observatory Ridge under heavy snow, and published his *Mountaineering Art*. But these records too passed from memory, for still there were no young climbers in sufficient number to act on them. The situation was aggravated by the lack of clubs for potential climbers to join, for the SMC qualification was beyond them. A generation gap had been made by war.

At this point the SMC gave three valuable services. They published guides to Ben Nevis and Skye, which kept the records alive, built and opened in 1926 a stone hut for climbers at the foot of the Nevis cliffs, this in memory of Charles Inglis Clark, who had been killed in the war, and in 1925 half a dozen of their members established the Junior Mountaineering Club of Scotland, open to all men of seventeen or over. No experience was demanded. The essential purpose was to give young men the mutual companionship and training they needed, in the hope that in course of time they would revitalize Scottish climbing. No controls were imposed, on the principle that the adult young thrive best when self-responsible.

The club grew slowly for a year or two, but more and more of the war-time generation were discovering mountains; enthusiasm grew and membership increased. They were exploring new routes in Glen Coe in 1928, and in 1931 the Devil's Cauldron in the Chasm of Buachaille Etive Mor was climbed by J. G. Robinson and I. G. Jack. Later in the 1930s, the trickle of routes was to become a flood, augmented from new clubs, the most important of which were the Ptarmigan Club formed in 1929 by J. B. Nimlin, who made eight new climbs on the Cobbler; the Creag Dhu Club in 1930, whose members kept high rock-climbing standards; the Lomond Mountaineering Club in 1933; and University Clubs. All these clubs tapped a new source for recruits from a rich but moneyless stratum of society. In the Cairngorms, a mere handful of routes had been done on Lochnagar when Henry Alexander's guide was published by the SMC in 1928. But G. R. Symmers and Ewen of the Cairngorm Club opened a campaign that added a dozen routes by the end of the decade.

Practice: Aids to more difficult climbing had been introduced since 1920. Boots designed with narrow welts and sewn-in tongues replaced the old hobnailers. At 25 shillings they were available to all. Tricounis (serrated edge-nails) gave better grip on hard snow and on small, incut holds; windproof anoraks with hoods, designed from close-woven cotton for Arctic and Everest expeditions, ousted tweeds and greatly aided the pressing of climbs in adverse weather conditions. The normal allowance of rope between climbers was doubled to 60 feet, often to 80 or 100 feet for the leader, and these longer run-outs were accompanied by shoulder-belays to protect the moving climber on rock, to which the belayer also anchored himself by hitching on to a rock-spike.

1930–1940

Summer: Scottish climbing received a great accession of strength from Dr J. H. B. Bell and Dr Graham Macphee, two of the outstanding mountaineers between the wars. Their exploratory enterprise both in summer and winter became the most powerful influence since the days of Raeburn and Collie, and they invited young climbers to join their ropes. Bell ranged across the whole Highland area. Some of his more important climbs were Diamond Buttress of Bidean nam Bian, the Eagle Ridge and Parallel Buttress of Lochnagar, and the complex of Orion routes on the west face of the North-East Buttress of Ben Nevis – most notably his *Long Climb*. Macphee concentrated most effort on Ben Nevis, climbing eleven new routes in 1935 while editing the climbers' guide published in 1936. Two of the best routes on Nevis were led by A. T. Hargreaves: Route I on Carn Dearg and Rubicon Wall on Observatory Buttress. The latter when made in 1933 was the hardest climb on the mountain.

In the Cairngorms, a remarkable double first ascent on the Mitre Ridge of Beinn a' Bhuird was made in 1933 by two Cambridge University parties led by E. A. M. Wedderburn of the SMC and by M. S. Cumming of the JMCS. In Glen Coe, a momentous advance was inaugurated by G. C. Williams in 1934, when he opened the Rannoch Wall of Buachaille. His Route I, although not severe, went up an intimidating wall, continuously sheer and exposed, of a kind hitherto avoided. Second ascents were made by the Glasgow JMCS, who from 1936 were responsible for the development of the face until the second war. J. F. Hamilton climbed Agag's Groove, a longer route than the first, and I. H. Ogilvie followed with several harder climbs. Rubbers (plimsolls) were used on all these climbs (except when W. M. Mackenzie, W. H. Murray, and J. K. W. Dunn climbed Agag's Groove in the winter of 1937 using nails). An important broadening of technique came from Bell, whose championing of loose and vegetatious rock as a satisfying climbing medium brought numerous good climbs, both by himself and through his strong influence over young climbers of the period. A side-effect in Glen Coe was the first ascent of Clachaig Gully (1700 feet) in 1938 by Murray's party, but the main effects were long term, seen in the development of climbing on Lochnagar and the Cairngorms in general by Aberdeen climbers from the late 1940s onward.

1935–1940

Winter: The Renaissance: The revival of ice-climbing which began in 1935, was heralded in 1934 by P. D. Baird's lead up the S.C. Gully of Stob Coire nan Lochan in Glen Coe. A short note of this in the *SMC Journal* drew attention to the 70-foot ice pitch but led to no immediate repetition. Next year, a brief article in the *Journal* written by Williams vividly described Graham Macphee's lead up Glover's Chimney on the Tower Ridge of Ben Nevis. The huge icefall masking the lower rocks, the severe traverse on iced rocks to regain the gully, the iciness of the final chimney to Tower Gap, and the two run-outs of 130 feet of rope on the first and last pitches, fired the imagination of JMCS climbers. This was the kind of climbing they wanted, and for which the Highlands, they were already realizing, made ample provision. They had enjoyed good practice on the short, uncomplicated ice-climbs of Stob Ghabhar and Ben Nevis, now they went out to look for better things, and one of their first discoveries was Crowberry Gully. They were unaware of Raeburn's ascent, or of his climb up Green Gully on the Comb – buried in 30-year-old records. The leaders of the new movement (in order of arrival) were J. F. Hamilton, W. M. Mackenzie, and W. H. Murray, with several others from the JMCS; and from the SMC, Macphee and Bell. Mackenzie was the pre-eminent iceman of the time. He and J. K. W. Dunn, A. MacAlpine, and Murray formed a team devoted at first to numerous reascents of the great buttresses and ridges of Ben Nevis and Glen Coe, as well as the ice-holding gullies like S.C. Gully, Arch Gully, and Crowberry Gully. Snow and ice conditions on such climbs varied so greatly from month to month and year to year that they were climbed often in freak conditions, for example when successive snow-falls, thaws, and frosts had covered the rocks in massive ice never recorded in Raeburn's time. The development had been made possible by better roads and cheap second-hand motor-cars, which allowed sustained weekly access. Hotels charged only 9s. 6d. for supper, bed, and breakfast; barns and caves were free. Cheap lightweight tents and eiderdown sleeping bags – by-products of the Everest expeditions – allowed camping at the base of the cliffs. The consequence was a rapid rise in the standards of climbing.

Practice: From 1936, the leaders used slater's picks with a 14-inch shaft (short ice-axes were not made), to ease the wrist-strain of prolonged one-handed cutting at high angles (63 to 90 degrees) and to allow cutting in chimneys. Ice-axes, shortened from 39 inches to 31–33, were used on pitches where the quality of ice would often allow better finger-holds to be cut faster with the adze than the pick after the pick had burst the top ice. Head-torches were introduced by the Mackenzie–Murray ropes in order to continue climbing after dark on snow or iced rock (but only where the route was known – they were no aid to route-selection). Pitons, snap-links, and rope-slings were carried but used only as belays to secure retreat or advance in exposed situations where natural rock-spikes were buried in ice or non-existent. Alpine climbers all had ten-point crampons, but never carried them at home; they were clumsy on rock and impractical on near-vertical ice. Step-cutting was an art to be enjoyed. Boots nailed with tricounis (after 1920) gave neat movement and safer hold, especially on thin ice-notches, which if brittle split off under crampon-spikes. Rope-lengths were greatly increased, for a leader on ice might expect to run out 120–150 feet to find a stance. Full-weight rope was never used in winter, its weight being too great a drag on a delicately balanced leader. The lighter lines carried were manilla and hemp of 1-inch or $1\frac{1}{4}$-inch circumference (called 'piano-wire' when wet or frozen). The shoulder belay was largely succeeded by the waist belay, which gave the belayer much greater stability when saving a fall.

The standards of earlier climbers were thus first re-established and then, by more frequent advantage taken of hard conditions, greatly exceeded before evidence appeared in print. Ice climbs that broke new ground and set higher standards were Garrick's Shelf on the Crowberry Ridge, a prototype of the modern ice-climb, and the Deep-Cut Chimney of Stob Coire nam Beith, climbed in 1937 and 1939 by Mackenzie and Murray (leading through). Green Gully was reclimbed by J. H. B. Bell at this time, and Comb Gully climbed by F. G. Stangle, the latter route becoming for a while the hardest of the Nevis ice-climbs. Lochnagar was neglected; it was wrongly thought that ice in quantity did not form there. Zero and Point Five Gullies of Ben Nevis were being reconnoitred by Murray and R. G. Donaldson when the second war stopped further winter development.

1940–1950

The Lull: The second war did not, like the first, make an end of mountaineering. There were no developments, but important events mainly on granite. In 1940 Scroggie and Ferguson of Dundee made a severe direct start to Eagle Ridge on Lochnagar, to which Bell added a direct finish, transforming the ridge into one of the best in Scotland – hard, sound, and airily narrow. This with Bell's further climbs on Lochnagar and Creag an Dubh Loch revealed as never before the potentialities of the Cairngorms, soon to be exploited by enthusiastic Aberdonians. J. F. Hamilton gave a similar service in Arran when he made a superb route up the south ridge of Rosa Pinnacle, which Townend and Curtis followed with many others. Granite climbing was suddenly given its rightful place after long neglect, and more widely enjoyed. On Ben Nevis, Brian Kellet's numerous climbs culminating in Gardyloo Buttress and Minus Two Buttress, came as a further reminder of opportunities waiting.

When the war ended in 1945 the lull (a relative term) continued three years longer. The best of the old climbs were repeated in summer and winter, and new ones added. An extraordinary surge of interest in mountains by men leaving their teens occurred, perhaps in relief from war-time curbs on freedom of activity. Many were stimulated by Murray's *Mountaineering in Scotland*, first published in 1947. At the same time, a flood of ex-WD clothing and equipment came on the market, enabling them to kit out at cut prices. As numbers increased, the accident rate to hill-walkers rose too. The SMC had formed a Mountain Safety Committee in 1936 to organize and set up rescue posts, equipment, and teams drawn from the clubs. Now local teams began to form, reinforced by the RAF mountain rescue teams first formed in 1944. A new Mountain Rescue Committee for Scotland was formed in 1950 and has since been re-formed on a much broader base to include the Clubs, the RAF, British Red Cross, Scottish Youth Hostels Association, Scottish Council of Physical Recreation (now the Sports Council), Police, and others. It has become an autonomous and charitable body, receiving money grants from climbers and all interested persons, from the Department of Health for rescue-post equipment, and more recently from police funds.

Clubs sprang up all over the country. The British Mountaineering Council had been formed in 1944 to look after their wider interests, followed by the Association of Scottish Climbing Clubs in 1946 (now the Mountaineering Council of Scotland). A few training schools were established, both to meet a need and create a demand for instruction, or to try to realize the now disputed idea that character is developed by mountain adventure, as in Outward Bound schools.

This latter ideal was the origin of the Glenmore training centre in the Cairngorms, until the SCPR took it over for strictly technical instruction in outdoor pursuits.

During the lull, rock-climbing standards rose sharply. John Cunningham and W. Smith of the Creag Dhu made many very severe routes on the Rannoch Wall and North Buttress of Buachaille, notably Gallows Route and Guerdon Grooves, the latter far in advance of its time. Murray's preparation of the SMC's first rock-guide played no small part in spurring exploration in Glen Coe, which fell away markedly after publication in 1949.

Practice: Important technical developments were the introduction of vibram soles and nylon rope. Vibrams, named from Vitale Bramani, who invented them in 1935, were moulded rubber soles, which from 1947 gradually replaced nailed soles, but only after long controversy. They were less effective than nails on wet grass and lichenous rock, and on hard snow and ice. But they gave a good grip on most rocks, were lighter and warmer, and needed less repair. Advantages were held to exceed disadvantages, so that nails gradually vanished. The winter deficiencies of vibrams were so great that ten-point crampons had to be carried for safe movement on ice and hard snow, hence the best ice-climbers of Aberdeen continued to use nails into the late 'fifties. The limitations of vibrams, by enforcing crampon-use, were to lead nearly twenty years later to a revolutionary change in tools and technique. Nylon rope ousted manilla as soon as it became available in 1946–7. Its greater strength and elasticity gave additional safety, and its water-shedding property gave new suppleness. In former days, climbers caught in foul and freezing weather had to wear the frozen rope sometimes after reaching their cars, tents, huts, or hotels, before they could untie. These days were now gone. Continental tension-climbing was introduced to the Cobbler in the late 'forties by members of the Creag Dhu. (The leader ties on to two ropes. He drives a piton into a crack above his head, clips a rope to it with a snap-link, and his second man tensions that rope, holding the leader to the rock while he climbs up a step or two and repeats the process with the other rope. Holdless rock may be climbed and overhangs surmounted by attaching foot-slings to the pitons. A single rope may suffice for short tension movements.) The technique had many refinements and its early years were experimental.

1950–1960

Summer: The next decade was the most eventful of the last hundred years, both in summer and winter. More than 800 new climbs were made (146 in winter). A widely ramifying exploration of new rock-climbing areas, and of corries where investigation had not hitherto been thorough, was carried out by several groups of which the principal were the Aberdeen school, led by W. D. Brooker, Len Lovat's parties from Glasgow, Dan Stewart's from Edinburgh, and more importantly in the later 'fifties by the very strong school of Edinburgh climbers emerging under the leadership of J. R. Marshall. While winter climbing was to be the more remarkable development, it was backed by and in some ways depended on the advances in summer rock-climbing.

In the Cairngorms, Brooker's ascent of Black Spout Pinnacle in 1949 was followed by a systematic development of cliff after cliff on Lochnagar, Creag an Dubh Loch, the corries of Beinn a' Bhuird, Coire Sputan Dearg, Coire Etchachan, the Loch Avon basin, and the Garbh Choire of Ben Avon. The leading climbers were Brooker, Tom Patey, Jerry Smith, G. Annand, J. Y. L. Hay, Ken Grassick, Graeme Nicol, M. Taylor, and R. Sellers. Some of their notable routes were Labyrinth Edge, the first on the great slabs of Creag an Dubh Loch; Crimson Slabs of Coire Etchachan; the Citadel and Sticil Face of Shelter Stone Crag; Parallel Gully B on Lochnagar; and most significantly the Pinnacle Face of Lochnagar in 1955 by Jerry Smith, wearing rope-soled shoes. His climb marked the increasing abandonment of nails for summer use and set a new standard for future ascents. Climbs of comparable character on steep open rock followed, of which examples were Djibangi and Talisman on Coire Etchachan, and the Link on Lochnagar. Many of the best routes were promptly followed by winter ascents. At the close of the decade, the Cairngorms had more routes than Skye.

On Ben Nevis the most important development was the finding of ways through the great overhangs and overlapping slabs of Carn Dearg Buttress. The potentialities were revealed by another English incursion, when Joe Brown and Don Whillans in 1954 climbed Sassenach. Whillans followed this with Centurion and The Shield in 1956. These long and splendid routes, together with very hard climbs made in Glen Coe by John Cunningham, W. Smith, P. Walsh, and M. Noon – climbs like Whortleberry Wall on Buachaille (the hardest on Rannoch Wall), Slime Wall (North Buttress), and Carnivore on

Creag a' Bhancair – inspired other Scottish climbers to realize the potential of rocks in the west.

The Edinburgh climbers, now one of the dominant forces in mountaineering, had been putting up rock-climbs all over Scotland. Their outstanding product was Robin Smith, aged 18 in 1957, when he began making numerous very severe routes. In 1958 they set to work in Glen Coe. Some of their long, formidable climbs were Smith's Shibboleth on the North Buttress of Buachaille (a line up the centre of Slime Wall), Kneepad on the nose of Gearr Aonach by Haston, Yo Yo on Aonach Dubh North Face by Smith, Big Top by Smith, and Trapeze by Marshall. These and a few others like them were thought to be a grade more difficult than Sassenach. In 1959 they went to Nevis, where Smith, Haston, Holt, and Marshall climbed The Bat, a magnificent route between Sassenach and Centurion, superior to its famous neighbours in situation and severity. This work required the most modern techniques and toughness in using them. J. R. Marshall wrote: 'It is this quality which is the surprising product of the modern age, that the routes penetrate the great "impossible" walls by tenuous thread-like weaknesses, inducing the greatest concentration on route-finding and technique, with a commensurate heightening of the appreciative senses. Completion of one of these great routes is somewhat akin to the sensation of emerging from engulfment by a great piece of music or painting.'

Other important events of the decade were the opening up of the 2-mile-long cliffs (hornblende schist) on Ben Lair in 1951, and of the granite slabs of Beinn Trilleachan above Loch Etive in 1954. The latter was a most valuable discovery by Eric Langmuir and others, who climbed Sickle and Spartan, two very severe routes of nearly 600 feet. This introduced a new type of slab climbing on a site offering much further development, which was taken up in the next two years by Noon, W. Smith, Cunningham, and E. Taylor, who made a series of 9 remarkable climbs, of which Swastika (685 feet) was Noon's best, Agony (540 feet) the first use of artificial climbing on a big scale in Scotland, and Long Wait (1000 feet) by Cunningham and Robin Smith, the longest. Another 4 were added by the Edinburgh climbers in 1960.

In Wester Ross the gneiss cliffs of Carnmore Crags above Fionn Loch were developed largely by M. J. O'Hara around 1957. He took part in nearly 40 routes out of a total of 86. In Skye, Robin Smith climbed the 1000-foot Thunder Rib in Coire Tairnealar, and Brooker and C. M. Dixon discovered the Coireachan Ruadh face of Mhic Coinnich, where they climbed the Crack of Dawn, to which R. Barclay and Brooker added Dawn Grooves in 1958 – two of the hardest routes in the Cuillin. In 1957 Ian Clough arrived on the Scottish scene (from Yorkshire), and recorded new routes by the score – at least 40 in 1959 alone, some of them very severe climbs of great length, like Astronomy (955 feet) on the North-East Buttress of Nevis. These are no more than examples from the greatest outburst of climbing that Scotland had yet known. A phenomenal feature of this decade and the next was the output of new routes by Dr Tom Patey; nothing like it, so long sustained in such volume, and so widely spread, had been seen before in the history of Scottish rock-climbing.

The ascent of Everest in 1953 gave mountaineering a new prestige and stimulated the accession of recruits to clubs and training schools, more of which were founded. In England, Education Authorities began to think of extending physical training to hills by setting up adventure centres – an idea that spread to Scotland ten years later. The greater numbers involved in mountaineering led to rapid extension of rock-climbing by more men of natural skill, but produced too a larger crop of accidents to the unskilled. Rescue services had to be repeatedly expanded and developed in efficiency. The quality and range of clothing and equipment were much improved.

Winter: The extraordinary expansion of winter climbing (146 new routes) started in the Cairngorms in 1950. The principal events were the opening up of Lochnagar and Creag Meaghaidh, which seemed to emerge from the mists of time into sunlight, and the development of long ice-climbs on Ben Nevis, giving a new dimension to winter climbing there.

Cairngorms: The Lochnagar clearance was heralded by Brooker's Giant's Head Chimney, followed promptly by Tom Patey's winter ascent of Douglas Gully. Patey was 18 years old. His climbing of the 200-foot pitch was a *tour de force* without parallel in Scotland – the first grade 5 climb. A spate of great winter routes immediately followed, not only by Patey and Brooker but by a growing number of Aberdeen climbers inspired by their example. The routes were better climbs than Douglas Gully, equally hard but of greater variety. Examples were Scorpion (700 feet) on Carn Etchachan by Patey, Nicol and Grassick; Eagle Ridge (650 feet) by Patey, Brooker and Taylor; Mitre Ridge on Beinn a' Bhuird, by Brooker and Patey;

Polyphemus Gully (600 feet) by Grassick; Parallel Buttress (700 feet) by Patey, Brooker, and J. Smith; the Sticil Face of Shelter Stone Crag (700 feet), another *tour de force* by Grassick and Nicol; and two fine climbs by R. Sellers: the Labyrinth of Creag an Dubh Loch (750 feet), and the South-East Gully of Beinn a' Bhuird. These explorations gave birth to the numerical grading of winter climbs, intended to compare not the technical difficulties, which widely fluctuate, but relative levels of formidability – length, time and demands on resource. From the middle 'fifties the Edinburgh climbers had been making routes of high standard on Ben Nevis, Creag Meaghaidh, and in Glen Coe; then in 1958 Marshall and Tiso (using front-point crampons) plucked that icy plum of Lochnagar, the Parallel Gully B (700 feet), one of the great ice-climbs of the decade and the culmination of the Lochnagar campaign.

Creag Meaghaidh: The campaign here opened in 1955, when Patey was making forays into Lochaber. His Central Pillar was the first of the modern classics in Coire Ardair. For the rest of the decade, the Edinburgh climbers virtually took over the corrie, Marshall, Ritchie, Haston, Stenhouse, and Tiso all participating in a series of climbs of which Left Hand Gully, Smith's Gully of Pinnacle Buttress (600 feet) and the 1959 Face Route (1000 feet), were notable examples. Creag Meaghaidh henceforth became one of the principal ice-climbing centres of Scotland.

Glencoe: One outstanding ice-climb was made up Raven's Gully by Hamish MacInnes in 1953.

Ben Nevis: A similar campaign opened on Ben Nevis in 1957. It fell to Hamish MacInnes, Patey, and Graeme Nicol to fire the first shot, and the bang was a big one; the first winter ascent of Zero Gully (1500 feet). The climb was an important break-through on Nevis, where Zero and Point Five Gullies, to either side of Observatory Ridge, had long been reconnoitred and attempted in vain by several strong parties, two of which had peeled off. The lower 400 feet of Zero is a vertical corner choked by big ice overhangs. MacInnes and Patey shared the lead through the maze, using single-rope tension from ice-pitons (Patey) and front-point cramponing between pitons (MacInnes) in combination with pick-and-axe work. In five hours they won a way to the plateau.

Point Five Gully (1000 feet) went unclimbed for two more years, for it seldom came into climbable condition, being a natural drainage line subject to avalanche from above; Patey's parties had been turned back seven times for this reason. In 1959 the first ascent was made by siege tactics, when Ian Clough and others spent five days on the climb, roping off to the CIC hut each evening and leaving fixed ropes for the next day's ascent. The first genuine ascent was made in the following winter by Robin Smith and Marshall, who climbed the whole in seven hours – a first-class demonstration of technique and pace. Two remarkable climbs done among others in 1959 were Minus Two Gully (900 feet) and the Orion Face (1000 feet), the first by Marshall, Haston, and Stenhouse, and the face by Robin Smith and Holt. The latter was an important advance: a route up a great face demanding a wide range of climbing skills, and this seemed to augur the shape of things to come.

Practice: In this decade, standards had soared beyond those of the 'thirties. At first this showed less in what was done as in the pace at which it was done – a change less in new techniques than in confidence. A psychological barrier had fallen. This had loomed high in the 'thirties when the main body of mountaineers had thought long ice-climbs over rock an 'unwarrantable hazard'. Pioneers are always a small minority. They had jumped the barriers in the 'thirties and accepted too the use of artificial aids in case of need, but still wanted to keep that use minimal. By the 'fifties, all hesitations had gone. Men knew what they wanted and moved faster. The technical changes were not numerous. Initial practice had favoured a 30-inch ice-axe and a short hammer-axe (with pick) both with slings. On ice walls the long axe tended to be too little used and the hammer-axe much used, but over-use of the latter was time-wasting where better finger-holds could often be cut with an adze (as noted earlier). Therefore practice in the 'fifties changed to favour a shorter ice-axe (18–25 inches) and a hammer-axe, both without slings to allow quick hand-to-hand change.

In the late 'fifties the Edinburgh climbers began using crampons, still with ten points but with the front two projecting forward ('lobster-claws'), as adjuncts to vibrams. The front points could be used for two or three quick kick-ins up to each previously cut hold, thus reducing step-cutting. They were awkward on rock and troublesome on ice-walls, so that tricounis were still preferred by the Aberdeen climbers: Patey used them even in Zero Gully. Their conversion to crampons followed the evolving technique in front-pointing, which had been aided by the stiffening of vibram soles with inner plates of steel or fibre-glass to support the foot (initially

223

for summer rock-work on small holds). Long ice-pitons were normally carried and occasionally used with slings or *étrier* (a ladder either of cord with two to four alloy rungs or else of wide tape). A leader could drive in a piton ahead, clip on a sling to take his weight, and thus leave his hands free to cut more holds or drive a peg. Double ropes were used to make tension traverses. Another device borrowed from summer rock-climbing was the attachment of runners (slings) to spikes, chockstones, or pitons, as running belays in the middle of a pitch. The active rope, clipped to these with snaplinks, gave the leader protection and renewed confidence. In gullies, ice-axe belays were discontinued wherever a rock-spike could be cleared or a piton driven, or an ice-bollard made. With such aids and the increase in skill and pace, much harder routes were climbed. New techniques, skills, and standards come from individual men and women with ideas and the vigour to carry them into effect. The most influential men of the period were W. D. Brooker, Dr Tom Patey, Hamish MacInnes, J. R. Marshall, and Robin Smith.

1960–1970

Summer. Rock-climbing again increased throughout the 'sixties. More than 1,000 new routes were made of which 778 were on summer rock. Most of this activity was in the North Highlands (196 routes), Skye, the Cairngorms, Glen Coe, and the Central Highlands: notably the latter, where only 14 routes had been made in the 'fifties but 109 in the 'sixties. This unusual rise was caused by exploration of the Loch Laggan area: Creag Meaghaidh, the cliffs of Binnein Shuas (a new find), and Creag Dubh near Newtonmore.

At the start of the decade, much effort was concentrated on Ben Nevis, to which a new guide was being written by Marshall. Some of the outstanding climbs there between 1961 and 1964 were Bullroar (525 feet) by Marshall, Torro (800 feet) by J. McLean, King Kong (1020 feet) by Brian Robertson, and Orgy (2000 feet) by Clough, all on Carn Dearg Buttress; and Gardyloo Buttress (350 feet) and Minus Three Gully (520 feet) by Marshall. After 1965 Ben Nevis was neglected relative to other areas (in regard to new routes).

In the Northern Highlands, new climbs of every grade were discovered in all parts, even on the Fannaichs where Patey found an 800-foot hard severe climb on the Geala Buttress of Sgurr nan Clach. He was indefatigable in exploration. One of his best contributions in 1960, the Nose of the Cioch (600 feet) on Sgurr a'Chaorachain

36. Loch Toll
an Lochain,
An Teallach.
*Torridonian
Sandstone*

37. Loch Broom from Ben Mor Coigach.

38. Pinnacles of Stac Polly, Coigach.

in Applecross, while not hard is considered the most enjoyable climb on Torridon sandstone. In Skye that same year, he and Bonington climbed King Cobra (700 feet) on the Coireachan Ruadh face of Mhic Coinnich, which they regarded as unequalled in the Cuillin for situation and difficulty. The sea-stacks and cliffs of the North Highland coast were the scene of a principal development in which Patey played a leading part. Others had been there before him (at the Duncansby stacks, for example), but his climbs on Am Buachaille at Sandwood Bay, on the Old Man of Stoer off Assynt, the Old Man of Hoy in Orkney, and his sensational crossing from Handa to the Great Stack (climbed in 1969 by MacInnes), attracted followers by the very difficulty of access to picturesque sites. His death in 1969 on the Maiden, a stack off Whiten Head, closed the most influential career in Scottish climbing history.

Much of the new climbing made use of artificial (or tension) techniques, which had been thoroughly mastered, even if used only on short stretches of rock on mainly free climbs. In the Cairngorms they were used on The Giant (430 feet) on the Central Gully Wall of Creag an Dubh Loch, by Bathgate, Ewing, and Brumfitt; and on Cougar and King Rat by Rennie, Williams, J. Bower and Alan Fyffe. Likewise on the Trilleachan Slabs, where numerous routes were added from the middle 'sixties onward. New climbers of great ability were then emerging. Among them from Dumbarton were R. Carrington, Fulton, J. R. Jackson, and Ian Nicholson; from Edinburgh, K. Spence and J. Porteous; and from Dundee, Neil Quinn, Douglas Lang, and J. Bower. Their best routes included Carnmore Corner on Beinn a' Chasgein Mor by Carrington and Jackson; The Pinch on Trilleachan Slabs by the same party; and on Shelter Stone Crag, The Pin by Carrington, and Steeple by Spence and M. Watson. Much good climbing was done by many others like J. McArtney, Fyffe, and MacInnes. From 1968 many overdue second ascents were made of the Glen Coe routes that had marked the Edinburgh school's peak of climbing there. A first advance on them was Kingpin on the Church Door Buttress in 1968 by J. Hardie and W. Thompson. The standard of free climbing was again rising. At the opening of the decade, only a few climbers had been capable of doing very severe routes; by the end there were many. This change had been caused by a spread of confidence based on the security given by free use of artificial aids. A fall by a leader was no longer unacceptable.

Practice: PA's (lightweight canvas boots with smooth rubber soles designed by Pierre Allain) were widely used; many of the more severe climbs could hardly have been done without them. Nylon tape for slings and loops now became common, replacing rope and cord for certain uses. Crash hats had been introduced to protect the head, but not everyone used them. A multitude of pitons, differently designed and of different metals for insertion in differing kinds of cracks and rocks, and a great number of other artificial aids like assorted nuts for insertion as chockstones in cracks to take runners, wooden wedges and metal 'bongs' for wider cracks, and 'sky-hooks' of flattened metal for use in tiny flakes or edges, were made and carried, until some too serious climbers were like mediaeval knights weighed down by excess metal. Many other devices were introduced, some from North America, some from Europe, some from England. The use of tension climbing was reduced by the leader's using a short loop 'cow's tail' to clip or hook himself to a piton while driving the next one, then operating the pulley system himself, or better, by using only a single rope and dispensing with tension by more careful *étrier* technique. This gave more speed by removing two-rope confusion. The use of artificial aids has been the subject of continuing controversy. In Scotland they have rarely been employed to excess; free climbing has flourished.

Schools: A very different kind of development occurred in 1965, when the SCPR in co-operation with the Mountaineering Council of Scotland and the Scottish Education Department instituted the Scottish Mountain Leadership Training Board. This was conceived (initially in England) to meet a new situation of danger caused by youth leaders and school teachers taking children on to hills. Some by lack of experience in navigation and of mountain weather and its severities were leading their parties into serious trouble. The Board's purpose was to provide training for adults in charge. It was neither possible nor desirable to eliminate danger from mountaineering, but feasible to reduce it. Residential courses at the Glenmore National Centre in the Cairngorms (spreading to other outdoor centres) concluded with an assessment of candidates and the grant (or otherwise) of a mountain leadership certificate. Provision was made for a winter certificate of higher standard, and later for mountain instructor's certificates. The courses had a valuable effect at a time when hill-walking was becoming an extension of physical training at schools. The 'leadership' certificate was much criticized by mountaineers on one count: that it vouched for knowledge of safe method but not of leadership qualities, in which respect it was misnamed and misleading.

In the later 'sixties, county education authorities established numerous outdoor training and adventure centres in the Highlands. Like Glenmore Centre they provided a range of courses for children and adults in hill-walking, elementary rock and snow climbing, skiing, sailing, and canoeing. Glenmore has been outstanding for the very high quality of instruction given in mountaineering, winter survival, and rescue techniques.

Clubs: The clubs proliferated. Their expansion not in size but in number was most beneficial, for the most appreciated merit of the club system in Scotland has been the more intimate companionship that clubs give. From that has sprung the whole development of mountaineering. Mass instruction at schools had a real but strictly limited value; for any continuing progress in mountaincraft and performance and techniques depends on the opportunity for pro-longed learning-by-example among friends, while climbing when and where they choose. The clubs in providing these opportunities for team-forming, individual initiative, and the exchange of ideas, have become mountaineering's essential backbone – a framework on which tradition and development naturally hang and grow.

An important element in all climbing development has been the dissemination of information through the *Journal* of the SMC and through the club's twenty-three volumes of district and rock-climbing guides.

Winter. These ten winters produced 233 new climbs in all parts of the Highlands with further advances in technique and standards. In the early years, three grade 5 ice-climbs, which had defeated previous attacks, were made on Creag Meaghaidh: the North Post (1500 feet) by Patey, the South Post Direct (1200 feet) by Mac-Eacheran and Knight, and the Centre Post Direct (1500 feet) by Brian Robertson, Cairn, and Harper. The outstanding climbs on Ben Nevis were the Orion Face Direct (1500 feet), Gardyloo Buttress, and Minus Three Gully, all by Robin Smith and Marshall; in the Cairngorms, Djibangi (500 feet) by McArtney and Barclay, and Talisman (500 feet) by Grassick and Light, both in Coire Etchachan.

An historic event came in February 1965: the first winter traverse of the Cuillin main ridge by two ropes – Patey with Brian Robertson, and MacInnes with David Crabbe. They enjoyed perfect snow-ice conditions and spent two days on the ridge.

In the second half of the decade numerous good climbs were again made on Creag Meaghaidh. Three grade 5 climbs were done by the Dundee climbers – Ritchie's Gully Direct (500 feet) by Hunter and Quinn; The Wand (700 feet) by Crichton, Hunter, Lang, and Quinn, and The Pumpkin (1000 feet) by R. McMillan, G. Peet, and Quinn. In 1969, his last year, Tom Patey made his solo crab-crawl on Creag Meaghaidh, an 8000-foot girdle traverse grade 3–4, in the astonishing time of five hours. More important was his discovery of the winter climbing opportunities on Ladhar Bheinn, where he climbed Viking Gully (1200 feet), and reported that winter possibilities there were as numerous as Creag Meaghaidh's. Meantime, an enormous number of new climbs were being made in the Northern Highlands. In the Cairngorms, Cunningham and W. March were responsible for a large number of routes, of which the best was The Chancer (300 feet) on Hell's Lum Crag, for which they used a front-point technique with daggers. On Lochnagar, Rennie and Keir climbed Tough-Brown Direct (600 feet), and Grassick, Light, and Nicol climbed Pinnacle Face (550 feet). Again, all these were grade 5 routes. The extraordinarily high standard of ice-climbing now prevalent is best illustrated by the fact that by 1965 Point Five and Zero Gullies were being regularly climbed in 8 to 10 hours.

Practice: Hiduminium-shafted ice-axes and hammers were designed and produced in Glen Coe by Hamish MacInnes and were much stronger than wood-shafted axes. The ice-axe belay on steep snow had always been a doubtful safeguard. If wood it could snap, but if metal, be plucked out. A new belay-tool for snow called a 'deadman' was introduced (from the Antarctic) in the later 'sixties. This was a flat alloy plate with a wire sling. Driven into snow at an angle of 40 degrees to the slope it proved most effective.

On ice, the main contributory factor in faster climbs was the development of crampon techniques. Traditional practice had found no way around the need to cut hand and foot holds on steep ice, which was slow and tiring however skilful. Therefore, to gain speed lobster-claws with front spikes angled down and kept sharp had been brought in from Europe in the 'fifties, and improved in the 'sixties by increase of the claws to twelve. They allowed one to climb steep ice on the front points only, as exemplified in the good times made around 1965 in Point Five and Zero Gullies, but to the end of the decade and beyond much time had still to be spent in cutting handholds. This curtailment of front-pointing was countered by a widely adopted method, of which Tom Patey and Hamish MacInnes were pioneers, of front-pointing with aid of two short axes, relying on the driven picks for hold, or at higher angles for balance. It was only a partial solution, for there was a limit to the angle at which picks could thus be used without pulling out. MacInnes from 1965 tried to find the answer by designing a special drop-head axe, but without as yet finding the best angle for the pick. As early as 1937 Dr J. H. B. Bell had used pitons as hand-daggers to save cutting holds on an icy traverse in the Centre Post of Coire Ardair. Such primitive tools were replaced with heavier daggers made with handles. The climber could better drive them into ice above his head and move up a step or two very quickly. But this dagger technique made a big demand on his confidence even if he took protection from screw-in pitons (safer in ice than other types). The method had been used successfully, for example by Cunningham and March on The Chancer in 1970, but neither daggers nor twin axes were yet providing the answer: they were far too precarious at high angles.

1970–1975

Winter

Practice: An impasse had been reached. It was overcome by a unique team-effort of Cunningham, the American Yvon Chouinard, and MacInnes. Two pairs of revolutionary tools were devised and made. The first, by Chouinard, were a hammer and axe with down-curved picks; the second, by MacInnes, were a hammer and axe with straight picks inclined sharply down (55° to the shaft) and called Terrordactyls (from their pterodactyl shape). All four hooked into the ice and held it so well that weight could be put on them. The shafts were now the handholds, so the wrist-strain of gripping them had to be eased by reintroduction of wrist-loops (like ski-stick loops). The theory was simple: drive in the picks above, front-point up to them till they came to shoulder-level, and repeat. In fact, long-drawn experiment and practice, in which Cunningham, Chouinard, and MacInnes were all involved, were required to evolve the tools and technique. In climbing, the foot had to be given a decisive kick-in but not moved thereafter; the heel could not be raised or dropped without dire consequence, and so on. The curved Chouinards could be troublesome to extract if driven too hard, but the Terrordactyls, which were easier to extract, could even support the climber if he clipped to the hole in the shaft and let his arms drop while he leaned back and rested. Some time elapsed before the tools and exacting technique were accepted. That they were, was largely due to the work of Cunningham and March in proving them on long, fast ascents from 1971 onwards. Their demonstrations both on ice and in print finally converted the Scottish icemen. Most of them today do not carry a conventional ice-axe at all; they use adze and hammer Terrordactyls. The rope carried for two climbers on a big route may be two lengths of 200-foot nylon ($1\frac{1}{4}$-inch circumference) used double.

Recent routes: From 1970 there had been a marked falling off in climbing in Glen Coe due to successive mild winters, which were now too rarely providing the good conditions that had encouraged the revival of ice-climbing in the 'thirties. In the west, Creag Meaghaidh and Ben Nevis drew most of the action – a good winter's day can now be enough to bring two or three hundred climbers on to either mountain. Excellent routes were made in the Cairngorms: Bower Buttress (350 feet) on Creag an Dubh Loch by Bower and Simpson; Bugaboo Rib on Braeriach (500 feet) by Strange and Findlay; and the Winter Face (750 feet) of Black Spout Pinnacle by Quinn and Lang. On Ben Nevis, Astronomy on the Orion Face was climbed by Fyffe, MacInnes, and Spence; Slav Route (1480 feet) by Lang and Quinn, a feature of their ascent being the use of a long rope for repeated run-outs of up to 190 feet to save belays in taking stances; Minus One Gully (1000 feet) by K. V. Crocket and C. Stead – the last of the great gully climbs on Nevis; and Minus Two Buttress (900 feet) by B. Dunn, C. Higgins, and D. McArthur. These were some of the hardest routes among a multitude of good climbs. There had been a heavy production of the more useful grade 4 routes, where most hard climbing is done, and a turning from gullies to the formidable mixed climbs on the big buttresses. This trend had been accelerated by the demonstration of front-point technique in Point Five Gully, which Cunningham and March climbed in 1971 in $2\frac{3}{4}$ hours. More astonishing was the performance given in 1973 by Ian Nicholson, who finding the rare perfect conditions climbed solo both Zero and Point Five Gullies in 3 hours. Using a Terrordactyl and a Chouinard hammer, he achieved rhythm of movement and found steepness no problem up to the vertical. The excellence of the new equipment was now beyond dispute, and the move to the harder buttress faces where the most varied skills are required is certain to continue.

Other effects of the technique are to make winter climbing more comfortable by removing much hard work and long waits at belays; to bring the big climbs within the scope of many more climbers; and to alter grades. The Douglas Gully terminal wall, for example, is becoming almost a commonplace climb on front-points. Most of the high standard rock routes, like Eagle Ridge and Mitre Ridge, retain their winter calibre as they are not susceptible to front-pointing, and the Pinnacle Face of Lochnagar has only twice been climbed. It remains to be seen to what further use Terrordactyls may be put. While mainly for pure ice, they are versatile, and can be used on ridge and buttress climbs to hook on to nicks, whether on a mere pocket of ice or in rock. The climber can then clip on a sling or *étrier* and stand on it. The tool can be jammed in cracks or driven into a little runnel of ice, providing good hold where almost none had existed. These extensions of use have not been fully exploited at the time of writing, and already MacInnes is devising improvements both to lobster-claws and the Terrordactyl.

Ever since the late 'thirties, the notion that any route climbed in summer could be done in winter has gained ground. It has been fully realized on Lochnagar, where rock at all angles can sometimes be so well coated in frozen snow that any route can be made to go, but elsewhere remains an ideal. On Ben Nevis, Carn Dearg Buttress has not yielded up its wintry heart; there will be no shortage of other great climbs awaiting icemen.

11 The Development of Scottish Skiing

Nordic and Alpine Origins

Scottish skiing began in 1890 as a direct introduction from Norway. As a means of transport on level and upland ground, skiing had flourished in Scandinavia over the previous 5,000 years. It had developed as a sport in Norway only from the middle of the nineteenth century, and then not on mountains but as cross-country racing. Since time was gained or lost across country on the soft snow of flat and uphill ground, the refinement of technique had been concentrated on that, not on downhill running on hard snow. Thus when central Europeans made their first attempts to ski on steep Alpine slopes in the 1880s, they had problems to solve. The Nordic turns were the telemark (a one-foot steered turn with all weight on the leading ski) suitable only for deep soft snow, and the christiania (a swing turn with skis held near to parallel) of which little was known. The Alpine pioneers had to find a way of traversing steep mountain slopes using the ski-edges in a series of descending curves across the fall line. The method was found and evolved by Matthias Zdarsky, the Austrian father of mountain skiing. He developed the stemming turn (snow plough) from 1895, using a long bamboo pole not only to aid the turn, but to brake. This marked the first departure from Nordic skiing.

Zdarsky's slow and clumsy stem-turns were much criticized. The followers of Nordic methods appealled for straighter running and a return to a freer style by the abandonment of sticks for turning and braking. His answer was the stem-christiania, which started as a stem and ended as a christiania. The turn was adopted everywhere from 1910, when Alpine skiing finally broke with original Nordic and developed its own technique and equipment. The stem-christiania demanded a firm binding of boot to ski, and Zdarsky had already invented steel cables and toe-caps. The turn's principle of weight-shift and body-swing became the basis of later developments in racing turns, such as parallel christiania (middle 'thirties) and wedeling (short linked swings down the fall line).

1890–1914

The earliest Scottish skiers were mountaineers and mostly members of the Scottish Mountaineering Club. All were brought up in the Nordic tradition. Their imagination had been fired by the publication of Nansen's *First Crossing of Greenland* (1890). W. W. Naismith began practising skiing in the Campsies in 1890–2; Harold Raeburn used ski in 1892 while climbing in Norway, and several other members of the club were experimenting. Raeburn was not impressed. He could move faster on foot with far less trouble. The early Scots skiers saw ski as a means of travel rather than upright tobogganing. Their goal was ski-touring, which appealed to men who wanted to get off the beaten track – like Fridtjof Nansen. Ski were of ash, plane, or pine, 7 feet long and narrow with thong bindings. They were not thought suitable for steep-sided mountains, and Zdarsky's Alpine work was not appreciated.

In 1904 W. Rickmer-Rickmers, an evangelist for the Alpine school, came to the SMC's Easter meet on Ben Nevis and tried to convert members. He presented twelve pairs of ski to the club, designed by Zdarsky. Harry MacRobert (introduced to skiing on the Pentlands by Raeburn) reported: 'They were short, rigid, and heavy, and the metal soleplate hinged at the toe was controlled by a powerful steel spring. The idea was that short ski were essential for steep mountain slopes.' But the style was so slow and clumsy that members were neither enamoured nor wholly convinced. They persisted with long ski while accepting the stem. All skiing was then on soft snow, which except after a snowfall was not the usual condition on Scottish mountains. No Scots could ski as they do today. They could run fast and straight, and achieve a telemark or a stem turn, but hard snow technique was unknown.

The first Alpine ski clubs had formed from 1890, and the Ski Club of Great Britain in 1903. In 1907 Scottish mountaineers played a prominent part in founding the Scottish Ski Club. Its hundred members continued in the Nordic tradition that ski were for travel over snow-clad country. Nansen was their first honorary member. From 1909 to 1914, mountaineers were taking their ski to club meets on Ben Nevis, the Monadh Liath, the Drumochter and Tyndrum hills, and especially in the Cairngorms, where skiers included Dr A. M. Kellas, J. A. Parker, Sir Henry Alexander, MacRobert, Naismith, and Raeburn. At the SMC meet at Aviemore in 1913, one party crossed Cairn Gorm and Macdhui to Glen Derry and returned

233

over Carn Ban and Sgoran Dubh – 40-odd miles in 2 days. The Scottish skiers, using waxes or sealskins for cross-country work, now went over fairly steep slopes, down which, with aid of sticks and stemming, they were able to run slowly even over hard crust. More attention was paid to technique, and Naismith prophesied: 'In the Alps, it is not unlikely that the sport may eventually become popular.'

In the Alps the free Nordic style, in which turns and swings were made without aid of a big stick, returned around 1910 but adapted to Alpine conditions by evolution of the stem-christiania. The change in style and outlook greatly favoured the development of skiing in Scotland, where hard-packed and icy snow of all kinds was common. The Scottish Ski Club membership had doubled by 1914. But for the war, skiing would now have made swift progress. Instead, like climbing, it died.

1920–1939

Any enthusiasm that survived the war was damped by a 10-year succession of snowless winters. Raeburn wrote gloomily in 1920: 'It is unfortunate that the long snow-skates are so heavy and clumsy, else they would be more useful . . . snow conditions will always prevent us from becoming really expert at home. . . . Even on the highest hills conditions are usually bad. . . . Then by April the mountain snow-line has already run up to 2,000 feet or higher. To carry a pair of long, heavy planks several miles to an altitude from 2,000 to 3,000 feet above our hotel is likely to prove too exhausting for the enthusiasm of most. Some do this. They are occasionally rewarded by some very fine running.'

The enthusiasts were too few at first to re-found the Ski Club, but the huge development of the sport in Switzerland slowly provided a potential membership. Its revival came in 1929, for which members of the SMC were largely responsible (supplying the first president, secretary, and treasurer). A succession of good snow years providentially followed. The sport for the first time grew popular. This was attributable to the motor-car, improved roads, and the rise in standard on hard snow, to which the introduction of steel-edges greatly contributed in the early 'thirties. The popular resort was Ben Lawers, where the Lochan na Lairige road crossed the pass to Glen Lyon at 1,800 feet. This became the centre of the club's activities. A hut was built in the corrie at 2,500 feet between Beinn Ghlas and Meall Corranaich. Everyone who had not already mastered the stem-christiania was learning it, and each winter week-end skiers were out on the Pentlands, Campsies, Braes of Angus, and Lochaber, or at Bridge of Orchy, Dalwhinnie, Glen Shee, Braemar, and Aviemore. A few mountaineers favoured Meall a' Bhuiridh. With new skills and equipment, skiers were able to enjoy the best conditions, when the April snow high up had became hard *névé*.

1940–1960

During the second war, many Scottish skiers and climbers continued or learned to ski in Canada, the Lebanon, and Scotland while serving with the mountain commandos. After the war, an infectious enthusiasm for the sport spread. Wooden ski with flexible bindings and boots were still used, and with these the skier had wide choice of movement, to climb uphill, tour the plateaux, walk, or concentrate on the pistes. But the scene was changing. To pack in practice – and more exhilaration in less time – tows powered by small engines were installed on Lawers and then on the Cairngorms above Glen Clunie and the Spittal of Glenshee. In 1956 the first permanent uplift was built by the Scottish Ski Club on the north face of Meall a' Bhuiridh, Glen Coe. This was taken over by the White Corries Company, who added a chairlift and improved tows. Similar developments followed in the north corries of Cairn Gorm and Glen Shee, with full supporting facilities: access roads, hill-chalets, snack-bars, ski-schools, equipment-hire, and hotels providing *après ski* entertainment. Skiing in the 'sixties became big business, and developments on the ground no longer dependent on clubs, but promoted by development companies, local government authorities, the Sports Council, the Scottish Tourist Board, and the Highlands and Islands Development Board. The latter bought Cairn Gorm.

Alpine techniques and downhill-only skiing prevailed on the beaten pistes; high racing standards were achieved; and while the technique was appropriate to Scottish snow-conditions, the developments brought in equipment specially designed for speed but inappropriate for touring – like rigid boots and ski soled with plastic, metal, or fibreglass. Laminated ski (invented by the Norwegians) and safety bindings were most valuable innovations, but piste-boots and bindings limited the downhill skier to the piste. Few are now able to ski on soft snow, but all on hard, which they prefer for they learn on it and their turns are made for it – the reverse of the original position. At Easter 1975, fifteen thousand skiers visited the

Cairngorms. Aviemore captured two-thirds. The development of other centres, such as Aonach Mor in Lochaber or Ben Wyvis in Cromarty, appears imminent.

Some mountaineers, those who, like the early skiers, want to get off the beaten track, have come to think of downhill-only as a folly of the tourist industry, grossly expensive, plagued by crowds and clatter and technical fetish; but they and a few others (beginning to grow in number) have learned to make the best of both worlds: the narrow piste for its thrill of speed; the open plateau for its many-sided demands on awareness – an ever-changing surface under the ski; the sense of possession of a white wilderness, utterly remote from city-civilization; route-finding; the freedom of an indefinite land-space and sky; and silence. They use for touring light and flexible ski with loose bindings that leave the heels free to move up and down. They can still ski in the Nordic style, use skins or waxes for climbing, and travel far through the hills from Clova and Mar to Drumochter, or from Strathspey to the Derry burn.

Bibliography

Topography and Geology: Chapters 1 and 2
1865 Geikie, A., *Scenery of Scotland*
1897 Geikie, A., *Geology*
1928 Tyrrell, G. W., *Geology of Arran*
1941 Harker, A., *The West Highlands and Hebrides*
1948 Phemister, J., 'The Northern Highlands', *British Regional Geology*
1952 Meteorological Office, *Climatological Atlas*
1956 Charlesworth, J. D., 'Later Glacial History of the Highlands', *Trans. R.S.E.*, vol. LXII, part iii, No. 19, 1954–5.
1964 Bullard, E. C., 'Continental Drift', *Journal of the Geological Society*, London, No. 120
1964 Richey, J. E., *Scotland: The Tertiary Volcanic Districts*
1965 Craig, G. E., ed., *Geology of Scotland*
1967 Sissons, J. B., *The Evolution of Scotland's Scenery*
1968 Hurley, P. M., *Confirmation of Continental Drift*
1972 Mintz, L. W., *Historical Geology* (Plate Tectonics)
1973 Murray, W. H., *The Islands of Western Scotland*
1974 Nethersole-Thompson, D., and Watson, A., *The Cairngorms: Their Natural History and Scenery*

Colonization by Plant and Animal Life: Chapter 3
1888 Harvey-Brown and Buckley, *Vertebrate Fauna of Scotland*
1945 Ford, E. G., *Butterflies*, revised 1957
1952 Manley, Gordon, *Climate and the British Scene*
1956 Durnie, S. E., 'Pollen Analysis of Peat Deposits', *Scot. Geog. Mag.*, May 1972
1962 McVean, D. N., and Ratcliffe, D. A., 'Plant Communities of the Scottish Highlands', *Monograph* of the *Nature Conservancy*
1962 Brown, P., and Waterston, G., *The Return of the Osprey*
1964 National Trust for Scotland, *Ben Lawers and its Alpine Flowers*
1964 McVean, D., 'Prehistory and Ecological History', in *Vegetation of Scotland*

1964   Smith, Malcolm, *British Amphibians and Reptiles*
1964   Stephen, David, *Scottish Wild Life*
1966   Lamb, H. H., *Changing Climate*
1967   Fitter, R., *Penguin Directory of British Natural History*
1967   Rayner, D. H., *The Stratigraphy of the British Isles*
1968   Matthews, Harrison, *British Mammals*
1969   Darling, J. Fraser, and Boyd, J. Morton, *The Highlands and Islands*
1969   Fitter, R., ed., *Book of British Birds*
1972   Ford, E. B., *Moths* (3rd edn.)
1973   Murray, W. H., *The Islands of Western Scotland*
1974   Ratcliffe, D. A., 'The Vegetation', in *The Cairngorms*

Man in the Highlands: Chapter 4

i. Prehistory:

c. 685   Adomnan, *Life of St Columba*, ed. A. O. Anderson and M. O. Anderson, 1961
1856–7   Stuart, John, ed., 'The Ancient Sculptured Stones of Scotland', *The Spalding Club*
1876–80   Skene, W. F., *Celtic Scotland*, 3 vols.
1881   Drummond, J., 'Sculptured Stones of Iona and the West Highlands', *Soc. of Antiq. of Scot.*
1903   Allen, J. Romilly, *Early Christian Monuments of Scotland*
1928   Royal Commission on Ancient and Historical Monuments, *The Outer Hebrides, Skye, and the Small Isles*
1935   Childe, V. Gordon, *The Prehistory of Scotland*
1940   Simpson, W. D., *St Ninian and the Origins of the Christian Church in Scotland*
1946   Childe, V. Gordon, *Scotland before the Scots*
1949   Piggott, Stuart, *British Prehistory*
1954   Lacaille, A. D., *The Stone Age in Scotland*
1954   Wainwright, F. T., *The Problem of the Picts*
1957   Dibby, G., *Testimony of the Spade*
1958   Piggott, Stuart, *Scotland before History*
1962   Piggott, Stuart, ed., *The Prehistoric Peoples of Scotland*
1963   Henshall, Audrey S., *The Chambered Tombs of Scotland*, vol. 1
1963   Feachem, R. W., *A Guide to Prehistoric Scotland*
1964–70   Domhnull Gruamach, *The Foundations of Islay*, 2 vols., Graham Donald, Islay

1964   Mackie, Euan W., 'Monamore Neolithic Cairn, Arran', in *Antiquity*, March 1964
1965   Mackie, Euan W., 'Brochs and the Hebridean Iron Age', in *Antiquity*, 39
1965   Mackie, Euan W., 'Dun Mor Vaul Broch', *Antiquity*, December
1965   Mackie, Euan W., 'The origin and development of the broch and wheelhouse building cultures of the Scottish Iron Age', *Proc. Prehist. Soc.*, xxxi
1966   Rivet, A. L. F., ed., *The Iron Age in Northern Britain*
1967   Henderson, Isobel, *The Picts*
1967   Thom, A., *Megalithic Sites in Britain*
1968   Thom, A., 'Cup and Ring Marks', in *Systematics*, VI, 173
1969   Case, Humphrey, 'Neolithic Explanations', in *Antiquity*, XLIII, 171
1969   Mackie, Euan W., 'The Historical Context of the Origin of the Brochs', *Scot. Arch. Forum*
1970   Mackie, Euan W., 'The Scottish Iron Age', in *Scot. Hist. Review*, XLIX, 147
1972   Henshall, Audrey S., *The Chambered Tombs of Scotland*, vol. 2 (The Hebrides)

ii. Historical and General:

1549   Monro, Donald, *A Description of the Western Islands*
1582   Buchanan, George, *Rerum Scoticarum Historia*, 4 vols., trans. James Aikman, 1827
1695   Martin Martin, *Description of the Western Islands*
1754   Burt, Captain, *Burt's Letters from the North of Scotland*, reprint 1974
1746–75   Forbes, Robert, *The Lyon in Mourning*, Sc. Hist. Soc., 3 vols., 1894–96, ed. Henry Paton
1755   Webster, A., *An account of the number of people in Scotland in 1755*, Nat. Lib., Edin.
1771–5   Pennent, T., *A Tour in Scotland and the Western Isles*, 3 vols.
1775   Johnson, Samuel, *Journey to the Western Islands of Scotland*
1782   Flategan and Frisian MSS, *Haco's Expedition against Scotland, 1263*
1785   Boswell, James, *A Journal of a Tour to the Hebrides with Samuel Johnson*

1787   Knox, John, *A Tour through the Highlands and the Hebride Isles in 1776*
1791-8   Sinclair, John, *The Statistical Account of Scotland*, 21 vols.
1793   Statistical Account of Scotland, *Argyll, Inverness, Ross and Cromarty, Sutherland*
1800   Garnett, T., *Tour through the Highlands*
1808   Walker, J., *An Economic History of the Hebrides and Highlands*
1819   MacCulloch, J., *Description of the Western Islands*
1824   MacCulloch, J., *Highlands and Western Islands*, 4 vols.
1826   Sinclair, John, *Analysis of the Statistical Account of Scotland*
1827   Chalmers, Robert, *Picture of Scotland*
1831   Logan, James, *The Scottish Gael*
1845   New Statistical Account of Scotland
1850   Anderson, *Guide to the Highlands and Islands*
1856   Ross, Donald, *Letters on the Depopulation of the Highlands*
1857   MacLeod, Donald, *Gloomy Memories in the Highlands*
1857   Reeves, William, ed., *Adomnan's Life of St Columba*
1867   Skene, W. F., *Chronicles of the Picts and Scots*
1874   Miller, Hugh, *Cruise of the Betsy, 1846*
1876-80   Skene, W. F., *Celtic Scotland*, 3 vols.
1881   Gregory, D., *History of the Western Highlands and Isles*
1884   Royal Commission, *Report on the Highlands and Islands; and Evidence taken by H.M. Commissioners of Inquiry into the condition of crofters and cottars in the Highlands and Islands, 1883*, 5 vols.
1887   Hennessy, W. M., ed., *The Annals of Ulster*
1887-92   MacGibbon, David, and Ross, T., *The Castellated and Domestic Architecture of Scotland*, 5 vols.
1895-7   Stokes, W., ed., *The Annals of Tigernach*
1896   MacGibbon and Ross, *The Ecclesiastical Architecture of Scotland*, 3 vols.
1897   MacDonald, David, 'The National Dress', *Celtic Monthly*, vol. 5 No. 9
1897   Fraser, J. A. Lovat, 'The Highland Chief', *Celtic Monthly*, vol. 5 No. 4
1906   Mackenzie, W. C., *A Short History of the Scottish Highlands*
1909   Brown, P. Hume, *History of Scotland*, 3 vols.
1910   Henderson, G., *The Norse Influence on Celtic Scotland*
1916   Mackenzie, W. C., *Races of Ireland and Scotland*
1920   Ritchie, J., *The Influence of Man on the Animal Life of Scotland*

1922 Anderson, J. G. C., ed., *Tacitus: Agricola*
1924 MacBain, Alexander, *Place-names of the Highlands and Islands*
1925 Press, M. A. C., *Laxdaela Saga*
1926 Watson, W. J., *History of the Celtic Place Names of Scotland*
1929 Kellett, E. E., ed., *Northern Saga*
1930 Nicolson, A., *History of Skye*
1932 Laing, S., ed., *Heimskringla* (The Norse King Saga)
1935 Jones, G., ed., *Four Icelandic Sagas*
1938 MacLeod of MacLeod, *The Book of Dunvegan, 1340-1920*, 2 vols., Spalding Club, Aberdeen.
1943 McClintock, H. F., *Old Irish and Highland Dress*
1949 Dwelly, Edward, *Illustrated Gaelic Dictionary* (superior to all others in recording 100,000 words with more meanings including the obsolete)
1949 Salaman, R. W., *The Social Influence of the Potato*
1952 Grant, I. F., *The Clan Donald*
1952 Haldane, A. R. B., *The Drove Roads of Scotland*
1955 Darling, J. Fraser, *West Highland Survey*
1957 Dasent, G. W., *Njal's Saga* (*c.* 1250)
1957 Jirlow, R., and Whitaker, I., 'The Plough in Scotland' *Scot. Studies*, vol. 1, Univ. of Edin.
1959 Simpson, W. Douglas, *Scottish Castles*
1961 Arbman, Holger, *The Vikings*, trans. A. Binns
1962 Haldane, A. R. B., *New Ways Through the Glens*
1963 Cruden, Stewart, *The Scottish Castle*
1963 Prebble, John, *The Highland Clearances*
1964 Domhnull Gruamach, *Foundations of Islay*, vol. 1, Graham Donald, Isle of Islay
1964 Richardson, James, *The Medieval Stone Carver in Scotland*
1964 Third Statistical Account, *Argyll*
1965-75 Highlands and Islands Development Board, *Annual Reports*, Nos. 1-10
1966 Murray, W. H., *The Hebrides*
1967 Moncrieffe of that Ilk, *The Highland Clans*
1968 Crofters Commission, *Recommendations for the Modernizing of Crofting*, Report to the Sec. of State
1968 Thomson, D., and Grimble, I., eds., *The Future of the Highlands*
1969 Highlands and Islands Development Board, *Development of Fisheries*, Special Report No. 2

1970   Glen, I. A., 'Illicit Stills', *Scot. Studies*, vol. 14
1972   Greig, M. A., *A Study of economic impact of the HIDB's investment in Fisheries*, HIDB
1972   Russell, W., *In Great Waters*, HIDB, Special Report No. 7 on Fisheries
1973   Murray, W. H., *The Islands of Western Scotland*

The Highland Districts and Mountains: Chapters 5 to 11

Scottish Mountaineering Club Guides. Publication dates are not quoted since these guides are in constant course of revision.

Andrew, K. M., and Thrippleton, A. A., *Southern Uplands*
Bennet, D. J., *Southern Highlands*
Steven, C., *Central Highlands*
Watson, A., *Cairngorms*
Johnstone, G., Scott, *Western Highlands*
Strang, T., *Northern Highlands*
Slesser, C. G. M., *Island of Skye*
Tennent, N. S., *Islands of Scotland*
Donaldson, J. C., *Munro's Tables*

Rock Climbing Guides
Johnstone, J. M., *Arran*
Houston, J. R., *Arrochar*
Marshall, J. R., *Ben Nevis*
March, W., *Cairngorms*, vol. I, *Loch Avon and the North Corries*
Strange, G. S., *Cairngorms*, vol. II, *Ben Macdhui, Coire Etchachan, and Beinn a' Bhuird*
Fyffe, A., *Cairgorms*, vol. V, *Creag an Dubh Loch, Glen Clova*
Fyffe, A., *Cairngorms*, vols. III and IV in preparation
Simpson, J. W., *Cuillin of Skye*, vol. I, *Glenbrittle*; vol. II, *Coir' Uisg, Sgurr nan Gillean, Blaven*
Lovat, L. S., *Glencoe and Ardgour*, vol. I, *Buachaille Etive Mor*; vol. II, *Glencoe, Beinn Trilleachan, Garbh Bheinn*
Rowe, I. G., *Northern Highlands*, vol. I, *Letterewe, Easter Ross*
Turnbull, D. G., *Northern Highlands*, vol. II, *Torridon, Applecross, Achnasheen*
1890–1975   Scottish Mountaineering Club, *Journals*, 30 vols.
1908   Abraham, A. P., *Rock Climbing in Skye*
1920   Young, G. Winthrop, *Mountain Craft*
1920   Raeburn, H., *Mountaineering Art*

1923 Baker, E. A., *The Highlands with Rope and Rucksack*
1928 Alexander, H., *The Cairngorms*, SMC
1933 Scottish Mountaineering Club, *General Guide*
1939 Borthwick, A., *Always a Little Further*, 3rd edn. 1969
1947 Murray, W. H., *Mountaineering in Scotland*
1950 Bell, J. H. B., *A Progress in Mountaineering*
1951 Murray, W. H., *Undiscovered Scotland*
1952 Humble, B. H., *The Cuillin of Skye*
1957 Clark, R. W., and Pyatt, E. C., *Mountaineering in Britain*
1966 Milne, M., and Heller, Mark, *Book of European Skiing*
1966 Murray, W. H., *The Hebrides*
1968 Murray, W. H., *Companion Guide to the West Highlands*, 5th
      edn., 1973
1968 R.A.F., *Mountain Rescue* (Training handbook), HMSO
1970 Blackshaw, Alan, *Mountaineering*
1970 Slesser, C. G. M., *Scottish Mountains on Ski*
1971 Patey, Tom, *One Man's Mountains*
1971 Penberthy, L., 'Equipment and Technique', in *Alpine Journal*,
      77, No. 321
1972 Cunningham, J., and March, W., 'New Ice Climbing Tech-
      niques', in *Alpine Journal*, 77, No. 321
1973 Langmuir, Fric, *Mountain Leadership*, Scot. Sports Council
1973 MacInnes, H., *Call Out*
1975 Cleare, John, *Mountains*, chap. 4

Magazines:
Mountain, Mountain Magazines Ltd.
Climber & Rambler, Holmes, MacDougall Ltd.

Appendices

1   LIST OF MUNROS

The list of Munros that follow should not be confused with Munro's Tables, which are separately published and list not only the 279 mountains of 3,000 feet and above, but also their 3,000-foot tops, both in order of district (with map references to each) and in order of height.

Since the first publication of Munro's Tables in 1891, they have been periodically revised by the SMC as new information and new methods of survey gave need. The latest revision by J. C. Donaldson was published in 1974. He gives metric as well as foot heights to take account of the Ordnance Survey's change to metric maps, which have now been issued. Foot heights have been taken from the latest 6-inch and 1-inch maps. The O.S. heights in these two series frequently differ, giving rise to apparent anomalies in conversion. In the list of Munros given below, heights marked M are taken from metric maps; marked * are from the nearest contour-line; marked + are conversions from 6-inch maps; and those unmarked are conversions from 1-inch maps. This new list gives 282 Munros.

Southern Highlands

	feet	metres
Ben Lomond	3192	974 M
Ben Narnain	3036	926 M
Beinn Ime	3318	1011 M
Ben Vane	3004	916 M
Beinn an Lochain	3021	920
Ben Vorlich, Loch Lomond	3092	943 M
Beinn Bhuidhe	3106	948 M
Beinn a' Chleibh	3008	917 M
Ben Lui (Laoigh)	3708	1130 M
Ben Oss	3374	1028 M
Beinn Dubhchraig	3204	977 M
Beinn Chabhair	3053	931 M
An Caisteal	3265	995 M
Beinn a' Chroin	3104	946 M

	feet	metres
Beinn Tulaichean	3099	945 M
Cruach Ardrain	3428	1045 M
Ben More	3843	1174 M
Stob Binnein (Am Binnein)	3821	1165 M
Ben Vorlich, Loch Earn	3231	985 M
Stuc a' Chroin	3189	972 M
Ben Chonzie	3048	929 M
Schichallion	3547	1083 M
Carn Mairg	3419	1042 M
Creag Mhor	3100*	975 +
Meall Garbh	3150*	975 +
Carn Gorm	3370	1029 M
Ben Lawers Range		
Ben Lawers	3984	1214 M
Meall Greigh	3280	999
Meall Garbh	3661	1116
Bheinn Ghlas	3700*	1118 +
Meall Corranaich	3450*	1076 +
Meall a' Choire Leith	3033	924 M
Meall nan Tarmachan	3421	1043 M
Meall Ghaordie	3410	1039 M
Stuchd an Lochain	3144	958 M
Meall Buidhe	3054	931 M
Beinn Heasgarnich	3530	1076 M
Creag Mhor	3387	1032 M
Beinn Chaluim	3354	1025 M
Meall Glas	3139	957 M
Sgiath Chuil	3000*	919 +
Beinn Dorain	3524	1074 M
Beinn an Dothaidh	3267	996 M
Beinn Achaladair	3404	1038 M
Beinn a' Chreachain	3540	1079 M
Beinn Mhanach	3125	953 M

Central Highlands

Cruachan Range		
Ben Cruachan	3695	1126 M
Stob Diamh	3272	997 M

	feet	metres
Beinn a' Chochuill	3215	980 M
Beinn Eunaich	3242	988 M
Beinn nan Aighenan	3141	957 M
Ben Starav	3541	1078 M
Glas Bheinn Mhor	3258	993 M
Stob Coir' an Albannaich	3425	1044 M
Meall nan Eun	3039	926 M
Stob Ghabhar	3565	1087 M
Stob a' Choire Odhair	3058	932 M
Meall a' Bhuiridh	3636	1108 M
Clach Leathad	3602	1098 M
Creise	3596	1100 M
Buachaille Etive Mor		
Stob Dearg	3345	1022 M
Buachaille Etive Beag		
Stob Dubh	3129	958 M
Bidean nam Bian	3766	1141 M
Sgor na h-Ulaidh	3258	994 M
Beinn Fhionnlaidh	3145	959 M
Beinn Sgulaird	3059	932 M
Beinn a' Bheithir		
Sgorr Dhearg	3361	1024 M
Sgorr Dhonuill	3284	1001 M
Aonach Eagach		
Sgor nam Fiannaidh	3173	967 M
Meall Dearg	3118	951 M
Sgurr Eilde Mor	3279	1008 M
Binnein Mor	3700	1128 M
Na Gruagaichean	3442	1055 M
Binnein Beag	3083	940 M
An Gearanach	3200*	985 M
Stob Coire a' Chairn	3219	983 M
Am Bodach	3382	1034 M
Sgurr a' Mhaim	3601	1098 M
Stob Ban	3274	999 M
Mullach nan Coirean	3077	939 M
Ben Nevis	4406	1344 M
Carn Mor Dearg	4012	1223 M

	feet	metres
Aonach Mor	3999	1219 M
Aonach Beag	4060	1236 M
Sgurr Choinnich Mor	3603	1095 M
Stob Coire an Laoigh	3650*	1115 M
Stob Choire Claurigh	3858	1177 M
Stob Ban, L. Treig Dist.	3217	977 M
Stob Coire Easain	3658	1116 M
Stob a' Choire Mheadhoin	3610	1106 M
Stob Coire Sgriodain	3211	976 +
Chno Dearg	3433	1047 M
Beinn na Lap	3066	937 M
Carn Dearg	3080	939 M
Sgor Gaibhre	3124	952 M
Beinn Eibhinn	3611	1101 M
Aonach Beag, Alder Dist.	3647	1112 M
Geal-Charn	3650*	1132 M
Carn Dearg	3391	1034 M
Beinn a' Chlachair	3569	1088 M
Creag Pitridh	3031	924 M
Mullach Coire an Iubhair	3443	1049 M
Ben Alder	3765	1148 M
Bheinn Bheoil	3333	1016 M
Sgairneach Mhor	3160	991 M
Beinn Udlamain	3306	1010 M
A' Mharconaich	3174	967 M
Geal Charn, L. Ericht	3005	916 M
Beinn a' Chaoruinn	3453	1053 +
Creag Meaghaidh Range		
Creag Meaghaidh	3700	1130 M
Stob Poite Coire Ardair	3460	1053 +
Carn Liath	3298	1006 M
Monadh Liath		
Carn Dearg	3093	945 M
Carn Ban	3087	942 M
Carn Ballach	3009	920 M
Carn Sgulain	3015	920 M
A' Chailleach	3045	930 M
Geal Charn	3036	926 M

	feet	*metres*
Cairngorms		
Meall Chuaich	3120	951 M
Carn na Caim	3087	941 M
A' Bhuidheanach Bheag	3064	936 M
Carn an Fhidleir or Carn Ealar	3276	994 M
An Sgarsoch	3300	1006 M
Beinn Dearg	3304	1008 M
Carn a' Chlamain	3159	963 M
Beinn a' Ghlo		
Carn nan Gabhar	3677	1121 M
Braigh Coire Chruinn-bhalgain	3505	1069 M
Carn Liath	3197	975 M
Glas Tulaichean	3449	1051 M
Carn an Righ	3377	1029 M
Beinn Iutharn Mhor	3424	1045 M
Carn Bhac	3098	946 M
An Socach	3059	944 M
Carn a' Gheoidh	3194	975 M
The Cairnwell	3059	933 M
Carn Aosda	3003	917 M
Glas Maol	3504	1068 M
Creag Leacach	3238	987 M
Cairn of Claise	3484	1064 M
Carn an Tuirc	3340	1019 M
Tom Buidhe	3140	957 M
Tolmount	3143	958 M
Cairn Bannoch	3314	1012 M
Broad Cairn	3268	998 M
Mayar	3043	928 M
Driesh	3108	947 M
Mount Keen	3077	939 M
Lochnagar	3789	1155 M
White Mounth	3650*	1110 M
Carn an t-Sagairt Mor	3430	1047 M
Ben Avon	3843	1171 M
Beinn a' Bhuird	3924	1196 M
Beinn Bhreac	3051	931 M
Beinn a' Chaorruinn	3553	1082 M

	feet	metres
Bynack More	3574	1090 M
A' Choinneach	3345	1017 M
Beinn Mheadhoin	3883	1182 M
Derry Cairngorm	3788	1155 M
Carn a' Mhaim	3402	1037 M
Ben Macdhui	4296	1309 M
Cairn Gorm	4084	1245 M
Braeriach	4248	1296 M
Cairn Toul	4241	1293 M
The Devil's Point	3303	1004 M
Beinn Bhrotain	3795	1157 M
Carn Cloich-mhuillin	3087	942 M
Monadh Mor	3651	1113 M
Mullach Clach a' Bhlair	3338	1019 M
Meall Dubhag	3268	998 M
Carn Ban Mor	3443	1052 M
Sgor Gaoith	3658	1118 M
Geal Charn	3019	920 M

West Highlands

	feet	metres
Sron a' Choire Ghairbh	3066	935 M
Meal na Teanga	3000*	917 M
Gaor Bheinn or Gulvain	3244	987 M
Sgurr Thuilm	3164	963 M
Sgurr nan Coireachan	3136	956 M
Sgurr na Ciche	3410	1040 M
Sgurr nan Coireachan, G. Dessary	3125	935 M
Sgurr Mor	3290	1003 M
Gairich	3015	919 M
Meall Buidhe	3107	946 M
Luinne Bheinn	3083	939 M
Ladhar Bheinn	3343	1020 M
Ben Sgritheall (Sgriol)	3196	974 M
The Saddle	3314	1010 M
Sgurr na Sgine	3098	945 M
Sgurr a' Mhaoraich	3365	1027 M
Gleouraich	3395	1035 M
Spidean Mialach	3268	996 M

	feet	*metres*
Creag a' Mhaim	3102	947 M
Drum Shionnach	3200*	987 M
Maol Chinn-dearg		
Aonach air Chrith	3342	1021 M
Maol Chinn-dearg (w. top)	3214	981 M
Sgurr an Doire Leathain	3250*	1010
Sgurr an Lochain	3282	1004 M
Creag nan Damh	3012	918 M
Five Sisters or Beinn Mhor Range		
Sgurr Fhuaran	3505	1068 M
Sgurr na Ciste Duibhe	3370	1027 M
Saileag	3100*	959
Sgurr a' Bheilach Dheirg	3378	1031 M
Aonach Meadhoin	3250*	1003 M
Ciste Dubh	3218	982 M
Mullach Fraoch-choire	3614	1102 M
A' Chralaig	3673	1120 M
Tigh Mor na Seilge	3285	1002 M
Sgurr nan Conbhairean	3634	1110 M
Carn Ghluasaid	3140	957 M
A' Ghlas-bheinn	3006	918 M
Beinn Fhada (Ben Attow)	3385	1031 M
Sgurr nan Ceathreamhnan	3771	1151 M
Creag a' Choire Aird	3150*	978
An Socach	3017	920 M
Mam Sodhail	3862	1181 M
Carn Eige	3880	1183 M
Beinn Fhionnlaidh	3294	1005 M
Tom a' Choinich	3646	1111 M
Toll Creagach	3455	1053 M
Carn nan Gobhar	3251	992 M
Sgurr na Lapaich	3775	1150 M
An Riabhachan	3696	1129 M
An Socach	3508	1069 M
Sgurr na Ruaidhe	3254	993 M
Carn nan Gobhar	3251	991 M
Sgurr a' Choire Ghlais	3554	1083 M
Sgurr Fhuar-thuill	3439	1049 M

	feet	*metres*
Sgurr nan Ceinraichean	3004	915 M
Maoile Lunndaidh	3294	1007 M
Creag Toll a' Choin	3250*	1006 M
Sgurr a' Chaorachain	3455	1053 M
Sgurr Choinnich	3276	999 M
Bidein a' Choire Sheasgaich	3102	945 M
Lurg Mhor	3234	986 M
Moruisg	3026	928 M

Skye

The Cuillin

Bla' Bheinn (Blaven)	3044	928 M
Sgurr nan Gillean	3167	965 M
Am Basteir	3050*	936
Bruach na Frithe	3142	958 M
Sgurr a' Mhadaidh	3014	918
Sgurr a' Ghreadaidh	3197	973 M
Sgurr na Banachdich	3167	965 M
Sgurr Dearg	3254	986 M
Sgurr Mhic Choinnich	3107	948
Sgurr Alasdair	3257	993
Sgurr Dubh Mor	3089	944 M
Sgurr nan Eag	3037	923

Island of Mull

Ben More	3169	966

Northern Highlands

Maol Chean-dearg	3060	933 M
Sgorr Ruadh	3142	960 M
Beinn Liath Mhor	3034	925 M
Beinn Alligin	3232	985 M
Liathach	3456	1054 M
Beinn Eighe	3309	1010 M
Slioch	3217	980 M
A' Mhaighdean	3173	967 +
Beinn Tarsuinn	3070	936 +
Mullach Coire Mhic Fhearchair	3326	1019 M

	feet	metres
Sgurr Ban	3194	989 M
Ruadh Stac Mhor	3014	918 M
Beinn a' Chlaidheimh	3000*	914 M
An Teallach	3483	1062 M
Fannaich District		
A' Chailleach	3276	999 M
Sgurr Breac	3100*	1000 +
Meall a' Chrasgaidh	3062	934 M
Sgurr nan Clach Geala	3581	1093 M
Sgurr nan Each	3026	923 M
Sgurr Mor	3637	1110 M
Beinn Liath Mhor Fannaich	3000*	954 M
Meall Gorm	3109	967 +
An Coileachan	3015	923 M
Fionn Bheinn	3062	933 M
Am Faochagach	3120	954 M
Cona' Mheall	3150*	980 M
Beinn Dearg	3547	1084 M
Meall nan Ceapraichean	3150*	977 M
Eididh nan Clach Geala	3039	928 M
Seana Braigh	3040	927 M
Ben Wyvis	3433	1046 M
Ben More Assynt	3273	998 M
Conival	3234	987 M
Ben Klibreck (Cleith Bric)	3154	961 M
Ben Hope	3042	927 M

Note. As a result of the revised heights shown on the O.S. metric maps issued since the latest revision of the *Munro's Tables* was published in 1974, three new Munros are included in the above list, namely, Creise, Maoile Lunnaidh and Sgurr nan Ceinraichean.

2 MOUNTAIN CODE FOR SCOTLAND

Mountains are dangerous. Warning advice on safety and survival in both condensed and lengthy forms has been issued over the years by the SMC and other clubs, the Mountain Rescue Committee for Scotland, the British Mountaineering Council, the police, and by many others through pamphlets, books, and magazines. Experience has been that these warnings are not widely read unless kept brief. Large numbers of people, who do not aspire to be mountaineers, venture on to the hills during holidays only, or on impulse when finding paths or chairlifts, almost always in ignorance of the conditions of terrain and weather, and so without equipment essential to safety or survival. Frequent rescue and search operations have to be mounted on a large scale at great expense.

In 1972 the Countryside Commission for Scotland sponsored a highly condensed code, prepared by members of the Mountaineering Council for Scotland and the Scottish Mountain Leadership Training Board, and issued to the public by the Scottish Sports Council.

BEFORE YOU GO
Learn the use of map and compass
Know the weather signs and local forecast
Plan within your capabilities
Know simple first aid and the symptoms of exposure
Know the mountain distress signals
Know the Country Code

WHEN YOU GO
Never go alone
Leave written word of your route and report your return
Take windproofs, woollens, and survival bag
Take map and compass, torch and food
Wear climbing boots
Keep alert all day

IF THERE IS SNOW ON THE HILLS
Always have an ice-axe for each person
Carry a climbing rope and know the correct use of rope and ice-axe
Learn to recognize dangerous snow slopes.

Recommended reading on these points, approved by the Mountaineering Council for Scotland, is:

Mountaineering, by Alan Blackshaw (Penguin)

Mountain Leadership, by Eric Langmuir (Handbook of the Mountain Leadership Training Board). From Scottish Sports Council, 4 Queensferry Street, Edinburgh, EH2 4PB

Winter Climbing in Scotland, by W. H. Murray (from Scottish Sports Council)

Mountain Rescue and Cave Rescue (The Mountain Rescue Committee)

Exposure (British Mountaineering Council, Crawford House, Precinct Centre, Booth Street East, Manchester, M13 9RZ)

3 THE MOUNTAINEERING COUNCIL FOR SCOTLAND AND MEMBER CLUBS

The Council was formed by the mountaineering clubs of Scotland to foster mountaineering, to promote the clubs' interests, and to cooperate with other bodies concerned with mountainous land. It works closely with the Scottish Countryside Activities Council, the Mountain Rescue Committee for Scotland, the Scottish Mountain Leadership Training Board, and together with these bodies is the voice of mountaineers in Scotland to central and local government, and to all others having responsibility for mountainous land. It works in partnership with the British Mountaineering Council, which gives a similar but wider service in England and Wales. The member clubs are listed below. Secretaryships are liable to change, therefore anyone wishing to approach the clubs might best do so by writing first to the honorary secretary of the MCS, 11 Kirklee Quadrant, Glasgow, G12 oTS, for an up-to-date address, enclosing a stamped addressed envelope.

Members
Aberdeen M.C.
Aberdeen University Lairig M.C.
Association of Wardens of Mountain Centres
Braes o' Fife M.C.
Cairngorm Club, Aberdeen
Caithness Mountain and Ski Club
Caledonian Climbing Club, Fife
Carn Dearg M.C., Dundee
Civil Service (Rosyth) M. and S.C.
Coire Club (Aberdeen College of Education)
Creag Dhu M.C., Clydebank
Desperadoes M.C., Glasgow
East Kilbride M.C.
Edinburgh M.C.
Ëtchachan M.C., Aberdeen
Ferranti M.C., Edinburgh
Fife M.C.

Findhorn Wayfarers M.C., Moray
Forfar and District Hillwalking Club
Galloway M.C., Dumfries
Glasgow Fire Service M.C.
Glasgow Glenmore Club
Glasgow University M.C.
Grampian Club, Dundee
Greenock M.C.
Heriot Watt University M.C., Edinburgh
Holiday Fellowship M.C., Glasgow
Inverness M.C.
Jacobite M.C., Edinburgh
Junior Mountaineering Club of Scotland, Edinburgh
— Glasgow
— Lochaber
— Perth
— London
Ladies Scottish Climbing Club
Lang Craigs Club, Dumbarton
Lomond M.C., Glasgow
Microwave Electronic Systems Ltd. Lochend M.C., Edinburgh
Moray House M.C., Edinburgh
Moray M.C.
New Corriemulzie Club, Glasgow
Ochil M.C., Perthshire
Ross-shire Hillwalking Club
Rucksack Club, Dundee
St Andrews University M.C.
Scottish Mountaineering Club
Starav M.C.
Stirling University M.C.
Strathclyde University M.C., Glasgow
Strathspey M.C., Aviemore
Upperward M.C., Biggar

4   OUTDOOR ACTIVITIES CENTRES

Scotland has approximately eighty Outdoor Activities Centres. At least half of these are run by the Regional Education Authorities, mostly exclusively for pupils, but some Authorities will hire the centre out to other organized bodies when it is not required for their own courses. Apply to the Youth Organizer at the District Education Department. Most other centres are for Scouts, Guides, and Youth Clubs.

There are seven main centres offering a published programme of courses of instruction in hill-walking and climbing. They are:

GLENMORE LODGE, Aviemore, Inverness-shire. Apply to the Scottish Sports Council, 4 Queensferry Street, Edinburgh.
LOCH EIL CENTRE, Achdalieu, by Fort William, Inverness-shire. Apply to Loch Eil Trust, 10 Palmerston Place, Edinburgh.
JOHN RIDGWAY SCHOOL OF ADVENTURE, Ardmore, Rhiconich, by Lairg, Sutherland.
GARRY GULACH ADVENTURE CROFT, Garry Gulach, Invergarry, Inverness-shire.
WEST HIGHLAND SCHOOL OF ADVENTURE, Applecross, Ross-shire. Apply to the Field Officer, Outward Bound Trust, Iddlesleigh House, Caxton Street, London, SW1H 0PU.
MORAY SEA SCHOOL, Burghead School of Adventure, Moray. Apply to the Field Officer, Outward Bound Trust, as above.
GLENCOE MOUNTAINEERING SCHOOL, Kinlochleven, Argyll.

In addition to these main centres, the Scottish Youth Hostels Association runs courses in hill-walking, climbing, and skiing at four centres:

GARTH, Fortingall, Perthshire.
BALQUHIDDER, Stirlingshire.
LOCH MORLICH, Glenmore, Aviemore, Inverness-shire.
GLEN BRITTLE, Isle of Skye.

Applications go to the SYHA, National Office, 7 Glebe Crescent, Stirling, SK8 2JA.

5 PUBLIC AND VOLUNTARY BODIES CONCERNED WITH THE HIGHLANDS

OFFICIAL OR PUBLIC BODIES, with responsibilities for conservation:

1. All District and Regional Authorities.
2. *Countryside Commission for Scotland,* Battleby, Redgorton, Perth. *Objects:* Conservation of natural beauty and provision of facilities for enjoyment of the countryside.
3. *Forestry Commission,* 231 Corstorphine Road, Edinburgh, EH12 7AT.
    North Conservancy, 60 Church Street, Inverness.
    East Conservancy, 6 Queens Gate, Aberdeen AB9 2NQ.
    West Conservancy, 21 India Street, Glasgow, G2 4PL.
    Objects: Timber production. Conservation of wildlife and landscape. Provision of access.
4. *Highlands and Islands Development Board,* 27 Bank Street, Inverness. *Objects:* Promotion of industries and enterprise.
5. *Nature Conservancy,* 12 Hope Street, Edinburgh, EH9 2AS. *Objects:* Scientific advice on conservation and control of flora and fauna. Establishment and management of Nature Reserves. Research.
6. *Red Deer Commission,* Elm Park, Island Bank Road, Inverness. *Objects:* Conservation and control of red deer.
7. *Scottish Sports Council,* 4 Queensferry Street, Edinburgh, EH2 4PB. *Objects:* Encouragement of physical recreation.
8. *Scottish Tourist Board,* 2 Rutland Place, Edinburgh, EH1 2YU.

VOLUNTARY ORGANIZATIONS, with a concern for conservation:

1. *Association for the Preservation of Rural Scotland,* 20 Falkland Avenue, Newton Mearns, Renfrewshire, G77 5DR.
2. *British Mountaineering Council,* Crawford House, Precinct Centre, Booth Street East, Manchester, M13 9RZ.
3. *Conservation Society,* 8 Esslemont Avenue, Aberdeen. *Objects:* Conservation of wildlife, natural resources, and human cultures.
4. *National Trust for Scotland,* 5 Charlotte Square, Edinburgh,

EH2 4DU. *Objects:* Preservation of places of historic or architectural interest, and of natural beauty.

5. *Royal Scottish Forestry Society*, 26 Rutland Square, Edinburgh, EH1 2BU.

6. *The Royal Society for the Protection of Birds*, 17 Regent Terrace, Edinburgh, EH7 5BN.

7. *Scottish Countryside Activities Council*, 15 Main Street, Dundonald, Kilmarnock, Ayrshire. Coordinating body for the principal outdoor organizations engaged in recreation but concerned with amenity (includes the Mountaineering Council for Scotland). *Objects:* To collect information relating to use of the countryside for leisure activities; to spread knowledge of the countryside; to reconcile conflicting interests in its use; and to represent agreed interests to all persons and authorities having responsibilities for the countryside.

8. *Scottish Landowners Federation*, 26 Rutland Square, Edinburgh, EH1 2BT.

9. *Scottish Rights of Way Society*, 6 Abercromby Place, Edinburgh, EH3 6JX.

10. *Scottish Wildlife Trust*, 8 Dublin Street, Edinburgh, EH1 3PP. *Objects:* Conservation of wildlife, habitats, and natural beauty.

11. *Scottish Woodland Owners Association*, 6 Chester Street, Edinburgh, EH3 7RD.

12. *Scottish Youth Hostels Association*, 7 Glebe Crescent, Stirling, SK8 2JA.

Mountain rescue is organized in Scotland by the Mountain Rescue Committee of Scotland, whose members are representatives from the civilian Rescue Teams, the RAF, the Chief Police Officers, the Red Cross, the Scottish Mountaineering Club, the Mountaineering Council for Scotland, the Scottish Sports Council (Glenmore Training Centre), the Scottish National Ski Council, the MRC of England, and the SYHA. The Honorary Secretary is Hamish MacInnes, Glen Coe, Argyll (tel. Kingshouse 225 or Ballachulish 258).

Rescues are free. The rescued may, if they choose, make a contribution to funds.

Government makes important grant of funds in five ways: by support of RAF teams; Service helicopters; payment for equipment at Rescue Posts, which are sited and maintained by the MRCS; payments direct to the Committee for equipment of voluntary teams; and by Police services. The Police provide teams, insurance of civilian teams, some necessary equipment, transport and radio, replacement of damaged or lost equipment, and reimbursement of lost wages. The MRCS also receives donations from climbing clubs, industry, charitable bodies, and individual men of good will. The teams raise money by their own efforts.

RESCUE: GO DIRECT TO RESCUE POST IF KNOWN, OR TELEPHONE.
DIAL 999.   ASK FOR POLICE.

RESCUE TEAMS AND POSTS

Southern Highlands

Teams	*Posts and Grid References*
Isle of Arran	Police Station, Brodick, Arran.
Benmore Adventure Centre, Holy Loch, Cowal	Succouth Farm, Arrochar. NN 295 053
Arrochar	The Hawthorns, Drymen, Stirling-shire. NS 475 886

Teams	Posts and Grid References
Killin	Police Station, Crianlarich, Perth-
Lomond	shire. NN 387 253
Ochils	National Trust for Scotland,
Argyll Police	Visitor Centre, Car Park, Ben
Falkirk Mountaineering Club	Lawers. NN 609 379
	Dounans Camp School, Aberfoyle

Central Highlands

Glencoe	Achnambeitach, Glencoe. NN 140
Argyll	566
Rannoch School, Loch Rannoch	Kingshouse Hotel. NN 260 546
Fort William Police	Scottish Ski Club, Meall a' Bhuiridh
Lochaber M.R. Association	hut. NN 270 520. Manned winter
	only
	Police Station, Fort William.
	C.I.C. Hut, Coire Leis, Ben Nevis.
	NN 167 723
	Steall, Glen Nevis – stretcher only.
	NN 177 684

Cairngorms

Overlapping heavily with North, West, Central, and South Highland Districts.

Aberdeen	Nature Conservancy Hut, Derry
Braemar	Lodge. NO 041 933
Scottish N.–E. Counties'	Spittal of Muick, Glen Muick.
Constabulary	NO 307 849
Inverness Police	Police Station, Braemar. NO 148
Cairngorm MRT	914
Glenmore Lodge	Police Station, Ballater
Gordonstoun School, Elgin	Police Station, Aviemore. NH 895
Moray	127
Grampian Club	Glenmore Lodge. NH 986 095
Carn Dearg M.C.	White Lady Shieling, Coire Cas,
JMCS, Perth	Cairn Gorm. NH 995 053
Kirkcaldy M.C.	Aberärder Farm, Lochlagganside,
Falkirk M.C.	by Newtonmore. NN 479 875

Teams	*Posts and Grid References*
Angus Constabulary	Central Police Office, West Bell Street, Dundee
Rannoch School, Loch Rannoch	Glen Doll Lodge, Glen Clova, Angus. NO 278 763

West Highlands

Kintail	Camusrory, Loch Nevis. NM 857 957
Skye	Kintail Lodge Hotel. NG 938 197
	Doctor's House, Glenelg. NG 815 194
	Glen Lichd House, Kintail – first aid kit in bothy. NH 005 173
	Police Station, Portree, Skye
	Glenbrittle House, Skye. NG 411 214
	Coruisk Hut – stretcher and first aid. NG 487 196

Northern Highlands

Dounreay	Glen Cottage Hostel, Torridon. NG 930 565
Ross and Sutherland Constabulary	Dundonnell Hotel. NH 090 881
Torridon	Inchnadamph Hotel. NC 252 217
Dundonnell	Police Station, Thurso
	Police Station, Rhiconich, Sutherland. First aid kit and stretcher.

For more detailed information, refer to *Mountain and Cave Rescue*, the handbook of the MRC, 9 Milldale Avenue, Temple Meads, Buxton, Derbyshire, SK17 9BE.

7 GLOSSARY OF GAELIC AND NORSE WORDS AND PLACE NAMES

(Part I. List of common words from which most place names are constructed.

Part II. List of place names that cannot readily be reconstructed from Part I.)

Names are listed alphabetically from the first noun or adjective following the prefixes Glen, Loch, River, Ben, or their Gaelic equivalents, which are Gleann, Ghlinne, Loch, Allt, Abhainn, Amhuinn, Beinn, Bheinn, Bidean, Bidein, Binnein, Carn, Cnoc, Creag, Maol, Meall, Sgor, Sgurr, Spidean, Sron, Stob, Stuc, Tom, Torr.

Pronunciation: g and th are always hard; ch is guttural as in loch; fh is silent; bh and mh are aspirated (as V in English).

The definite article: this varies for gender, case, number, and first letter of the noun: an, am, a', an t-, nan, nam, na, na h-.

An, the, is used before consonants except b, p, f, when it changes to *Am,* and except before aspirates, when it changes to *a'* (*a' bhrathair,* the brother). Before vowels and vowel-sounds it changes to *an t-* (Meall an t-Suidhe, pronounced Mellantee, hill of the seat).

Hills: The physical characteristics usually but not invariably implied by the hill-titles are:

Tom and *Torr,* low; *Cnoc,* fairly steep, but never one of the highest; *Meall,* gently rounded or shapeless; *Maol,* bald bluff top; *Carn,* high and stony; *Bidean, Bidein, Binnein, Stob, Sgurr, Stuc,* and *Spidean,* always bold, often peaky if not pinnacled; *Creag,* cliffed or craggy; and *Beinn* (however spelt), can be any shape or size.

Part I

aber, abha, abhair, river's mouth, sometimes a confluence
achadh, field, plain, meadow
aid, piece, portion
aird, height, high point
airidh, airigh, shieling
allt, burn, river

266

amhainn, amhuinn, river
aonach, ridge, steep height (if at low level, a meadow)
ard, height, high point
ath, ford

bad, spot (place)
baile, township
ban, bhan, white, bright, fair
barr, top, point
beag, small
bealach, pass
beith, birch-tree
ben or **benn,** anglicization of *beinn,* hill or mountain (gen. *beinne*),
    and of *beann,* peak or top (gen. pl. *beann*). Also *bheinn.*
bidean, bidein, peak
binnein, peak
bo, cow, pl. *ba,* cattle
bod, tail, penis
bodach, old man
bothan, hut, bothy
braigh, brae, hill, top
bran, raven; name of Fingal's dog
braon, shower, gen. *bhraoin*
breac, breacan, speckled
brochan, porridge
buachaille, herdsman
buidhe, yellow
buiridh, bellowing (of stags), gen. *bhuiridh*

cailleach, old woman
caisteal, castle, a fastness
cam, crooked
camas, bay
caol, caolas, strait
caor, rowan, pl. *caoran*
caora, sheep, gen. *caorach, caoraich*
capull, horse
carn, cairn, hill, or pile of stones
carr, rock-ledge, broken ground
cas, steep
cat, wild cat

267

cean, ceann, head
ceathach, mist
choinneach, mossy place, bog
chrois, cross or crossing place
cill, cell or church
cioch, pap, gen. *ciche*
cir, comb, gen. *chir*
ciste, chest, coffin
clach, stony
clachan, small township
cleit, cliff, crag, reef
cnap, cnoc, hillock
coille, wood
coire, corrie
corran, low cape tapering to a point
creachan, rock
creag, crag, cliff
croit, croft
cruach, chruach, hill
cuach, cup, deep hollow
cul, back
curra, marsh, bog

da, two
dail, field
damh, stag, gen. *daimh*
darach, oakwood
dearg, red
diollaid, saddle
diridh, the divide
dobhar, burn
donich, brown
dorlin, dhorlin, isthmus covered at high water
dorus, strait, gate
drochaid, bridge
drum, druim, ridge
dubh, dark, black
dun, fort

each, horse
eag, notch

eagach, notched place
ear, east
eas, waterfall
eighe, file, notched
eileach, rock
eilean, island
eun, bird, gen. *eoin*

fada, long, gen. *fhada*
faochag, whelk
fas, level place
fearn, alder
fiadh, deer
fionn, white, clear, bright
frith, deer forest, gen. *frithe*
fuar, cold

gabhar, goat, gen. *ghabhar*
gaoth, wind, gen. pl. *gaothaich*
garbh, rough
garbhanach, rough ridge
gartan, gartain, enclosed field; also name of person
geal, white
gearanach, walled ridge
gearr, short
gille, young man, boy, pl. *gillean*
glac, hollow, trough
glais, burn
glas, ghlas, grey or green
gleann, glen
glomach, chasm
gorm, blue
greadadh, torment, blast, gen. *ghreadaidh*

ime, butter-making
inbhir, inver, confluence
innis, inch, island, or meadow
iolair, eagle

ken or **kin,** from *cean*, head
knock, from *cnoc*, hillock
kyle, from *caol*, strait

ladhar, hoof, fork
lag, lagan, hollow
lair, mare
lairig, pass
laogh, calf, gen. *laoigh*
laroch, dwelling place
lax (Norse), salmon
leac, slab, stone
leathad, a slope
leathan, broad, broad slope
leis, lee, leeward (*Coire Leis* – corrie to leeward)
leitir, slope
liath, grey
lochan, small loch

maighdean, mhaighdean, maiden
mairg, rust-coloured
mam, rounded hill
maol, headland, mull, bare hill
meadhon, middle, gen. *mheadhoin*
meall, hill
moin, mhoin, moine, bog or moss
monadh, hill, range (usually heathery)
mor, mhor, big
muc, pig, gen. *muic*
muileann, mill, gen. *mhuilinn*
mullach, top, summit

ness, (Norse) point or headland

ob, bay, dim. *Oban*
odhar, dun-coloured
or, boundary (old Gaelic), gold
ord, conical hill

poite, pot
pol, farmstead (from Norse *bol*)
poll, pool, pit
puist, post

righ, king
ron, seal

ros, ross, promontory, moor
ruadh, red
rubha, rudha, promontory, point. Abbreviations *ru, rhu, row*
ruigh, shieling

sail, heel
scuir, peak
sean, old, gen. *sin* (pron. *shin*)
seileach, willow
sgeir, reef
sgiath, wing
sgurr, sgor, peak, usually rocky
sith, fairy
sithean, fairy hill
slochd, deep hollow, pit
sneachd, snow
spidean, peak
sput, spout, dim. *sputan*
srath, strath, broad level glen
sron, nose
stac, steep rock, sea-stack
steall, waterfall
stob, peak
stuc, steep rock, peak
subh, berry
suidhe, seat

tairneilear, thunderer
tarmachan, ptarmigan
teallach, forge, hearth
tigh, house
tioram, dry island accessible at low tide
tir, land, region
tobar, well
toll, hole
tom, hill
torr, small hill
tuath, north
tulach, hillock, dim. *tulachan,* pl. *tuilachean*

uaine, green

uamh, cave
uig, bay
uisge, water

vik, (Norse), creek

Part II

Abernethy, *Aber Neithich*, Mouth of the pure burn (here a confluence)

Achaladair, Field of the hard water

Acharacle, *Ath Dhorrcail*, Torquil's ford (near Shiel Bridge)

Achintee, *Ach' an t-Suidhe*, Field of the seat

Achlean, *Achadh Leathan*, Broad field

Achray, *Ath-chrathaidh*, Ford of the shaking

Achtriochtan, *Ach' Troiseachan*, Field (or big flat) of the crossing places

Affric, *Afraic*, from *ath*, ford, and *breac*, speckled

Aighean, Beinn nan, Hill of the hinds

Alasdair, Sgurr, Alexander's peak (Alexander Nicolson)

Alder, *All dhobhar*, rock water

Aline, Loch, *Alainn* (gen.), beautiful

Alligin, jewel

Alsh, Loch, *Aillse* (gen.), foaming

Altnafeadh, *Allt nam feith*, Burn of the bogs

Aonach Eagach, Notched Ridge

Appin, *Apdaine*, *Apuinn*, Abbey land

Applecross, *Aber Crossan*, Mouth of the Crossan (burn)

Arcuil, (Norse) *Ark-fjall*, Ark hill

Ardair, Coire, *Ar'dobhair*, high water (burn)

Ardgour, *Ard Ghabhar*, Height of the goats

Ardnamurchan, Point of the ocean

Argyll, *Earra-ghaidheal*, (pron. Erragyl), Coastland of the Gael

Arkaig, Loch, *Airceag*, steep, difficult place

Armine, Ben, *Beinn an Armuinn*, Hill of the hero

Arran, *Arainn*, *Arann*, possibly *Ar*, high, *In*, island, but is not thus spelt in early literature

Assynt, (Norse) *Ass*, Rocky district

Atholl, *Athfodla*, New Ireland, or Brit. *Aethwyddel*, gorse-brake

Avich, Loch, *Abhaich*, Place of the burn

Aviemore, *Agaidh Mhor*, Great gap

Avon, Ben and Loch, *Ath-fhinn*, Ford of Fionn (Fingal), or of *Fiann*, his followers

Badcall, *Bad*, spot (place), *call*, of hazels = Clump of hazels
Badenoch, *Baideanach*, from *Baithte-n-ach*, Drowned land (inundation by the Spey)
Ballachulish, *Baile a' chaolais*, Township of the narrows
Balloch, *Baile-loch*, Loch township
Barr More, Big top
Basteir, Am, The Executioner
Benderloch, *Beinn eader da loch*, Hill between two lochs
Beoraid, Loch, Beaver loch
Bharnais, bealach, Pass of the gap
Bheithir, Beinn a', (Ben Vare), Peak of the thunderbolt
Bhraoin, Loch a', Loch of the showers
Bhrochain, Coire, Corrie of the porridge
Bidean nam Bian, *Bidein nam Beann*, Peak of the bens (11 tops)
Bidein Druim nan Ramh, Peak of the ridge of oars
Black Mount, *Monadh Dubh*, Dark hills
Blaven, *Bla' bheinn*, Mountain of bloom
Bonar, *Am Bonnath*, The bottom ford
Braemar, *Braigh Mharr*, Hills of Mar
Braeriach, *Braigh Riabhach*, Brindled hill
Breadalbane, *Braghaid Alban*, The high land of Alban
Broom, from *Braon*, shower: *Loch a' Bhrain*, Loch of the showers
Bruach na Frithe, Hill of the deer forest
Bruar, river, glen, Bridge stream (spanned by natural arch)
Buachaille Etive Mor, Great Shepherd of Etive
Builg, Loch, Bog loch
Bute, *Bod*, Tail (of Cowal)

Caenlochan, *Cadha an Lochain*, Narrow pass of the loch
Caime, Coire na, Crooked corrie
Cairnbawn, Loch, *Cairn ban*, Loch of the white cairn
Cairn Gorm, *Carn Gorm*, Blue mountain
Caisteal Abhail, Ptarmigan's stronghold
Callater, glen and loch, *Caladair*, Glen of the hard water
Capel Mounth, *Monadh Chapull*, Hill of horses
Carn Eige, Cairn of the notch
Carn an t-Sagairt, Hill of the priest
Carn an Tuirc, Hill of the boar

Carron, *Carr*, rocky shelf

Ceathreamhnan, Sgurr na, Peak of the quarters

Chabhair, Ben, Hill of the antler

Chairn, Stob Coire a', Peak of the stony corrie

Chaluim, Ben, Malcolm's hill

Chaorachain, Sgurr a', Peak of the boiling torrent, or of the sheep-run

Chaoruinn, Beinn a', Mountain of the rowan-tree

Cheathaich, Ben, Hill of the mists

Chinn-dearg, Maol, *Cheann-dearg*, Bare, red-headed hill

Chleibh, Ben a', Hill of the chest

Chno Dearg, Red nut

Chochuill, Beinn a', Hill of the hood

Choinnich Mor, Sgurr, Big peak of the bog

Choire Claurigh, Stob, *Clarach*, bare: Peak of the bare corrie

Choire Leith, Spidean a', (pron. Spitean a Horrie Ley), Peak of the grey corrie

Choire Mheadhoin, Stob a', Peak of the middle corrie

Chonzie, Ben (pron. Ben-y-Hone), Hill of the deer-cry

Chralaig, a', The round place

Chreachain, Beinn a', Hill of the clam shell

Chroin, Stuc a', Peak of the cloven hoof

Chuirn, Beinn a', Hill of the cairn

Clachaig, Stony place

Clachlet, *Clach leathad*, Stony hill-slope

Claurigh, Stob Choire, *clarach*, bare: Peak of the bare corrie

Cleith Bric, Beinn, *Cleith bhreac*, Hill of the speckled cliff

Cluanie, Clunie, glen, river, and loch, *Cluanaidh*, meadow

Cnoc Coinnich, Boggy hill

Cobbler, *An greasaiche crom*, The crooked cobbler

Coe, glen and river, *Comhann*, Shrine (not now known)

Coigach, Place of the fifths (Celtic division of land)

Coilessan, Wood of the waterfall

Coireachan Ruadh, Red corries

Coire na Ciche, Corrie of the pap

Coire Dhorrcail, Torquil's corrie

Coire Domhain, Deep corrie

Coire Easain, Stob, Peak of the corrie of waterfalls

Coire Gabhail, Corrie of booty (cattle)

Coire Ghrannda, Corrie of the ugly cliff

Coir' a' Ghrunnda, Floored corrie

Coiregrogain, Awkward corrie
Coire an Iubhair, Corrie of the yew-tree
Coire an Lochain Uaine, Corrie of the green lochan
Coire Mhic Fhearchair, Farquarson's corrie
Coire Sgriodain, Stob, Peak of the scree corrie
Conon, river, *Abhainn Chonainn*, Hound river
Corriemulzie, *Coire Mhuillidh*, Mill corrie
Corrievreckan, *Coire Bhreacain*, Speckled gulf, or Breacan's gulf (tide race)
Corrieyairack, *Coire Ghearreig*, Corrie of the short notch
Corronaich, Meall, Hill of the bracken corrie
Corrour, *Coire Odhar*, Dun-coloured corrie
Coruisk, *Coir' uisge*, Water corrie
Cowal, *Comhghall*, from Comgall, grandson of King Fergus
Coylum, *Cuing Leum*, Narrow leap
Crask, *Crasg*, A crossing over a ridge
Creach Bheinn, Bare hill
Creag an Leth Choin, Rock of the lurcher (dog)
Croe, glen, *Gleann crotha*, Enclosed glen
Cruachan, Ben, *Cruachan Beann*, Mountain of the peaks
Cruach Ardrain, High mountain
Cuillin, (Norse) *Kjölen*, Keel-shaped ridges
Cul Mor, Great back

Dalnacardoch, *Dail na Ceardaich*, Field of the smithy
Dalnaspidal, *Dail na spideil*, Field of the hospice
Dalness, *Dail an easa*, Place of the waterfalls
Dalwhinnie, *Dail Chuinnidh*, Champion's field
Dee, river, *Uisge Dhé*, Water of Deva (river goddess)
Derry, glen, *Gleann Doire*, Glen of the small wood
Devil's Point, *Bod an Deamhain*, Devil's penis
Dhorrcail, Coire, Torquil's corrie
Dirrie Mor, *Diridh Mor*, Great divide
Doire Duibh, Loch an, Loch of the dark wood
Don, *Deathan*, Devona (river goddess)
Dorain, Beinn, Hill of the otter
Dornie, *Dornach*, Pebbly place
Dornoch, *Dornach*, Pebbly place
Dothaidh, Beinn an, Hill of the Scorching
Driesh, *Dris*, Bramble thicket

Droma, Loch, Loch of the ridge
Druim nan Ramh, Ridge of oars
Drumochter, *Druim uachdair*, Ridge of upland
Duich, Loch, from St *Dubhtach* (Bishop of Ross, 11th century)
Dunoon, *Dun abhainn*, Fort of the burn
Durness, (1) Gaelic *Dubh rinn*, Black point (former name, anglicized
    to Durine)
        (2) Norse *Dyra Ness*, wild beast cape (wolf infested)
Duror, *Dur-dhobar*, Hard water

Earn, Loch, *Eireann*, Ireland's loch
Eas a' Chual Aluinn, (pron. Ess-kool-aulin), Splendid waterfall of
    Coul

Easain, Stob Coire, Peak of the corrie of waterfalls
Eask, glen, *Easg*, Bog glen
Eigg, Isle of, *Eag*, notch
Eighe, Beinn, Hill of the file (serrations)
Eilde, Lairig, Pass of the hinds
Eilde Mor, Sgurr, Big peak of the hinds
Eilean Donan, from St Donan of Eigg (*c.* AD 620)
Einich, glen, *Eanich*, Glen of the marsh
Eriboll, loch, Gaelic *earr*, butt end; Norse *bol.* farm, or alternatively
    from Norse *Eyndbol*, Elvind's farm
Ericht, loch, *Eireachd*, Assembly loch
Etive, loch and river, *Eite*, Horrid (stormy) one
Eunaich, Beinn, Fowling hill

Faindouran, *Feith an Dobhrain*, Burn of the otter
Fasnakyle, *Fas na coille*, Level place of the wood
Feshie, glen, *Feithisidh*, Glen of the level bog
Fhidhleir, Sgurr an, Fiddler's peak (pron. Scooraneelar)
Fiannaidh, Sgor nam, Peak of the Fianns (Fingal's army)
Fillan, Strath, *Faolan*, Little Wolf – name of 16 saints (also gives
    name to *allt*, *gleann*, and *inbhir Fhaolain* of Glen Etive)
Finnan, glen, from St Finan (d. AD 575)
Fionnlaidh, Beinn, Finlay's hill
Firth, Norse *fjoror*, an outer sea-loch, estuary
Foinaven, *Foinne Bheinn*, Wart mountain
Fortingall, *Farthair chill*, Fort church (fort is adjectival– commanding
    a bluff near church)

Foyers, *Foithear*, Terraced slope

Gaick, *Gaig*, cleft
Gairich, Peak of Roaring
Gairloch, *Gearr loch*, Short loch
Gaoith, Sgor, Peak of the wind
Garry, glen, *Garadh*, Glen of the copse
Gelder, glen, *Geal dhobhar*, Glen of the bright water
Ghlo, Beinn a', Hill of the veil (mist)
Ghreadaidh, Sgurr a', Peak of the high winds
Gillean, Sgurr nan, Peak of the young men
Gilp, loch, *Gilb*, chisel
Glas Maol, *Glas Mheall*, Green hill
Glencoul, *Gleann cul*, Back glen
Glenelg, *Eilg*, old district name
Glenfinnan, from St Finan (d. AD 575)
Glenshee, *Gleann sith*, Fairy glen
Gleouraich, uproar
Gloy, glen, *Ghlaoidh*, Glen of the glue (shining liquid)
Goat Fell, *Gaoth Bheinn*, Hill of the winds
Goil, loch, *Gobhal*, fork, or *goilin*, inlet
Grampians, *Gruaim peinnean*, Dark mountains (Old Gaelic)
Gruagaichean, Na, The maidens
Gruinard, Norse *Grunna fjord*, Shallow fiord
Gulvain, *Gaor bheinn*, Gore (piercing thrust) mountain

Hebrides, Norse *Hav-bred-ey*, Isles on the edge of the sea
Hope, Ben, Norse *Höp*, Inner bay

Inchard, loch, *Uinnseard*, Loch of the high ash-tree
Inchnadamph, *Inch nam damh*, Stag's meadow
Isles of the Sea, *Hinba* (O.G. *In*, island; *ba*, sea. H indicates plural.
   Pron. Eenba)
Iubhair, Coire an, Corrie of the yew-tree

Kildonan, *Cill Donnain*, Church of Donnan (of Eigg)
Killin, *Cill Fhinn*, Church of Fionn
Kincraig, *Ceann na creige*, Head of the rock
Kingussie, *Ceann a' ghiuthsaich*, Head of the pinewood
Kintail, *Cean da shaill*, Head of two seas
Klibreck, Ben, *Beinn Cleith bhreac*, Hill of the speckled cliffs
Knoydart, Norse, *Knutr's fjord*

Kylesku, *Caolas cumhang*, Narrow strait

Lagangarbh, Rough hollow

Lairig Gartain, *Gorton*, small field or garden; pass above small enclosed fields, or Pass of Gartan (personal name)

Lairig Ghru, *Dhru*, Pass of the Druie burn

Lap, Beinn na, Ben of the bog

Lapaich, Sgurr na, Peak of the bog

Lawers, Ben, from *Labhar*, loud and resounding, in reference to burn; plural added in reference to 3 divisions of the district of 'Lawers'

Laxford, loch, Norse *Lax fjord*, Salmon loch

Leac an Tuath, North stone

Lecht road, *Leachd*, declivity

Lennox, from *Leamhnach*, men of the district of Leven

Leven, river, *Leamhain*, Elm water

Liathach, The grey one

Lichd, glen, *Leachd*, declivity

Linnhe, loch, *Linne*, sound, channel

Lismore, *Lias Mor*, Great garden

Loch an Eilein, Loch of the island

Lochan Uaine, Green lochan

Lochnagar, *Lochan na gaire*, or *na gaoir*, or *nan Ghabhar*, Lochan of the noise, or sobbing, or goats

Lomond, loch, *Laomuinn*, from *laom*, blaze. Beacon. (The loch was formerly named Loch Leven)

Long, loch, Loch of the ships

Lorn, from Loarn, son of Erc of Dalriada

Loy, glen, *Laogh*, calf

Loyal, Ben, *Beinn Laghail*, from Norse *Laga-fjall*, Law-fell

Lui, Ben, *Beinn Laoigh*, Hill of the calf

Lyon, river, loch, glen, *Liomhunn*, grinding

Macdhui, Ben, *Binn mach Duibh*, (obsolete local vernacular) Dark hills. Could be from *Mhic Duibh*, MacDuff (Earl of Fife, who held land in Middle Ages)

Mairg, Carn, Rust-coloured hill

Mam na Cloich' Airde, Hill of the stony height

Mam Sodhail, *Sabhal*, Barn hill

Maree, loch, from St *Maelrubha* – *Mael*, tonsured, *rubha*, variant of *rudha*, red = tonsured red-head

Meaghaidh, Creag, *Mhigeaghaidh*, Crag of the bog-land

Mhadaidh, Sgurr a', Peak of the foxes
Mhaim, Sgurr a', Peak of the pass or breast
Mhic Coinnich, Sgurr, Mackenzie's peak
Mhic Fhearchair, Coire, Farquarson's corrie
Moidart, Norse, meaning lost
Moraich, Sgurr na, Peak of the sea-plain
Morar, *Mordhobar*, Big water
Morlich, loch, *Mor Leacainn*, Loch of the big slope
Morven, *Mor bheinn*, Big hill
Morvern, *A' Mhorbhairn*, Sea gap (originally name of Loch Sunart)
Morvich, Sea-plain
Mounth, from *Monadh*, Heathy hills
Muck, *Muc*, pig
Muick, glen, *Muic*, pig
Mullach nan Coirean, Hill of the corries

Naver, loch, strath, *Nabhair*, cloudy
Nevis, Ben, from *Neamh*, the heavens or clouds, and *bhathais*, the
     top of a man's head = Mountain with head in the clouds
Nevis, loch, Loch of Heaven
Newtonmore, *Baile Ur an t-Sleibh*, New town of the moor

Ochils, *Uchil*, high
Oich, *Obhaich*, Stream-place
Orchy, glen, river, *Ar-choill*, On wood (wooded)
Oss, Ben, Hill of the stag
Oykell, river, strath, Gaelic *Oiceil*, Norse *Ekkjall*, both from early
Celtic *Uxellos*, changing to *Uckel*, High bank

Parph, *Am Parbh*, Gaelic form of Norse *Hvarf*, Turning point

Quinag, *Cuinneag*, barrel (or churn)
Quiraing, *Cuith raing*, Pillared stronghold
Quoich, glen, loch, *Cuaich*, cup

Rannoch, *Raithneach*, Bracken region
Reay, originally *Meadhrath*, Mid-fort
Reigh, Allt an, *Ruigh*, Burn of the shieling
Rois-bheinn, *Froisbheinn*, Hill of the showers
Rothiemurchus, *Rata Mhurchuis*, Forest of Muirgus
Rowardennan, *Rudha-Eodhnain*, Adomnan's point
Rowchoish, *Rudha a' chois*, Point of the hollow

Rum, Gaelic *Rum* (Annals of Tigernach, ref. AD 676). Norse *Röm-ö*, Wide Island
Ruthven, *Ruadhainn*, Red place
Ryvoan, *Ruighe a' bhothain*, Shieling of the bothy

Schichallion, *Sidh Chailleann*, Fairy hill of the Caledonians
Scourie, Norse *Skoga*, copse; Gaelic *Airge*, shieling
Seana Bhraigh, Old hill
Seilg, Beinn na, *Seilge*, Hunting hill
Sgairne, Bealach A', Pass of rumbling
Sgiath Chuil, Back wing
Sgine, Sgurr na, Peak of the knife
Sgoran Dubh, Small black peak
Sgriol, Ben, *Sgreitheil* (and *Sgreamhail*), Dreadful mountain, or Ugly rind mountain (reference to big scree slopes)
Sgulaird, Beinn, meaning undiscovered
Sheallag, Strath na, Strath of the hinds
Shee, glen, *Sith*, Fairy glen
Shelter Stone (Cairngorms), *Clach Dhion*, Stone of Devona (river goddess)
Shiel, river, loch, *Seile* (O.G. *Sale*), meaning not known
Shieldaig, Norse *Sild vik*, Herring bay
Shin, loch, river, *Sin* (gen. of *sean*, old), Loch of the old one
Shira, glen, loch, river, *Siorabh*, Lasting river
Skye, Norse *Skuy-ö*, Cloud island. Gaelic *Eilean Sgiathanach*, Winged island
Sligachan, *Sligeachan*, Place of the clam shells
Slioch, *Sleagh*, spear
Smoo, cave, Norse *Smuga*, cleft
Spean, river, glen, *Spiathan*, dim. of *Spé* (Spey)
Spey, river, *Abhainn Spé*, Burn of the hawthorns
Stac Polly, *An Stac Poile*, Stack of the bog
Starav, meaning not known
Stobinian, *Am Binnein*, The pinnacle
Stoer, Norse *Staurr*, stake
Storr, Gaelic *Stor*, Decayed tooth, cliff
Struan, *Sruthan*, Small burn
Study (Glen Coe), *Innean a' Cheathaich*, Anvil of the mist (from which has come Scots *Stiddie*, (anvil)
Suilven, Norse *Sul*, Gaelic *bheinn*, Pillar mountain

Sutherland, Norse *Sudrland*, South land (relative to Orkney jarldom)

Tarbert, Tarbet, *Tairbeart* or *Tairm-bert*, 'an over-bringing' = Isthmus

Tarf, glen, *Tarbh*, bull

Tarmachan, Meall nan, Ptarmigan's hill

Thearlaich, Sgurr, Charles's peak (Pilkington)

Tomintoul, *Tom an t-Sabhail*, Hillock of the barn

Torridon, loch, *Toir-bheartan*, Bountiful loch

Toul, Cairn, *Carn 'n t-Sabhail*, Barn hill (pron. Towl)

Treig, loch, *Treag*, Loch of death (haunt of fierce water-horses)

Tromie, glen, *Tromaidh*, Glen of the dwarf elder

Trossachs, *Na Troiseachan*, The Crossing place (between Loch Katrine and Loch Achray)

Tulaichean, Beinn, Knolly hill

Tummel, river, loch, *Abhainn Teimheil*, River of darkness

Ulaidh, Sgor na h', Peak of the hid treasure

Ullapool, Norse *Ulli-bol*, Ulli's steading

Vane, Ben, *Mheadhoin*, Middle hill

Venue, Ben, *Bheinn Uaimh*, Peak of the caves

Vorlich, Ben, originally *Ard Mhur' laig*, Height of the sea-bag

Wells of Dee, *Fuaran Dhé*, Wells of God

Wrath, Cape, Norse *Hvarf*, Turning point

Wyvis, Ben, Awesome mountain

8   THE PRIVILEGE OF ACCESS

All land in the Highlands, except a minute urban fraction, is owned or tenanted by people who either try to earn a living from it or give employment. No man who owns land can survive financially today unless he turns his land to some good use. His hill lands are under sheep, cattle, deer, grouse, and trees. He employs shepherds, cattle-men, stalkers, gillies, gamekeepers, ponymen, and others to maintain the stock, tracks, gates, fences, houses, bothies, and plantations. The living environment that he helps to maintain attracts visitors in large numbers.

Visitors, whether tourists, walkers, campers, or climbers can injure Highland life by carelessness. The management and culling of livestock, and the money-earning sports of stalking and grouse-shooting, require a seasonal control of access.

Deer-stalking. The normal season is from 1 September to 20 October, when stag-culling ends. Hinds are culled from then until 15 February.

Grouse-shooting. Grouse are shot from 12 August to 10 December.

The passage of a walker can clear a glen of its deer, and a moor of its grouse, for that day. The deer may not move back for weeks unless driven by weather, thus the walker may disrupt a season's stalking. While stalking is for many a sport like mountaineering, for others who run hill farms the venison exports are essential to keep marginal enterprises solvent. Therefore, before taking to the hills or to grouse moors, inquire at the estate office if you know where it is, or at the nearest farmhouse, or ask the local owner or keeper, if deer are to be stalked or grouse shot that day. The courtesy will be greatly appreciated. An alternative route may be offered to you should the need arise.

The problem of access to deer forests or grouse moors in late summer and autumn may be avoided if you go instead to mountain ranges held by the National Trust for Scotland in Arran, Ben Lawers, Glen Coe, Kintail, and Torridon.

Sheep. In the lambing months of April and May, take no dog on to sheep grazings. Pregnant ewes can suffer injury if forced to run. If a sheep is found on its back, approach quietly, place it on its feet gently, and stand by until it can move steadily. Do not try to 'rescue' sheep apparently stuck on ledges: if approached by a stranger they may jump off and fall to their death. Instead, report to the farmer.

Fire and Litter. Great damage to plants, trees, birds, and animals is done annually in the Highlands by fire, and to mammals by litter. It is urgently important that everyone should observe the Country Code:

Guard against all risks of fire
Fasten all gates
Keep dogs under proper control
Keep to the paths across farm land
Avoid damaging fences, hedges, and walls
Leave no litter – take it home
Safeguard water supplies
Protect wildlife, wild plants, and trees
Go carefully on country roads
Respect the life of the countryside

Index

Compound place-names are listed alphabetically from the first noun or adjective following the prefixes Glen, Loch, River, Ben or their numerous Gaelic equivalents.